Trial Lawyer

Praise for *Trial Lawyer*

"Richard Zitrin is a great storyteller, and this book is filled with wonderful accounts of many of the fascinating cases that he has handled as a lawyer. At the same time, Zitrin is raising profoundly important questions about the ethical duties of a lawyer and how to achieve justice. Zitrin gives a real sense of what it is to to practice law with passion and compassion."

– Erwin Chemerinsky, Dean & Distinguished Professor of Law, University of California, Berkeley

"I don't think I can adequately describe how absorbed I was in reading what Richard wrote. He put into words not only what was happening and what we did, but more importantly provided it in a real living context."

– Johnny Spain of the San Quentin Six

"Richard Zitrin has written a powerful, moving and deeply human memoir, replete with gripping, heartbreaking and inspiring stories, about his life as a criminal defense attorney and the people he has represented. The institutionalized inequities of the legal system, especially as they relate to race and the treatment of Black people, are vividly laid bare, as are Zitrin's noble attempts to confront them. Zitrin offers a timely example of what it truly means to be antiracist, and how this by necessity entails personal risk, ethical grounding, and an unswerving commitment to justice."

– Chad Williams, Chair of the Department of African and African American Studies, Brandeis University

"Richard Zitrin is a great lawyer because he is a great storyteller. These are his best stories. They are compelling not only because they are true but also thanks to the behind-the-scenes details which bring to life what an advocate must do for his cause and his client. Any lawyer or law student would benefit from this book. Anyone interested in law and justice will enjoy it too. Zitrin has brought the law to life."

— Frank H. Wu, President of Queens College, City University of New York, and the author of *Yellow: Race in America Beyond Black and White*

"Richard Zitrin's book should be read by every lawyer, everyone who wants to be a lawyer, and anybody who wants to understand why lawyers do what they do."

— Steven Lubet, Professor & Director, Bartlit Center for Trial Advocacy, Northwestern University Pritzker School of Law

TRIAL LAWYER

A Life Representing People Against Power

RICHARD ZITRIN

political animal
P R E S S

Political Animal Press
Toronto • Chicago
www.politicalanimalpress.com

Distributed by the University of Toronto Press
https://utpdistribution.com/

Cataloguing data available from Library and Archives Canada

ISBN 9781895131611 (paperback)
ISBN 9781895131628 (ebook)

Typeset in Adobe Garamond, designed by Robert Slimbach and URW DIN Condensed, from URW Type Foundry

To Charlotte and Victoria, my touchstones,
and David and Cat, my mentors

Contents

Author's Note

Throughout the text of this book, I have used the real names of clients only when I have those clients' permission. Elsewhere, I have altered clients' names and backgrounds sufficiently to ensure their anonymity. This protects the sanctity of the attorney-client confidential relationship. I have not used a hard and fast rule for other people in this narrative. With two exceptions, Chapters 1 and 12, where I have used only real names, I have generally altered the names of judges and counsel I've criticized. I have also altered the names of "lay" (as opposed to expert) witnesses, and alleged victims. Most other names are unchanged.

– RZ January 2022

"We may not always know what the truth is,
but we know what's a lie.
"We don't always know what's fair,
but we know what's unfair."

–Ethicist Michael Josephson, in conversation
with Richard Zitrin, 1997

Introduction

This is a book of reflections on the most compelling cases that I encountered during my life as a trial lawyer. They're mostly cases of ordinary people who found themselves in extraordinary circumstances, some of their own making, some caught in the web of society's perceptions, many a combination of both. In addition to trying dozens of cases, I spent over forty years teaching legal ethics. So, I've also chosen cases that lay bare the ethical and moral dilemmas that I routinely encountered throughout my career. These cases underscore what I've learned about the inherent biases of the legal system – towards people of color, the poor, the less educated, and those who just don't appear to fit the mold of whatever society happens to consider "normal".

Far too many dilemmas in my life as a trial lawyer have meant choosing between an ethical requirement of the justice system and my own understandings of basic fairness and morality. Lawyers are sworn to serve justice, and yet defining "Justice" itself can be elusive; attempts to do so take many different forms depending on a person's perspective. At the same time, lawyers also swear allegiance to their clients – a fiduciary duty to vigorously represent them, always putting the clients' interests ahead of their own.

What happens, then, when a lawyer's duty to the justice system conflicts with the lawyer's duty to the client? Especially when it appears to the lawyer that the system is not being fair to that client? In such circumstances, how should I as a trial lawyer balance these two sometimes irreconcilable interests? I have come to see these as ever-present, fundamental questions.

I found that the answers to these questions were not just about the client vs. the system and were far more complex than a matter of good against evil. One principal reason for this is that no understanding of a lawyer's responsibilities can begin to be complete without addressing issues of race, class, and what renowned journalist Isabel Wilkerson has called "caste." In my very first case, while still a law student, I saw six Black and brown men herded into the courtroom, chained as if they were headed to the auction block. There was no question in my mind that these people were being treated as sub-humans mostly because the justice system was imbued with racism. Over the years, my law practice has put me together with many clients whose backgrounds and experiences never gave them a fair shot. So, in the last three decades of my law school ethics courses, the most important classes I taught were on racial and gender bias. Not only do race and class disparity affect justice, but they almost always affect *access* to justice. The "equal protection of the law" promised by the Fourteenth Amendment to the Constitution has rarely been applied equally to all.

For most all my clients, access was a central issue. In criminal cases, I largely represented marginalized individuals against the huge power of the state. In civil cases, my opponents were large, monied corporations, insurance companies, and law firms. But in civil cases, while the other side had the money and power, our side had *the facts*, at least if I had chosen my cases carefully enough. In criminal cases, on the other hand, the facts were often far from favorable, and aligned against us were not just money and power but also public perception. Most people, of whatever political persuasion – at least most white people – generally assumed that those charged with a crime were guilty of something.

When it comes to criminal cases, there have been two questions I've been asked more than any others from the beginning of my career: "How can you justify representing clients who are guilty? Even worse, how can you actually try to get those people off?" Ironically, the justice system that I often found myself at odds with in representing my clients is, at least at its theoretical core, the same system that protects those same clients. It's the system created by the United States Constitution, requiring that every accused have "due process of law" and "the effective assistance of counsel," so that people are innocent until proven guilty "beyond a reasonable doubt."

The reality is that a major part of the job of the criminal defense lawyer at trial is to make every effort to convince the jury to acquit a client who has committed a crime. The public may ask, "How can you work to get that guilty person off?" But our theoretical justice system's protections will result in a few guilty people going free in the interests of providing the same due process for everyone. To most experienced criminal defense lawyers, then, that question is old news. Indeed, our most sacrosanct hero, Abraham Lincoln, knew the answer to it. In his highly celebrated case, the defense of "Duff" Armstrong, Lincoln used an almanac to prove that the key eyewitness could not have seen by the light of the moon because the moon had already set when the crime took place. What is often omitted in the telling of this tale is that "Duff" Armstrong had almost certainly committed the crime. But this in no way deterred Lincoln. The defense attorney's sworn duty of advocacy remains the same today: to do anything within the bounds of the ethical rules to get a client acquitted. It's a fact of life from their very first day on the job.

And to be clear, the justice system and the Constitution foster – indeed require – this attitude. Our justice system is in part a reaction to the restrictions on freedom in 17th and 18th century England, where alleged heretics such as Quaker William Penn were repeatedly imprisoned for espousing views contrary to the Church of England. In 1670, Penn was tried for unlawful public speaking. Despite the judge directing a guilty verdict against him, the jury acquitted him. When they would not reconsider, the jurors themselves were imprisoned for refusing to convict. But in colonial America things improved. When John Peter Zenger was accused in 1735 of criminal libel after his newspaper published articles strongly critical of New York's governor, Zenger was ultimately acquitted because his lawyer convinced a jury that anyone was free to speak the truth. Times had changed, and our Constitution reflected those changes.

Unfortunately, the theoretical protections of the justice system do not always – or even usually – manifest themselves in practice. My average criminal client was just fighting for survival, and had little in common with Penn and Zenger, both patricians fighting for lofty ideals. But the justice system only succeeds when *all* people are afforded the same "due process," the same right to freedom unless and until a case is proved beyond a reasonable doubt.

Practically speaking, though, our justice system is filled with the same inequities that characterize society as a whole. While all criminal defendants are provided a lawyer, the stream of justice does not flow equally for accused and accuser. The vast majority of criminal defendants are poor, and they are disproportionally people of color. Poorer people are less likely to make bail and thus remain incarcerated while their cases are pending, putting pressure on them to plead guilty just to gain release. That often means being swept into the post-incarceration probation and parole system, which for many is impossible to escape. By now, it's a well-known and immutable fact that for the same class of crime, from petty offenses to murders, Blacks get harsher sentences than whites. And law enforcement bias against minority groups in general, and Black men in particular, not only continues but has been underscored by recent events in this country.

Usually, prosecutors are far better funded than public defenders. While it varies from state to state, appointed criminal counsel are often small firm or solo practitioners with little office backup who must petition – essentially beg – the courts for enough money out of their own budgets to investigate, conduct forensic tests on evidence, and provide psychological evaluations and testimony. Almost uniformly, criminal courts seem more interested in efficiency and just moving cases along than they do with dispensing truly equal justice. Thus, in a few states, including Texas, murder cases in which a defense attorney falls asleep during the trial are not reversed if the lawyer dozed at supposedly unimportant moments. After all, re-trials are expensive.

And it's not much better for poor people in the civil justice system. In my practice, I was able to choose my clients – and the favorable facts that went with them – so I had a luxury that the big-firm lawyers on the other side generally did not: picking my battles. This meant that the facts were usually on our side. But with the other side having unlimited funds and platoons of young lawyers to throw at a case, we could never compete in the amount of money spent or lawyer hours expended. Ordinary people have no right to a lawyer if they must defend themselves after they are sued, and if they bring their own cases against a powerful defendant, they are likely to face scorched-earth litigation, which is often prohibitively expensive. Since I could hardly expect my average civil plaintiff to have enough disposable income to fund an expensive case against a well-heeled defendant, I had to build up a substantial "war chest" so I could take on those costs myself – at the risk of losing that money if we lost the case.

Deeply entrenched in this legal world, where racism and other biases abounded, I felt that I knew such things when I saw them. And until the spring of 2020, I *thought* that I had a good understanding of white privilege. I mean beyond the super-obvious stuff: Black friends being mistaken for "the help"; Black drivers being arrested for resisting arrest when supposedly routine (and often illegal) traffic stops (broken taillights, failure to signal a lane change) escalated; role assumptions continuing to be made in courtrooms and boardrooms.

I've certainly been aware that my own privileged background gave me an unfair advantage over many, indeed most, people, and led me to much of the work I've chosen to do trying to even up the score. I remembered my white privilege every time I jogged from my law office through downtown San Francisco streets and needed a bathroom. I knew that despite my slovenly and sweaty t-shirt and shorts, I could still duck into a fancy hotel, give a nod of familiarity to the doorman, and make a beeline for the men's room, while my Black friend Cedrick, the accomplished high school math teacher and basketball coach who favored hoodies outside the classroom, would be stopped before he ever got inside.

But despite my own evolving understanding and my experiences with bias in the legal system, it was only when I returned to this memoir in the spring of 2020 and was reflecting deeply on the events of the day, that I realized I had so much more to learn about the pervasiveness of systemic racism. The murder of George Floyd and other events during the COVID-19 pandemic caused me to question basic assumptions about how well I understood society – and myself. I knew there was pervasive racism, but was knowing that enough? I knew I was an anti-racist, but wasn't there more if I dug deeper? My very first case had given me a leg up in understanding the grossly unfair treatment of those six men of color. Countless cases since had reinforced that lesson. But neither the treatment of those six prisoners nor all my subsequent cases fully translated to a clear understanding of the larger picture. I realized that what I had seen were just iceberg-tip examples of the systemic racism that governs most everything in our society.

Though I have long known that Black folks must walk a much more challenging path than I've had, whether they are poor laborers or lawyers who went to Stanford, I know today that I had grossly underestimated the extraordinarily pervasive nature of racism. I walk around the streets of San Francisco without fear. My Black friends, women and men, do not. Ever. I spend a fair amount of time in the impoverished, homeless-ridden Tenderloin neighborhood, and never think that a cop is going to stop me. Not so Cedrick. And especially not so Cedrick's teenaged son. My Black lawyer friends and the law students I mentor faced, and overcame, that more challenging path. But until 2020, I didn't fully appreciate that they *still* face it, no matter who they are, every day, in so many small ways that are cumulatively huge, running the gauntlet of society each day of their lives. I am learning that events like Professor Henry Louis Gates, Jr. getting busted on his own front porch are commonplace, almost expected occurrences for people of color.

On January 6, 2021, our Capitol was attacked. As I watched rioters storm the building with little police resistance, I remembered the previous June 1, one week after George Floyd died, when a group of peaceful protesters was forced out of Lafayette Park by police in riot gear using tear gas and other aggressive means, all so that President Donald Trump could have a Bible-holding photo-op. Had January's crowd of law-breaking rioters instead been a peaceful march of largely

Black protesters, there likely would have been far more police aggression and violence. That's the truth in Black and white.

But that isn't all. As a lawyer who has represented scores of clients from racial minorities to ensure their access to the legal system, I've also had to consider my role as a "white savior." Was I insensitive to how my efforts might affect the people I was trying to help? I knew that I was far from acting out the savior tropes that appear in *The Help* and *Green Book*, two movies I disliked precisely because they featured egregious examples of white saviorism. I knew that I tried to avoid "teaching" Black people a "white" way of doing things. And I've tried – not always successfully – to help only when asked.

And yet, I recognized that there were some occasions in which I was a "voice for the voiceless" without being *invited*. Even if the offense is unintended, an uninvited voice can be seen as showing a lack of respect for the fact that white people are not going to "save" Black people, something I surely knew. When I was appointed by the court to represent someone, I was invited to be that voice, but only for that one client, never for the group or groups that the client was part of. Indeed, I could not have written these words had I not been asked by Eva Paterson, the Bay Area's foremost civil rights leader, to write about moving beyond my own mere antiracism. When I asked Eva about the acceptability of being a white spokesperson, she reassured me that there is still a role for white folks to speak out and to help spread a message that, if only spoken by Black people, might appear to be self-serving. But there's a fine line between that and Savior City.

Pervasive bias, of course, has many forms, and I've seen it used against all kinds of people. A young Vietnamese man whose family repeatedly faced racial targeting and hostility, and who was then accused of a serious crime just for talking about protecting his family. An indigenous woman who became an addicted street hooker because her life experience left her so few choices. A teenager from a Middle Eastern background who was racially profiled by a cop in an upscale white, suburban town. A poor Latina whose truthfulness was disputed because of her language skills and status – and because her community's Fourth of July celebration of our nation's birthday occurred at a local bar instead of a country club. Each one of these stories, all amplified in these pages, had its own lessons, and each was essential to my growth as a lawyer and a person.

I've been fortunate to have had twin careers as a trial lawyer and a law professor. One came by choice, the other by happenstance – the offer from a friendly law school dean to teach a class in legal ethics at the University of San Francisco. That's how, at the age of thirty, I experienced two important events in rapid succession. On a Wednesday evening in early December 1977, I held the final class of my first semester of teaching. The next morning, I gave the closing argument in my first murder case. I'd been a lawyer for just under three years. In the decades since, I've tried cases before dozens of juries and taught hundreds of legal ethics classes. Putting aside that both trial lawyers and law professors are attorneys, on the surface there doesn't seem to be much in common between the two occupations. But for me, I have always seen my teaching through the dual prisms of practical application and basic human morality. For me, these two paths are symbiotic.

When I wrote my first book over twenty-five years ago, I was concerned less with the literal meaning of the codified ethics rules – those propounded by our justice system that lawyers are required to follow – than with those places where two different tenets must be balanced lest they lead to opposite results, such as where loyalty to the client clashes with a duty to a court, or where the codified rules clash with common social morality. A few cases have caused me to undergo life-altering experiences of self-examination. Perhaps unsurprisingly, most of the important lessons concerned matters not written in those black-letter rules. For example, many young trial lawyers, particularly if they're successful, are puffed up with ego. I was no exception. But experience has taught me to develop at least a reasonable degree of humility to dilute the hubris. Humility is a quality that actually makes us much better trial lawyers – and people.

There's the equally important lesson of developing – *earning* – a client's trust. A client's trust in a lawyer's judgment may be the most valuable currency the lawyer has — more than legal skills, experience, intelligence, or knowledge. Most of my clients came from a totally different world than the one I grew up in, so earning trust and carefully nurturing it was rarely easy, but it was always important. Trust means that lawyers speak the truth to their clients, so that in a criminal case, the client should know that no matter what, they will never get back to even. It means keeping clients informed, disclosing everything possible, and doing it in plain English (or whatever is the client's preferred language). After all, clients don't speak "legalese." It means being both tough and honest. Lawyers often want to round off the sharp corners of the truth, and sometimes that makes matters more palatable. But clients need — and most want — to hear much more than "Don't worry, I got this." Trust means remembering to represent the *person*, not just the case, and that sometimes, what's important to the client may go well beyond winning or losing. Finally, as I learned in my very first case, it means acknowledging that the lawyer can never presume to walk in the client's shoes. Most people, lawyers included, are tempted to say, "I know exactly how you feel." But they *don't* know. I can empathize with clients, I can get it intellectually, and I can appreciate their circumstances and pain. But I have not been where they have been.

An issue closely related to this – and to hubris vs. humility – is helping clients to develop their own autonomy, so they can make decisions that work best for them, rather than for their lawyer. I was fortunate that just as I was beginning to teach ethics, I had a case that centered on precisely this issue. I came to a clear-eyed view of who ultimately gets to make decisions, lawyer or client. Or put more bluntly, whether I am the client's mouthpiece or savior. This dilemma doesn't mean shying away from the best advice I can give a client, or even from pushing hard if I feel strongly that one course is clearly the best. But for me, overwhelming a client's will, as if I somehow have all the answers, is a mistake.

When it comes to the ever-present balance between the interests of the client and those of the court, I've tried to err on the side of the client whenever possible. Judges are generally not wild about this approach. I particularly found myself at odds with those jurists who like to maintain strong control of their courtrooms. But by always showing respect in the face of disagreement, I found that most judges would see my efforts as "nothing personal." Sometimes, though, I found it necessary to take a judge on directly when the judge was in the wrong. Many lawyers fear this; they have to work with these judges each day of their professional lives. But when a judge needed to be challenged, even strongly, I felt I had no right to back down, so long as I was respectful and within ethical bounds. My job was to do my best for the client, not make nice with the judge, even if that made the judge angry or led to contempt. I felt that lawyers who don't meet that challenge out of fear of judicial disapprobation put their own interests ahead of their client's – a major ethical gaffe.

Finally, I learned a great deal about finding contentment. It almost goes without saying that trial work is stressful, and many who engage in it, me included, have felt that stress in unhealthy ways. Trials are flat-out hard work, sometimes sixteen-hours-a-day work with no days off. Despite their tendency towards large egos, many trial lawyers are not working those hours for the joy of winning, but out of the fear of losing. That was me too. When I lost, I was inadequate, and it was my fault. When I won, I was relieved. But happy? Not part of the equation. This is not at all to say that I hated the work, for what I did was endlessly rewarding. But it is telling that the case in which I learned the most about lawyering and life was one in which wisdom was delivered by a psychologist, not a lawyer.

Other than my first case, most of my cases didn't make many headlines, though they were no less important for it. Absent the constant media noise and the baggage that famous cases carry, these personal stories are about real people, not familiar tales known to all. Many of these stories have extraordinary features: thought-provoking, poignant, occasionally bizarre and laugh-out-loud funny. And they shine a bright light on the inherent unfairness and biases of the legal system. The odds were often stacked against these clients. The efforts we lawyers must make often require thinking – and acting – not merely outside the box, but off the wall, where the usual rules of the road sometimes yield to new, even untried, trial strategies. These strategies are impacted by each of the ethical conundrums described here, and they are explored through the cases of the real clients I was trying to serve.

Each chapter that follows is about a case with its unique cast of characters, strange-but-true facts, brilliant trial tricks and tactics—and not-so-brilliant ones that failed miserably. Each had its own lessons for me: about social justice, and about fairness, strategy, ethics, morality, and more. Perhaps about how to be a better lawyer, but also, I hope, how to be a better – and more aware – person in the world outside the courtroom.

1

Johnny Spain, David Mayer, and the San Quentin Six

People of the State of California v. Stephen Bingham, et al.

On August 21, 1971, six people, including Black Panther leader George Jackson, were killed at San Quentin State Prison. One of the most violent episodes in the history of American prisons, it has remained an enigma. The trial, when it finally occurred, was then the longest criminal trial in American history. The case lasted fifteen years from indictment to the last verdict. Yet despite verdicts on all six original defendants, the online county court record states that their dispositions are "not available." From the beginning, the case was filled with conspiracy theories. The law-enforcement theory was that the "Six" had conspired with radical lawyer Stephen Bingham to plan an escape that resulted in murder. The principal defense theory was that prison officials formed the conspiracy, setting up a scheme to kill George Jackson that got out of hand.

Today, little is remembered, less is clear, and much remains unknown and unknowable. Basic facts about the case on the internet and even mainstream media are full of factual inaccuracies. What is known is that three of the six Black and brown defendants were acquitted of all charges, and the one single person

who was convicted of murder had his conviction overturned twice
by an appeals court and was freed over thirty years ago. He was
my first client, Johnny Spain.

On a hot, sticky day in late June 1973, I found myself sitting
with my new boss David Mayer in one of two tiny, grimy
maximum-security visiting rooms reserved for prisoners like
Johnny Spain. The indignity of these rooms could not be lost
on anyone. I had never seen anything remotely like it, but I had
never even been in a local jail before, much less a high-security
prison. About the size of two phone booths back-to-back, the
two sides were separated by a plexiglass partition that went
from the ceiling to just above a narrow writing shelf. Below
the plexiglass was a four-inch-high heavy wire mesh screen.
Below the screen was about a one and one-half inch open
space through which we could pass papers back and forth.

The rooms were disgustingly – nauseatingly – filthy and
roach-infested. We were escorted into our side of the room by
a guard and locked in. On the other side, Johnny arrived with
an escort, chained around the legs and around the waist, with
another chain around his neck that made it look as if he were
heading to the auction block. Two short chains connected the
waist chain to handcuffs. In order to write, Johnny had to
contort his body sideways to get his hand close enough to the
pieces of paper in front of him.

The escort remained present, seated behind Johnny, not
more than three feet away. Privacy was a joke. For me, though,
the greatest indignity was how we "shook hands". After we
arrived, Johnny and David both extended their fingers through

the narrow bottom opening and "shook hands" by the tips of their fingers. Then I did the same.

A job with David Mayer

When I was twenty-six, I moved to San Francisco after completing two years of law school but with little idea about what I wanted to do. I was not particularly interested in practicing law, having first spent a few years after college working in politics. For a while in law school, I drove a taxi to earn money instead of the more traditional part-time law-clerk work.

But a week after arriving in June 1973, I had a stroke of good luck. My ex-college roommate Dave, who'd introduced me to my future wife – the reason I'd moved to the West Coast – told me he'd just been offered two jobs. One was working for a prestigious San Francisco boutique firm run by a former judge; the other was working in Marin County, north of the City, on the highly publicized and politicized "San Quentin Six" case. He chose the former and recommended me for the latter. And that was how my first legal work was as a five-dollar-an-hour law clerk in a six-defendant multiple-murder-charge case arising out of the events of August 21, 1971, at San Quentin State Prison.

I learned a lot about law and life from my mentor, David Ross Mayer, the guy who hired me for that job on first meeting. Before Vietnam, David had been a deputy DA in Southern California. Then he went into the Air Force Judge Advocate General Corps to do his required military service.

For his first two years, he was stationed in East Hampton, NY, on the south shore of Long Island, perhaps the cushiest assignment in the service. He learned to fly planes and hung out on the beach with his wife and young son. That was until he was sent to Okinawa, a key staging point for the American air assault on North Vietnam. It was 180 degrees from life in the Hamptons.

Fights, drugs, and crime were rampant on Okinawa, as was abuse of military power by both commissioned and non-commissioned officers. As a JAG officer, David could be assigned either to prosecute or to defend. After a couple of defense cases, he realized not only that he was very good at it but that the system was stacked against the little guy, who seemed to be presumed guilty in front of military courts. Because the Air Force had a policy of allowing defendants to choose their lawyer if available, David's successes meant that as the number of defendants requesting his services rose, he wound up doing nothing other than defending accused enlisted men.

By the end of his four-year commitment, the last thing David Mayer wanted to do was to return to a prosecutor's office. He had been radicalized by those last two years. He moved with his wife and son to Marin County in Northern California, started hanging out with some old-time "lefty" lawyers, and took on prison cases there and in Sacramento. Word spreads fast in the prison system, and by 1972 one of the "Six," Willie Tate, requested that David be appointed his lawyer. Because public defenders are only allowed to represent one co-defendant, five of the six defendants needed to have counsel appointed by the trial court and paid by the state.

David's representation of Willie was not to be, though, because in a move I can only understand as perverse, presiding trial judge Henry J. Broderick refused to appoint David to represent the client who wanted him. Instead, he appointed David to represent Johnny Larry Spain, the only Black Panther in the group and the one most closely tied to George Jackson.

Violence in prison

The San Quentin Six incident was the last in a series of violent events in and around California prisons during 1970 and 1971, each of which related to George Jackson. Jackson had entered the prison system after pleading guilty to robbing a gas station of $70, for which he received what was then called an "indeterminate sentence" of one year to life, the term to be determined by how the prisoner conducted himself inside. The "life" part of this sentence sounded as incredible then as it does today; in fact, it's now considered unconstitutionally cruel and unusual punishment. Back then, for George Jackson, it was a death sentence.

During his first stay at San Quentin, Jackson joined the Black Panther Party and learned Marxist theory from fellow prisoner W.L. Nolen. In early 1969, Nolen and Jackson were both transferred to Soledad State Prison not far from Monterey. A year later, in January 1970, a guard fired several shots into the Soledad prison yard, ostensibly to quell a riot. Three black inmates, including Nolen, were killed by a single guard. A grand jury quickly exonerated the guard, calling it justifiable homicide. Later that same month, a different

The "Soledad Brothers," from left, George
Jackson, Fleeta Drumgo & John Clutchette,
1970. Jackson is holding a copy of Life
Magazine picturing Angela Davis with the
caption "The Making of a Fugitive"

guard was killed after being beaten and thrown from a prison tier into the yard. Jackson was one of three prisoners accused of that guard's murder. In order to publicize what she believed were trumped up charges, his lawyer, Fay Stender, took a series of letters that Jackson had written to her and turned them into an instant best-selling book called *Soledad Brother*, the name given to Jackson and his two co-defendants. By the end of 1970, George Jackson was a celebrity. And he was shipped back to San Quentin, this time to the Adjustment Center.

On August 21, 1971, with the Soledad Brothers' trial just a week off, Jackson was shot and killed outside the Adjustment Center, while allegedly trying to escape after gaining possession of a 9mm Astra, a Spanish Civil War-era semi-automatic pistol. Five other people, three prison guards and two white "trusty" inmates – main-line prisoners assigned to deliver food to the AC – also died that day. Johnny Spain had followed Jackson outside the AC and was captured alive.

In the spring of 1973, with the case very much still in the pre-trial stage, David Mayer was appointed to be Johnny Spain's new attorney. A few months later, I joined the defense team.

In my first week on the job, David took me to the new Marin County Civic Center. This extraordinary building, the last major work designed by Frank Lloyd Wright, presented as two buildings built into the side of two hills at two varying levels, attached in the middle by an open-air rotunda. The circular motif existed throughout the building, replicated through arched entryways, rounded windows, and unusual circular-shaped courtrooms in which the jury, judge, defense, and prosecution sat as if in a theater-in-the-round.

It was there that I learned something of the Civic Center's non-architectural history. On August 7, 1970, after the deaths in Soledad Prison in January of that year, and a year before the San Quentin conflagration, George Jackson's seventeen-year-old brother Jonathan, well-armed underneath his trench coat, had entered one of those round courtrooms, where James McClain was being tried for assaulting a San Quentin guard. Jonathan freed McClain and two other prisoners from a holding cell. The four then fled the courtroom with four hostages – three women jurors and the trial judge, Harold Haley – after first taping a sawed-off shotgun around Haley's neck. In the courtroom corridor, they invited photographers to take pictures, while demanding the release of the three Soledad Brothers. Chief Assistant District Attorney Gary W. Thomas, who was prosecuting the case and whose wife was Judge Haley's niece, was either taken prisoner in the courtroom or ran out after the kidnappers as they headed towards an elevator to descend to their waiting van.

The sheriff's department officers held their fire as the group moved from the courtroom and down the courthouse corridor. But the ceasefire ended after the captors and hostages, now including Thomas, got in the van and began to drive off. Someone fired a shot, and a gun battle ensued in which Jonathan Jackson, McClain, and a third prisoner were killed, and the fourth, Ruchell Magee, was seriously wounded. Deputy DA Thomas was shot in the chest by a bullet later determined to have been from a San Quentin guard's gun. Judge Haley was killed – according to Thomas, shot by Magee, but according to forensics shot when the sawed-off shotgun around his neck went off, and another bullet, likely from outside the van, also hit him.

The shotgun and two other weapons, it turned out, had been registered to the flamboyant and outspoken Angela Davis, who had come to national attention for her radical political views. In the fall of 1969, with the strong support of then-governor Ronald Reagan, UCLA fired Davis for being a communist. A judge soon reinstated her, but UCLA fired her again in June 1970 for using "inflammatory language," such as calling cops "pigs" and "her statement that the [University of California] regents 'killed, brutalized (and) murdered'" free-speech demonstrators at Berkeley.

Less than two months later, Angela Davis, by now a celebrity, bought three weapons that wound up under Jonathan Jackson's trench coat. Davis immediately fled the area but was soon found, arrested, and charged with murder. Magee, who recovered from his wounds, was also charged.

My introduction to California

I didn't arrive in California until almost three years after the Marin County Civic Center shootout and two years after the deadly events at San Quentin. By then, Angela Davis had been acquitted of all charges, thanks in part to Howard Moore, Jr., who moved from Atlanta to join Davis's defense team. Back in Georgia, Moore had represented radicals Stokely Carmichael and H. Rap Brown, and had won a unanimous US Supreme Court decision to seat the elected Georgia state legislator (and future NAACP chairman) Julian Bond, which the Georgia House had refused to do. Meanwhile, the families of W.L. Nolen and the other two black prisoners killed in the Soledad yard won a $270,000 verdict against the prison and eight prison employees. And the two remaining Soledad Brothers, John Clutchette and Fleeta Drumgo, who'd been moved to the San Quentin AC with Jackson, were tried for murder and acquitted in early 1972.

Ruchell Magee, Angela Davis's co-defendant, widely regarded as a "jailhouse lawyer," cycled through a complex series of maneuvers, motions, and attorneys, including an effort to represent himself. He obtained several changes of the case's venue from one county to another: Marin to San Francisco to Santa Clara and back to San Francisco again. His case, two counts of kidnapping and one of murdering Judge Haley, finally went to trial in San Francisco in early 1973. But the trial settled nothing. In April 1973, after a dozen weeks of testimony, the jury was unable to reach a verdict: 11-1 to acquit on murder and kidnapping for extortion, but 11-1 to convict on simple kidnapping. A retrial date was set and was still pending when I arrived that June.

Meanwhile, the Six case itself had been on hold until shortly before I arrived. Right after the October 1, 1971 indictment, Judge Broderick held a hearing to appoint lawyers to represent the five defendants not represented by the Marin County Public Defender. The Marin Superior Court had no formal method then for appointing lawyers; mostly, judges simply picked from "respected" members of the local bar, a practice adhered to by Broderick. Before appointing a lawyer, the judge first asked each of the five remaining defendants the same question: "Do you have your attorney to represent you in this case?" When he got to Fleeta Drumgo, now a San Quentin Six defendant, Drumgo replied that he not only had a lawyer, but that he was present in court: Richard Hodge, a former DA who had tried both murder cases and prison cases. Hodge advised the court that he had agreed to represent Drumgo and was competent to do so. Broderick nevertheless ignored this request and instead appointed a lawyer named Richard Breiner.

Dick Breiner was a well-known local lawyer who later became a respected judge. But he had never tried a murder case, he was not in the courtroom that day, and he didn't solicit the appointment. And Drumgo didn't want Breiner, whom he had no reason to trust. The first thing Breiner did as Drumgo's counsel was what soon became the watchword for the defense in this unusual case – he "took a writ" to get Fleeta the lawyer of his choice.

Denials of motions happen all the time. The usual course is that an appeal of that denial waits for the end of the case. Not so for the San Quentin Six. There is a long-standing procedure that allows a party to petition the appeals court for a "writ of mandamus or prohibition," the first to mandate the trial court to act, the second to prevent the trial court from acting. Writ petitions are denied in a simple one-page, two-sentence order 95% of the time, but that leaves that remaining 5%. In the Six case, we all went for that 5%; almost every lost motion was followed by someone "taking a writ," petitioning the appellate court for relief.

Breiner's petition on behalf of Drumgo was one of the 5%; the Court of Appeal agreed to hear the matter, resulting in a stay of the trial court case in January 1972. Eventually, the appeals court unanimously agreed with Drumgo, noting that he had a competent attorney ready to accept appointment at the very beginning of the case, which would neither prejudice the prosecution nor delay the case in any way. But the prosecution appealed to the California Supreme Court, which reviewed the appellate decision, and found, 4-2 – one vote short of a 3-3 tie that would have upheld the lower court – that no indigent defendant had the right to choose counsel, even under these circumstances. Justice Stanley Mosk wrote this in his dissent: "Effective advocacy involves more than vigor, experience, and familiarity with the law. The attorney-client relationship contemplates trust and mutual cooperation, particularly when the attorney is defending the client's liberty." But the majority disagreed.

So it was that the Six case didn't return to the Marin court until the spring of 1973. By that time, some of the original court-appointed lawyers had begged off the case due to the press of other business or simply because they didn't want to be involved in a case so daunting and so highly charged with radical politics. Breiner, who had done his very best, was one who left. He was replaced not by Dick Hodge but by a conservative ex-DA, Michael Dufficy, a lawyer who seemed politically unsuited to such a task. And Johnny Spain also got a new lawyer: David Mayer.

San Quentin State Prison

San Quentin is set in a beautiful location, on the coastline of suburban Marin County overlooking San Francisco Bay. But San Quentin was not a nice place. At the time, it was still the notorious high-security fortress of film-noir fame. The famous gas chamber was there, with death row located on the third floor of the "Adjustment Center," the highest of high-security buildings in the prison system. The first tier, or floor, of the "AC" was the highest-security tier in the system, reserved for what the prison system called "administrative segregation" – better known as solitary confinement, and what prisoners and others called "the Hole." The Six were locked down for twenty-three-and-a-half hours a day, unable to exercise, and given just a couple of showers a week. I learned a lot about how cruel life could be from San Quentin State Prison.

By the end of my first week as David's law clerk, I had been inside San Quentin twice. It wasn't easy for us to get in. Even though I should have expected it, I was surprised by the extent of animosity the guards directed towards us – two people arriving to defend one of the men accused of killing three of their own. While they made some small effort to just follow procedure, the thinly disguised hostility was palpable.

When we approached the East Gate, our point of entry, armed with legal pads, pens, drafts of briefs, and court pleadings, we had to present all we had to the guards manning the gate. That's when the first game was played. The guards insisted on looking through our briefcases; David refused, noting that it was lawyer-client confidential and privileged information. After a while – ten minutes? a half-hour? – we were on to the next game: "Inmate Spain is not available." I can't remember what the reasons given for unavailability were on those first two visits, but there were many: He was eating lunch, or exercising, or "between gates," meaning on the way from one prison location to another and needed to wait for an escort to get to the visiting room, or no escort was available because they were short-handed. Or….

Eventually, though, we would be allowed to go through the metal detector, although that was the third game. That metal detector always seemed to be more sensitive when we walked through it. Other folks, the friends and relatives of main-line prisoners who entered through the same gate, seemed to have far fewer problems. For us, it usually took two or three attempts.

Once through, we were able to walk outside along a staff parking lot to the main prison visiting room, where "contact visits" took place between men and their families and friends at tables in a large, open room. All prisoners were entitled to legal visits. Those visits were supposed to be private, and separate rooms existed, but not for the San Quentin Six. Instead, we had our visits in one of the two tiny, disgustingly filthy rooms set aside for Adjustment Center prisoners.

I don't think I realized for years that during those earliest visits, I must have been partly in a state of shock. While I thought I was taking it all in stride, in hindsight, it was an otherworldly experience. And yet, it soon became the norm. Over the next several months, I made dozens of trips to these rooms, and I'm sure that after a while part of me became numb to the environment and what it symbolized.

Johnny

Over the next six months, as I researched and worked on all manner of motions. I spent many days out at San Quentin, often on my own, with my own special ID and an authorization letter from David. Talking with Johnny in that tiny, grimy little visiting room, I learned what he and his co-defendants faced every day on the AC's first tier. At least twenty-three hours locked down in single 6'x8' cells. One hour max of exercise time, five times a week – not much time to walk up and down the tier, stretch, visit with others, or play a quick game of dominoes. Showers two times per week, with the timing and water flow controlled by guards. Often, shower days meant no exercise that day. Tear gas routinely used when being removed from a cell. For first-tier prisoners, *no* outside time at all except when escorted through the prison yard to visits – so no fresh air. Only one personal or family visit a week. And when escorted, forced to wear leg irons, waist chains attached to handcuffs, and that chain placed around the neck.

More? Cell floors, especially those without drains, frequently flooded due to poor pipes, overflowing toilets, and water dripping down from the floors above. Habitual interference with mail. No TV. No radio. No academic or vocational study. And two "strip cells," reserved for those who in the eyes of the prison have misbehaved, with no wash basin, a hole in the floor for "waste elimination," and a 200-watt bulb controlled from outside the cell.

These conditions often dominated our conversations. They sounded so horrific – so devastating and dehumanizing – that I was sure that living with them had to have huge effects on Johnny both physically and psychologically. Instead of legal motions, Johnny would have preferred me to work on a *habeas corpus* petition showing that these conditions were unconstitutionally cruel and unusual punishment. But there was no hard-stop deadline for the petition, and there were rapidly approaching deadlines for all the motions that he and the others also wanted.

With a guard sitting right behind Johnny, when we got to any sensitive topic, we usually "spoke" by writing things down on yellow legal pads, showing them to each other through the plexiglass, then scribbling over them thoroughly with our ballpoint pens so that no one could read what we'd written. Johnny would hand his scribbles to me at the end of a visit so I could remove them from the prison. I grew to like him a great deal, and, indeed, admire him. I didn't think much then about whether he liked me, though in hindsight I believe I assumed it. But I was focused on helping him, not on being liked.

Still, during these visits, Johnny and I developed an easeful, trusting relationship that, sadly, David never had with him. Willie Tate, not Johnny, had requested David to be his lawyer. By pulling a switch when he appointed David to represent Johnny instead, Judge Broderick planted seeds of suspicion that Johnny never fully got over. How our own relationship of trust developed was a minor miracle, and a lesson that has stayed with me to this day. I restrained my natural inclination to talk and instead tried to be a careful listener. And although I was a total newbie, I had just enough life experience to know that I couldn't very well go into San Quentin State Prison, visit Johnny in a tiny, roach-infested visiting room smaller than a water closet, and say to him, "Trust me!" I was lucky to be in a situation where it was so obvious that trust had to be earned.

Not only was Johnny's prison experience beyond my emotional comprehension, so was his life story. I learned a lot about what it was like to be in Johnny's shoes, though I was aware I could never begin to know what it was like to walk in them myself.

Johnny read voraciously and was an intense student. When we first started meeting one-on-one, he had been inhaling everything he could read on what he called "miscegenetic children." He was obsessed with the issues facing these kids, whom today we'd call "biracial," and we spent hours discussing this over the course of many visits. His interest was understandable: The son of a white mother and her Black lover, he had grown up white in a white family in Mississippi until the age of six. His brothers and sisters were the white children of his mom and her husband. By age six, when he began looking too dark to pass for white, his mother arranged for him to be adopted by a Black family living in Watts, in L.A. He literally changed races from white to Black during his train ride to the West Coast.

From the beginning, Johnny emphasized the psychological dimension of his and the others' situations. He felt he was being treated like an animal. He was strongly taken with the work of a young Stanford professor named Philip Zimbardo, who in the summer of 1971 had divided male students into "guards" and "prisoners" in the basement of the Stanford psychology building. Zimbardo wanted to measure the effect on students having widely disparate power roles. The results were stark and dramatic. The more prisoners "misbehaved" – crying, depression, anger, a hunger strike – the more sadistic the guards became, putting prisoners in isolation, taking their cots and blankets, and so on. Zimbardo realized that such situations have a far more powerful influence over people's behavior than he thought. He closed the experiment early – ironically on August 20, 1971, one day before the San Quentin Six conflagration.

Johnny drafted a poem that closely fit with Zimbardo's lesson. He called it "frankenstein's monster, a poem for those" and it began like this:

> i am frankenstein's monster
> no matter how beautiful i may be
> i am ugly
> to those who created me

and ended this way:

> i am frankenstein's monster
> because i've turned
> on those who wanted me to turn
> on myself

Unfortunately, much as I wanted to fulfill Johnny's desire to challenge the conditions of confinement he and his co-defendants faced, I had to wait. Johnny understood that we had to put aside our concerns about those inhuman conditions in order to finish the trial motions. And for me to work on those motions, especially those that challenged the evidence and factual distortions, I needed to learn the relevant facts. To do that, I began by reading transcripts from the first court appearances in 1971.

Johnny and the judge

It was quickly apparent to me from reading those transcripts that Johnny was exceptionally bright, both a quick learner and an eloquent spokesperson. What struck me most clearly was that in the long colloquies between Johnny and Judge Broderick, Johnny had danced linguistic circles around the judge, to the point where Johnny largely controlled the agenda and the judge merely responded.

Johnny raised a huge number of issues at these early hearings, among them: his right to counsel of his choice; returning material taken from his cell; his need to receive certain books and keep them in his cell; preventing the prison from issuing disciplinary write-ups on a whim; even showing the judge the pencils he was permitted to prove they were "drawing pencils" instead of regular lead pencils. Johnny cited the judge with specificity to the judge's own ten-point order to the prison, noting that prison officials had failed to implement "numbers one, two, four, five, six, seven, nine and ten."

After about a half-hour back-and-forth at the case's second court hearing on October 15, 1971, Judge Broderick asked Johnny,

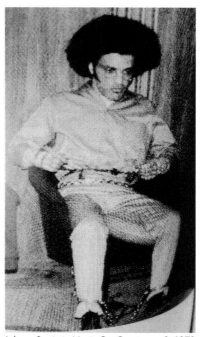

Johnny Spain in Marin Co. Courtroom 3, 1973

"All right, does that conclude the matter, Mr. Spain?" Johnny's answer was perfect: "Well, until I can think of something else." Two weeks later, Johnny had thought of several "something elses," leading the judge through another half-hour linguistic maze, including repeatedly objecting to the lawyer who'd been appointed to represent him by asking, "Who is this person?" Near the end of this colloquy, Johnny asked for books the judge had denied him that he said he needed for his defense:

JOHNNY: Quite evidently you didn't go over all the books.

THE JUDGE: No, I didn't read all the books.

JOHNNY: Well, then, how could you deny something if you did not read them? That's prejudice right there.

In reading these transcripts again, I consistently had the image of the courtroom, where I spent many days, brought to my mind's eye. Judge Broderick sitting on his elevated bench, dressed in black robes; Johnny, his huge afro bulging out, slumped in his chair because sitting erect was painful with the tight chains. And yet to me, from that position of gross inequality, it was clear that Johnny was more than the judge's equal.

The one issue Johnny repeatedly raised from the beginning was about his restraints: the leg irons and waist chains connected to handcuffs that all the Six were forced to wear. From the second court hearing:

> JOHNNY: I would like the Court to take a look at the handcuffs I have on.... My circulation has been cut off ever since I left San Quentin....
>
> THE JUDGE: All right, is there anything else that you wish to call to the Court's attention?
>
> JOHNNY: I wish the Court would look at these handcuffs and see how tight they are.
>
> THE JUDGE: I can look at them from here, and they appear to be shall I say snug ... but I'm not going to go down and inspect handcuffs....
>
> JOHNNY: Could I step just a few feet closer and you can see for yourself?

August 21, 1971

No one knows exactly what happened at the Adjustment Center on August 21, 1971, least of all me, even after reading every available report and transcript. But there are some things that we believed did not happen. One was the prosecution's story about how George Jackson had smuggled a gun into the AC. David and I jokingly described this to each other this way: George Jackson whips off his wig with one hand, grabs the nine-inch-long Astra from under the wig with the other hand, and with his *third* hand jams a clip inside the gun. Not likely. Or that Stephen Bingham, one of Jackson's lawyers, or his investigator, Vanita Anderson, smuggled that gun into the prison inside the casing of a tape recorder that was no bigger than the gun itself. Pretty implausible. Or there was a conspiracy among Bingham, the Six, and "other persons." But that was the core problem: *Who were these persons*, and how could we defend the case without knowing who they were?

As I started poring over the transcript of the grand jury testimony that led to the indictments. David needed more assistance to flesh out the details, so he signed on my old law school buddy Bill Balin, who'd just arrived in San Francisco, to do a blow-by-blow summary. The transcript was filled with mysteries. It was clear that George Jackson had gone to a legal visit with Bingham, and that he was searched before the visit. It was clear that Bingham had arrived for the visit hours earlier, at about 10:15 a.m., but – as we often had to do – he had to cool his heels for several hours before the visit began. It was clear that the visit ended at about 2:20 p.m. and that Jackson re-entered the AC at about 3:00 p.m. – a typical time lag from visit to return. It was clear that later, Jackson was shot and killed when he ran from the Adjustment Center, and that

Johnny followed him out and dove into some bushes as the shots took down Jackson. But that was about it.

What wasn't clear? First, the testimony about George Jackson's hair. Guards Urbano Rubiaco and Kenneth McCray searched Jackson before he left the tier. Both said they saw him fluffing out his Afro with an "afro-pick" comb. A sergeant on another tier said he saw Jackson's hair piled high on his head before the visit, while another guard saw nothing unusual. Edward Fleming, the officer who searched Jackson before placing him in the visiting room, saw nothing unusual about his hair and described it as "neatly combed." But in a statement outside the grand jury hearing, Fleming claimed he searched Jackson's "hair bed", because he was concerned Jackson was wearing a wig, and found nothing.

When Jackson got back to the AC, he was searched again by Rubiaco and McCray. Two other officers testified that his hair was "fluffed out" more than usual. A third said that from a higher tier, Jackson's hair looked different: frizzy, and plastered down in back. But neither Rubiaco nor McCray noticed any difference. Jackson was strip-searched, so that he had to remove all his clothing, which was also searched. Nothing.

But then, in this version, George Jackson produced the gun. Rubiaco and McCray both testified that Rubiaco asked Jackson to run his hands through his hair, which Jackson did. After that, the guards testified, Jackson pulled off a wig covering his hair, produced the pistol from under the wig, and inserted a clip – no testimony about where it had come from – into the butt of the gun. Rubiaco testified that Jackson had *two* clips, dropped one, and inserted the other. And then,

Jackson demanded the guards open the cells, which they did. McCray testified that Jackson said, "This is it; the Dragon has come!"

What happened after that was a blur. All the cell doors on the tier were opened, and prisoners and guards were everywhere. North side and south side prisoners who had never seen each other before because a "control corridor" in the middle blocked the sides from each other, mingled together. When the dust had settled, six people were dead, including Jackson, shot as he ran outside from the Adjustment Center. Johnny was retrieved from the bushes, handcuffed, and left on the ground. After the fact, several people reported shots fired inside the AC, and two guards died from gunshot wounds. But who fired the shots and with what weapon remained unknown.

To the defense team, the prison version of the story never made much sense. How could a 9" by 5" pistol fit into the casing of a small tape recorder? Or into Jackson's "wig"? How did Jackson produce a clip of bullets, much less two, after being strip-searched? And how did he negotiate wig, pistol, and clip(s) so smoothly? Prisoners' rights groups had an alternate theory: The prison engaged in a conspiracy to place a gun within Jackson's reach; created an implausible story about the gun traveling in a tiny tape recorder and then a hair wig; and then saw things go awry when all of the cell doors on the tier opened.

In several ways, this version seemed more consistent with logic, though to many of us on the defense team, it too, without more information, was vague on the details and thus not entirely convincing. Neither Johnny nor his co-defendants were at confessional, and anyway, none of them could know what was happening on the tier except in their immediate vicinity. For most, including Johnny, they said that the trauma of the events seriously impaired their ability to recall. We knew that under the law we didn't have to convince anyone, because the burden was on the prosecution to prove its case "beyond a reasonable doubt." But we also knew it would be hard to get a jury in largely white, wealthy Marin County to truly embrace this high degree of proof. We were stuck with too many unknowns.

Unfair unknowns in our view, because how could we defend against these most serious charges when neither the indictment nor the grand jury transcript of proceedings gave us even a hint of who the DA claimed did what? From our perspective, this allowed the prosecution to make up who Johnny's supposed conspirators were as they went along.

My job

Around the beginning of July 1973, I went to my first all-hands meeting at the prison: all the defendants, their lawyers, law students, and investigators. Because the case had been stayed so early in the proceedings, most of the pre-trial motions had never been briefed or argued. Judge Broderick set a September filing deadline, which seemed like next week to us, given all the motions that needed to be researched and briefed. I quickly learned that when you are faced with five murder counts and other assorted life-sentence accusations, you don't leave anything aside when it comes to filing motions. There were over a dozen of them.

The defense lawyers divvied up tasks among them. David took on way more than his share, as did Deputy Public Defender Frank Cox, David Johnson's lawyer, working solo, a one-man workaholic force of nature. Mike Dufficy, the conservative ex-DA appointed to represent Fleeta Drumgo, was the big surprise. He soon realized that things in the case simply didn't add up, and he took to his job seriously. With the help of junior lawyer Joel Kirshenbaum and, by the fall, Angela Davis's former lawyer, Howard Moore, Jr., he did his share. Lynn Carman, an iconoclastic solo practitioner with an odd manner but a sharp legal mind, represented Hugo Pinell and took on some of the more esoteric issues.

Lou Hawkins, Luis Talamantez's lawyer, and Ted Lachelt, who was supposed to represent Willie Tate, were with Dufficy the three remaining lawyers from the Marin "usual suspects" network. Lou didn't do much, and Lachelt did absolutely nothing and often couldn't even be found. By 1975, Lachelt's license had been suspended and he never practiced law again. Fortunately, John Hill, for Willie, and Ruchell Magee's old lawyer Bob Carrow, for Luis, came in for trial. And by September, Charles Garry, Johnny's lawyer of choice, had associated with David in the case. But though he signed the motions along with David, Charles did none of the day-to-day work.

The Six had become fixated on the idea that the grand jury was not a jury of their peers. They were black and Latino, young and poor. But the grand jurors, appointed by the Superior Court judges, were white, and well-to-do or upper middle class, just like the profile of most of Marin County – if the poor sections in Marin City and the San Rafael Canal area were ignored, as they often were. Several of the lawyers saw this as a real longshot, but in this case, no stone was left unturned. David, though, became passionate about the idea, immediately seeing the unfairness in having no one from the Six's backgrounds on the grand jury. So, David volunteered to take on this massive effort. This motion would take an incredible amount of work because he and our investigators would have to prove the disparity between the jurors and the population.

But that meant that when it came to the other motions on our plate, David turned to me. And what did I know? Next to nothing. I'd driven a taxi during law school instead of summering with a law firm. But David, understaffed, didn't have much choice, and he pointed to the fact I had written an award-winning "moot court" brief back at NYU. That, I thought, was just an exercise, a game. *This* was the real thing. Recently, I found my timesheets from that summer. It's hard to believe how much time I spent researching and drafting, just to make sure I didn't completely screw things up.

My main task was to attack the indictment on two related grounds: First came a "demurrer." Johnny, like every other criminal defendant under our Constitution, had the right to learn what he had been accused of from the transcript of testimony before the grand jury that indicted or charged him, or, as the US Supreme Court put it, how the indictment "sufficiently apprises the defendant of what he must be prepared to meet" to defend himself. But we couldn't possibly tell from that indictment what specific crimes Johnny – or anyone else

– was accused of committing, or what evidence supported those crimes. So how could we know what to defend against? The remedy for this situation is a demurrer. Because Johnny's first lawyer was the only one who hadn't filed a demurrer before the case was stayed on appeal, we could still file it, and it became our first motion.

In my research I quickly found a then-recent California case very similar to ours. In People v. Jordan, an appeals court "sustained," or granted, a demurrer on an eighteen-count indictment, and the case was never re-filed. Coincidentally, the "Jordan" in that case was Angela Davis's sister, Fania. I wrote that, as in Jordan, the grand jury transcript – ours was 379 pages and covered twenty-five witnesses – failed to explain anything about "the particulars of the offenses charged or the particular results of [Johnny's] own alleged activities with anything approaching the 'sufficient clarity' required" by the Constitution. The indictment didn't accuse Johnny of murdering anyone. In fact, none of the Six were accused of committing a murder. Rather, the indictment seemed to rely on the idea that it was enough to show that they assisted or conspired with "other persons," or "members of the conspiracy" without saying who those people were. I thought our brief was right on the money.

We lost. Within fifteen days of the mid-August decision, the time allowed by law, we "took a writ." We lost that too. We were angry but not surprised.

We moved on, this time to the second attack on the evidence: that the transcript of testimony before the grand jury didn't present enough evidence to meet the standard of "probable cause" – the level of proof the DA had to show to get to trial. Because the lawyers said I had done such a great job on the Spain demurrer (putting aside our resounding defeat) I was put in charge of this motion too, this time on behalf of all six defendants.

As we approached the September 14, 1973, motions deadline, our small team was going full-blast around the clock: Ruth Astle, a young law student working as an investigator, Cathy Kornblith, who had been Johnny's investigator from the beginning; Dorinda Whitley Lowe, a nice young Marin County native and David's loyal secretary, willing to work sixteen-hour days if necessary; Bill Balin, my old law school buddy, free of encumbrances so that long hours were fine with him. And me and David. There were days close to the deadline when we slept on the floor of our ratty little office at 710 C Street, San Rafael. David, Ruth, and Cathy focused mostly on the attack of the make-up of the grand jury. Bill wrote a forty-eight-page, twenty-three-incident summary of the grand jury transcript. And I wrote the motion to dismiss for lack of probable cause.

At the same time, we also ground out other motions – all well-reasoned and well-briefed, though we knew we were unlikely to prevail:

- motion for a speedy trial under the California and US constitutions;
- motion to suppress evidence found in Johnny's cell, including maps of the prison yard and George Jackson's legal folders, and to suppress blood samples of the

first-tier prisoners, because the guards failed to get a warrant;

- petition for removal to federal court – a constitutional right that lasted all of two days before a US district court judge ordered us back to Marin;
- challenge to remove Judge Broderick from the case for bias against Johnny and the others, by showing that Broderick sat in Judge Haley's old courtroom and had written the inscription on the Civic Center memorial to the slain judge;
- motion to change venue to another county; and
- motion to "unshackle" the defendants because there was no proof at all of the need for chains in the courtroom, which I worked on with Lynn Carman.

The most important motion for Johnny and the others was the unshackling motion. It was the first issue the guys brought up at every all-hands meeting. Many motions were directly about the evidence, but nothing was more important to the Six. Sitting at counsel table in the high-security courtroom built for the case, they were forced to wear leg chains, a chain around their waists, another shackle that attached the waist chain to their chairs, which in turn were bolted to the floor, and two eight-inch-long chains from the waist chain to the handcuffs, making it almost impossible for them to extend their arms long enough to take notes on counsel table. They wore these chains, twenty-five pounds in all, from when they left the Adjustment Center to when they arrived back that night. The Six felt, not without reason, that Judge Broderick had allowed the shackles merely because of the circumstances of the charges against them, and without any showing that they were necessary for courtroom protection.

We lost that motion in November. We lost the challenge to Judge Broderick, the speedy trial motion and the change of venue motion. We "took a writ" and lost those too.

On January 17, 1974, we lost the other motions except for a small victory in the motion to suppress when the DA agreed not to use the blood samples taken from Johnny. We were planning to take a writ on the other motions when we got a major surprise.

There was one motion that Judge Broderick couldn't decide – the motion to set aside the indictment because of the improper selection of grand jury members. Because the Marin County Superior Court judges had chosen the grand jurors, they were required to recuse or remove themselves from considering this motion – the one the Six most wanted and that David, Cathy, and Ruth worked so hard on. We hoped that we'd at least get a fair judge, unbiased by Marin County being home to San Quentin. A visiting judge from rural Nevada County named Vernon Stoll was brought in to conduct an evidentiary hearing on the issue of whether the grand jury's failure to have representatives of people of color and what he called "the low wage blue collar class" made the indictment constitutionally invalid.

At the beginning of the hearing, I was sitting in the courtroom when Judge Stoll did an amazing thing. The Six, chained and bolted to the ground as always, complained as they did at almost every hearing that their chains and handcuffs were too tight, and pleaded with the judge – as Johnny had since his second court appearance – to come down and examine the handcuffs himself without relying on the San Quentin guards. So, the elderly judge lifted himself off the bench and went to examine the defendants' wrists, then turned to the guard captain and told him to loosen the cuffs. The Six, to a man, loved this, grateful simply to be treated like humans. Had *nothing else* happened with that judge, he would have won the day.

But something else did happen, and on January 17, the same day that Judge Broderick denied all our other motions, Judge Stoll granted David's motion to quash the indictment. Once again, the case was immediately stayed. We were ecstatic. We knew the motion was a longshot, despite the logic of our arguments. But actually getting a complete dismissal? We could hardly believe it. All of us, defendants, lawyers, and the entire legal team were overjoyed.

Spain v. Procunier

By that time, I had finished up my final draft of the *habeas corpus* petition addressing the unconstitutional conditions in the Adjustment Center. Once the trial motions had been submitted and the writ petitions filed, in the last days of 1973, I was finally able to turn my full attention to this effort that was so important to the Six, with Johnny once again acting as spokesperson for the others. I'd been well prepped for this task not only from my conversations with Johnny and the other defendants, but by my having worked on the unshackling motion.

Outside *pro bono* lawyers, including the estimable Mark
Merin, had agreed they would step in to represent the Six once
the draft was completed, but the original filed petition, written by Ruchell Magee, made little sense despite his reputation
as a jailhouse lawyer. It needed a rewrite from scratch.

Just before I returned to work on the *habeas corpus*
petition, I got some help from an interesting place: a select
committee of the California Assembly. In the fall of 1973, they
issued a report titled "Administrative Segregation in California's Prisons," tellingly subtitled "Alias: The Hole, Lockup,
Solitary Confinement and the Adjustment Center." On page
2 of their report, their summary on adjustment centers stated
that "the Department of Corrections not only stumbled in
achieving their [social services] objective, but fell flat on their
face." They concluded that the department "not only segre-
gates these men, but oppresses and represses them as well." I
realized the obvious: This report could be a huge help.

It was also helpful to talk to Joseph Satten, MD, who was
then one of the nation's foremost forensic psychiatrists – the
chief of criminal psychology at the famed Menninger Clinic
and also the consulting psychiatrist at the federal penitentiary
at Leavenworth, Kansas, where he consulted with Truman
Capote on his non-fiction classic In Cold Blood. Satten had
just moved to California and, coincidentally and most help-
fully for me, "Sleepy Joe" (as everyone in his medical school
class called him for his thoughtful but very deliberate speech)
was a med school classmate and good friend of my dad's. He
had a wealth of knowledge about the conditions of confinement and the practical effects of deprivation that prisoners like
Johnny suffered.

The biggest help was being able to spend a lot more time going out to San Quentin to visit Johnny on my own in that grimy little visiting room. Johnny reminded me repeatedly of all the horrors of their confinement. We talked at great length about the sensory deprivation he faced, the psychological damage he suffered, and the institutional inevitability of the guards' brutality, just as Phil Zimbardo had witnessed. We discussed at length academic studies – some that he found, others I was given – that evaluated the effects of sensory deprivation, confinement in isolation, and limitations of motion caused by chains. He also had me read an "autobiography" he had hand-written, which brought home that he had been in a state of shock when moving from a white Mississippi home to a black Los Angeles one.

Johnny coordinated with me by drafting, by hand and in his own words, an extraordinary eight-legal-page, twenty-eight-paragraph declaration that was to accompany my final draft. No one edited this document; there was no need. And its eloquence spoke volumes. With so many issues, his declaration focused the most attention on being chained. It ended with this comment: "there is no case on record where a lower species animal has been chained up and placed in punitive conditions for over two years" as he had been. This resolute insistence that he was being chained like an animal would eventually be his path to freedom.

When my final draft in *Spain v. Procunier* was ready, in mid-January 1974, it was time to have it vetted by David and the other lawyers. It started with the formal prison "classifications" of Johnny's housing (the AC) and custody (maximum security) being "illegal and unconstitutional," "without due process of law," and "violative of the Department of Corrections' own procedures" because they were solely based on a case in which he was presumed innocent. Then the "Shackles and Restraints" section: cruel and unusual punishment; denying Johnny the effective assistance of counsel the Constitution requires, because they were so intrusive that they interfered with his ability to communicate with his lawyers. Then lack of exercise; unfair disciplinary write-ups; lack of visiting privileges and medical care. Then facts: details of the shackles; his history of good behavior; even that he couldn't wear prison-issue jeans to visits, and had to don a white jumpsuit instead. Then dates, times, and results of his hearings to try to leave the AC:

> September 18, 1973: "Subject's behavior while assigned to Segregation has been conforming" but criminal charges are noted and "Segregation is retained."
>
> October 19, 1973: (page A10): "Retain in Segregation pending legal procedures."
>
> December 17, 1973 (page A11): In its entirety: "Member of S.Q. 6. Militant."

Folded in and referenced throughout were the eloquent statements from Johnny's declaration, and my brief on the law.

But first, before showing the draft to the lawyers, I wanted to show it to Johnny. By the time I brought it to Johnny, he didn't feel the need to read it right then. Instead, we talked about other things: Zimbardo, his L.A. family, the last books he'd read. By then, I think, he trusted me to get it right.

One of the most important things I learned from my relationship with Johnny is the essential nature of trust. Trust is rarely earned easily, and almost never earned superficially. When you meet someone in that visiting room, just saying "trust me" is a pretty stupid thing to do. I mean, why should he trust me? As for the temptation to say, "I know exactly how you feel," that's even worse. I didn't know, and Johnny knew that I didn't know. Lawyers can empathize, "get it" intellectually. But can we put ourselves in the shoes of our clients? Johnny was locked up and locked down, chained, and literally enslaved, an African American man in a white-run prison system. No matter how empathic I might feel, his experience is not something I could ever fully "know."

As I finished the petition, I was readying for my last law school semester, where I'd spend fulltime in the Marin County courts and, under the rules that existed back then, be able to do contested hearings in criminal cases and get a real hands-on education. The Six case had been stayed, so while I was still in Marin County, it wasn't until the following January that I returned to Johnny's case. By then, the *habeas* case had morphed into a federal civil rights action before the Honorable Alfonzo J. Zirpoli. My job became to help on briefing and developing and preparing witnesses – psychiatrists and other experts on prisons and confinement – to testify at the upcoming trial set for the fall.

In December 1975 and January 1976, Judge Zirpoli issued two strong opinions. His December opinion described at length the facts relating to the confinement of the six plaintiffs

– for in this case they were plaintiffs and the prison system the defendant. His second opinion reached these determinations:

> That the use of neck chains constitutes cruel and unusual punishment and defendants ... shall immediately and hereafter desist and refrain from the use of neck chains;

> That the use of other mechanical restraints other than handcuffs constitutes cruel and unusual punishment unless an inmate ... present[s] an actual or imminent threat... and defendants ... shall immediately hereafter desist and refrain from the use of other mechanical restraints, except handcuffs...;

> That the denial of fresh air and regular outdoor exercise and recreation constitutes cruel and unusual punishment and plaintiffs [shall have] at least one hour a day of outdoor exercise or recreation for five days a week....

By the time of Judge Zirpoli's decision, I had moved on. In one form or another, *Spain v. Procunier*, stayed alive for thirteen years, allowing prisoners' lawyers to test the limits of the constitutionality of prison confinements before a series of federal judges.

The Six case eventually came back from the Court of Appeal once again, with Judge Stoll's decision to throw out the indictment overturned. Johnny succeeded in getting Charles Garry to be his counsel, and David was relieved of his responsibilities. During the hiatus in the case, I spend a good deal of time with Charles, and he offered me the job of "second chair" in the trial. But I was concerned about Charles' fading acumen, and decided, regretfully, that I would be better off taking up my mentor David Mayer's offer to be his partner. My law school classmate Dennis Riordan, who became California's best criminal appeals lawyer largely as a result of his efforts on behalf of Johnny, took my place. And I went back to 710 C Street, San Rafael, to learn how to be a trial lawyer.

EPILOGUE

People v. Stephen Bingham, et al., Marin County Superior Court Case #4094, commonly known as the San Quentin Six case, eventually went to trial and was, at that time, the longest criminal trial in the history of California, lasting seventeen months. Jury deliberations took over 100 days. The defense argued that it was the six defendants who were victims of a conspiracy – to kill George Jackson – and also put on a great deal of testimony about psychological harm and sensory deprivation. Philip Zimbardo was the first witness called by Charles Garry in Johnny Spain's defense.

The verdicts on the Six were rendered in August 1976. They resulted in convictions on only six of the almost fifty felony counts. Three defendants, Fleeta Drumgo, Luis Talamantez, and Willie Tate, were acquitted on all charges. David Johnson was convicted of a minor assault – kicking a guard – and was almost immediately released. Hugo Pinell, known to all as Yogi, faced testimony from two guards who testified that he had slit their throats. He was convicted of deadly assault by a life prisoner, punishable by life in prison.

Three of the Six have lived the rest of their lives quietly and under the radar. *Luis Talamantez* is a poet in Southern California. *Willie Tate* has also led a quiet life. Despite a Los Angeles Times story that he had died decades ago in prison, he is very much alive and still breaks bread with his lawyer and close friend John Hill once a month, COVID restrictions permitting. After *David Johnson*'s release, for a time he became an investigator with the Marin Public Defender's office, where his attorney Frank Cox worked until his retirement.

Fleeta Drumgo was shot and killed in November 1979, supposedly because of an alleged affiliation with prison gangs. *Yogi Pinell* spent the years after his conviction in continued solitary confinement, mostly at Pelican Bay, California's most secure prison. Two weeks after he was released to the "mainline," the general population in Folsom Prison in 2015, he was murdered, ostensibly by members of the white Aryan Brotherhood.

Stephen Bingham, the scion of a wealthy and politically prominent New England family (his grandfather was both a senator and governor of Connecticut) fled the country for thirteen years following the events of August 21, 1971. After returning to the States and surrendering, he was put on trial in the summer of 1986. While prosecutors pointed to his flight as proof of guilt, his lawyers argued that he was set up by a conspiracy within the prison to slip George Jackson a gun and kill him. Bingham was acquitted of all charges and returned to the practice of law. He retired in 2015.

Ruchell Magee eventually pled guilty to "simple" kidnapping just before his retrial. But that charge too carried a life sentence. Despite his repeated efforts to set aside his guilty plea, he remains in prison, where he has been since 1963. *Gary W. Thomas* was paralyzed from the waist down by the shots fired during the 1970 courthouse shootout. He returned to work only five months later and was soon appointed to the Marin County bench. He served on the Municipal and Superior Courts for twenty-six years. We tried to avoid bringing Black defendants into his court. *Angela Davis*'s career and celebrity flourished after her acquittal, and she remains today, at seventy-eight, an activist, feminist, writer, and thinker, still in great demand as a public speaker.

Charles Garry went from the Six case to defend what was left of the People's Temple – the cult led by Jim Jones that emigrated from San Francisco to Jonestown, Guyana, and then suffered over 900 deaths when Jones told his minions to commit "revolutionary suicide" by drinking a fruit drink laced with cyanide – resulting in the popular expression "drinking the Kool-Aid." Garry initially alleged a government conspiracy. After an ongoing quarrel with his co-counsel Mark Lane, he faded from the case. It was his last high-profile case. He went into semi-retirement and died at age eighty-one in 1991.

David Ross Mayer, after being replaced by Garry in the Six case, resumed a criminal defense practice in Marin County and later in San Francisco. I became his law partner on January 1, 1975, two weeks after my admission to the bar. David was one of those rare people who everyone – men and women – loved. He was also something *very* rare: a natural trial lawyer. His big-bear bushy beard, shaggy hair, tall physique and engaging smile not only allowed him to make friends easily but seemed to mesmerize jurors in the courtroom. He continued to be a superb prison-rights lawyer, responsible for many *habeas corpus* petitions that resulted in the release of prisoners, and successfully handling several prison murder cases. Included among them was the case of Earl Gibson and Lawrence Justice.

Gibson and Justice had also been accused of the 1971 murder of a San Quentin guard. They were convicted in 1973 but the conviction was reversed by a federal appeals court. In 1981, David, representing Larry Justice, and his co-counsel, Doron Weinberg, challenged the restrictions placed on the public's access to the Marin County courtroom where the trial would take place. Those restrictions did *not* include shackling the defendants, because in 1976, too late to help the San Quentin Six, the state Supreme Court had ruled that "the imposition of physical restraints in the absence of a record showing of violence or a threat of violence ... will be deemed to constitute an abuse...." But the Gibson-Justice trial judge signed an order allowing the Marin Sheriff's Office to use a metal detector at the courtroom door, pat-search all those entering as spectators, require proof of identification, and take a photograph of each person.

David and Doron took a writ. They argued that these restrictions denied their clients due process, including the right to a speedy and *public* trial. The appeals court agreed: the restrictions were not appropriate unless the defendants were allowed a full hearing to explore whether they were actually necessary under the specific facts of the case. The trial judge who was reversed was Richard Breiner, who in 1971 had represented Fleeta Drumgo on his right-to-counsel appeal.

David and I went on practicing law together for nine and a half years. By then we had both become bar-certified specialists in criminal law. I was beginning to branch out into other trial work. David was happier sticking to criminal law, and successfully defended Larry Justice, winning an acquittal. In 1984, he moved his office back up to Marin County, home to both him and San Quentin. In the years after we separated, personal challenges led David into dark periods of depression. After a couple of years of estrangement, I invited him to join me on a case I had in St. Louis. We went tromping off to federal court with our huge, hippie-style trial briefcases and our full beards, just like the old days. The judge definitely did not appreciate our Left Coast image, but it brought both of us great joy.

By 1988, though, David had sunk deeper into depression while litigating another prison murder case involving alleged members of the Black Guerilla Family, a group founded by George Jackson. This time he couldn't handle the pressure. I had to help him withdraw from representation. When I appeared for him, the judge on the case called me up to the bench to express her concern. David continued to spiral down despite the efforts of all his friends. Early in the morning on February 6, 1989, he climbed up a hillside overlooking the 101 Freeway a mile south of the Marin

David Mayer in Nicaragua, 1986

Civic Center. He dictated a ninety-minute-long cassette tape to me, and then shot himself in the head. He died instantly.

Johnny Spain was convicted of two counts of murder and one of conspiracy to commit murder. There was no proof offered that Johnny had killed anyone. Rather, the state argued that he had conspired with other persons. His close connection to George Jackson, membership in the Black Panther Party, and his run from the Adjustment Center were apparently enough to convince a jury that he must have done *something*.

The sufficiency of evidence in Johnny's conviction, a low threshold, was upheld in the California appeals courts. But Dennis Riordan, who came in to "second chair" the trial with Charles Garry and had moved on to do criminal appeals, took up the case. He filed a writ of *habeas corpus* in federal district court. District court judge Thelton Henderson threw out the conviction in 1982 because there had been improper private communications between the judge and one of the jurors that went to an essential issue. The federal appeals court agreed, but in December 1983, the US Supreme Court, in a highly unusual peremptory "By the Court" opinion, reversed the reversal.

Riordan, undaunted, went to Judge Henderson again, this time arguing that Judge Broderick's requirement that Johnny carry twenty-five pounds of chains during all court proceedings violated due process. Dennis had a huge amount of evidence, including expert testimony about the physiological, psychological, and humiliating effects of the chains. Doctors also verified injuries to Johnny's back and rectal area that were severely exacerbated by the chains. But the best evidence came from Johnny himself.

Johnny spent six years repeatedly raising the issue of his being chained in the courtroom: from his second court appearance to his sentencing, when he made an extraordinarily eloquent statement: He was an animal, rendered so by the chains he wore, to the extent that he was unable to participate in his own defense or to communicate with his lawyers.

On two occasions Johnny swore under penalty of perjury that he'd rather give up his constitutional right to be present at his own trial than sit in constant pain chained in the courtroom. On November 30, 1973, he submitted this handwritten motion:

> I would now like to move this court for an order allowing me to remain at San Quentin Prison rather than be brought to this courtroom. I am often chained for 9 or 10 hours a day while in court and I am physically unable and unwilling to endure the pain of the chains digging into my skin, and of having blood-flow infringed upon. … I'm under physical compulsion to make a decision, a choice between being in utterly unnecessary pain or giving up constitutional rights. I give them (the rights) up /s/ johnny spain.

On March 18, 1975, the week before trial, another handwritten plea:

> I, johnny larry spain, depose and say: …. First and foremost, I have been continuously subjected to anywhere from 7 to 10 hours of being chained and shackled, sometimes to the floor (if in the holding cell), and always to a fixed position if in the courtroom, while most of the time being in pain and/or under heavy medication; in either

instance I have found it almost impossible to understand the proceedings and the court has constantly refused to remedy ... the conditions.... [¶] I do not wish to be present at the hearing on March 18, 1975, which means, in sum: that I'm forced to select due process or severe pain....

Judge Henderson had extensive evidence taken and then, once again, threw out Johnny's conviction, on the grounds that not only were the chains unwarranted punishment and prejudicial for the jury, but the pain associated with the chains had indeed, as Johnny had long insisted, denied him his constitutional right to assist his counsel in his own defense. In August 1989, the appellate court again agreed: "Spain was forced to attend the trial for seventeen months in a physically and mentally debilitated condition." The majority opinion cited fifteen occasions even before the trial had begun when Johnny complained about pain, often asking to be removed from a hearing because of his discomfort.

Johnny & me, March 10, 1988, at a gas station in Fairfield CA on our way home.

On March 10, 1988, four days before Judge Henderson's second dismissal was argued on appeal, Johnny Spain walked out of prison in Vacaville, paroled by order of a Los Angeles judge. I was there to meet him along with my first wife, Naomi Weinstein, investigator Cathy Kornblith, and Dennis Riordan and his daughter. Cathy and Naomi and I had each put up our houses to get him released on bail. I drove Johnny down to San Francisco, where his parole plan was to live in our house.

Johnny's gradual transformation from prison radical to enlightened peacemaker was itself a remarkable story. It didn't happen overnight, but a bit at a time. A few months after his San Quentin Six conviction, Johnny was moved to the lower-security Duell Vocational Institute in Tracy, at the north end of California's Central Valley, the place where he had first been incarcerated. Tracy was in the midst of a race war, and Johnny was new to the general "main line" prison population. As a group of Black prisoners were moving on a smaller group of whites on his tier, Johnny found himself in the middle, taking a position with the Black group that he did not attack innocent people. He had nothing but his "rep" as a "hero"– Black Panther, brother to George Jackson, "guard-killer." That rep and the charismatic force of his presence were enough to quell the violence.

Johnny continued to evolve as he was moved from Tracy to the prison at Vacaville. Apprenticed to his electrician step-father as a kid, he became an electrician again. Among his jobs was fixing the cell lights after prisoners committed suicide by hanging, using a strip of bedsheet hung from the light fixture – something that happened far too often. Johnny figured out a way to install the lights so that nothing could be looped around them. After the prison authorities realized that, he was given more freedom to move about the prison on electrical jobs. He was a great athlete, and that plus the respect he was accorded enabled him to convince prisoners to field integrated football teams inside the prison walls – something virtually unheard of anywhere. He was soon Vacaville's most important peacemaker.

Importantly, he let go of the idea that when he killed Joe Long at a bus stop in 1967 – his original conviction – it somehow was not all his own fault, and he acknowledged it as the life he had taken unnecessarily. This is one topic we had never discussed at San Quentin. But when I came to visit him, often with my boys in tow so they could play basketball with him on a four-foot-high children's hoop in the visiting room, Johnny would talk about it freely and honestly. He had always been charismatic, but now the rest of his personality was channeled towards healing – both himself and others. And my kids loved the basketball games, always filled with laughter as Johnny swatted away their shots with a smile.

As his reputation among Black, white, and Latino prisoners grew, so did respect from the prison staff, even knowing his San Quentin history. When Judge Henderson overturned his conviction for the second time, all that stood between Johnny and freedom was parole from his original conviction. Cathy Kornblith went to work gathering letters in support of Johnny's parole. Many came from "important" people outside the prison system. But the most impressive letters were those from prison guards, over seventy in all, that lauded Johnny and his behavior. One guard who knew one of the men who died on that August day in San Quentin wrote that he would be proud to have Johnny come to dinner at his home with his wife and daughters.

Despite all this, the parole board hearings resulted in denials. So, Cathy and Dennis put together statistical proof that, virtually without exception, every prisoner convicted of a crime similar to Johnny's original offense had been released on parole. Dennis set a hearing in front of a Los Angeles judge and argued that it was time to let him go. The judge agreed.

Cathy and I had already set up bail on the Six case for Johnny with Judge Henderson, so we all took off for Vacaville to meet him. That night, we celebrated at my home. I know a lot of people were there – lawyers, investigators, many people from "the movement" – but outside of Johnny, Cathy, Dennis, and Angela Davis, I can't really recall who. Maybe too much alcohol.

My daughter, Maya, had agreed – to the extent that a two-year-old can agree to anything – to temporarily give up her room to Johnny. He had her giggling instantly and she loved him from the start. We got a phone installed for him so he could have some privacy. I remember he wanted to go downtown the very next day, so we handed him a map of the city but lost touch with him for several hours. He called from somewhere near Union Square. My wife asked, "Are you lost?" and he replied, "No, I know exactly where I am: right here!" After we stopped laughing, we managed to direct him back home.

March 10, when Johnny was released, was a Thursday. That Sunday, we did something we'd been talking about for years. I took Johnny with me to our Sunday morning pick-up basketball game at Miraloma Park. I insisted, for the only time in twenty-plus years playing in this game ruled by equitable behavior – no fights, no "winners" keep the court, everyone switches teams each game – that I be allowed to play with

Johnny posting me up,
Miraloma Park, SF, 1989

Johnny the whole morning. Not surprisingly, Johnny was the best player out there. Most surprisingly, I played the best I have ever played. Every perfect pass from Johnny resulted in a basket. Every screen, every give-and-go, worked. It was bliss! It was the first of many, many hoops Sundays, and Johnny became one of the most beloved players out there.

Johnny's years since his release have had ups and downs. He lectured at Stanford and became a counsellor at the San Francisco jail. He married a beautiful and accomplished photographer and was blessed with a precocious daughter. But when you go to prison as a teenager and remain there for twenty-one years, adjusting to life on the outside at almost forty is one of the most difficult things imaginable. At the toughest times, it seemed he had a unique ability to tread water in quicksand. But people loved him, and when times were roughest, they came to his aid. Once, twenty guys who played ball with him on Sundays came to my house to offer encouragement and a safe place. One, an assistant United States attorney who had just torn his Achilles tendon, limped up my steep stairs on crutches. Of all the things that happened that night, that was what impressed Johnny the most.

Today, Johnny remains as he was, trying his best and succeeding his fair share of the time. Now over seventy, he has a longtime life partner and decent contact with his kids, and he maintains his equanimity and curiosity about life. He remains close in my heart.

As for me: There's no question that my San Quentin Six experience had a huge effect on me. I changed from a liberal suburban white boy into a radicalized activist adult. In hindsight, though, I know that this was just the beginning of my evolution to better understanding, one that continues to this day. Part of this evolution centered on race, of course. But there were other eye-opening effects of this experience.

Perhaps the most significant was my feeling about judges and the justice system. In my privileged adolescent upbringing, judges were friends of my parents who joined them for evenings at the theater. If not all impartial, they were at least presumptively so, meting out justice as they saw fit in a dispassionate and objective way. I thought that the court system "bends towards justice," as Dr. King said. But I was blind to the first part of his quote: "The arc of the moral universe is long." The Six Case was a graphic demonstration of an arc not yet bent nearly enough. For there was little justice meted out in that case, managed by a judge who was neither impartial nor objective.

In hindsight, this seems both obvious and inevitable. The judges my parents knew were all white, mostly from similar immigrant backgrounds, brought up with a "liberal" philosophy of America as the promised land and the land of promise. They were, as we all are, products of their experience. And that

experience did not really provide much of a path to enlightenment. Of course, there were exceptions, like the kindly retired
Nevada County judge who stepped down from the bench to
examine the chains and handcuffs restraining the Six, and
especially Judge Alfonso Zirpoli, as "woke" a judge as existed
in the mid-1970's.

But even the most enlightened judge worked in a justice
system that was dysfunctional. The San Quentin Six case is a
textbook example of a justice system gone awry. The indictment accused the defendants of conspiring with a person or
persons unknown to commit murder and assault, impossible
charges to defend when the co-conspirators are phantoms.
The state went to extraordinary lengths to prosecute this case
to the fullest, including building a high-security courtroom
at the Marin County Civic Center, with a bulletproof plexiglass screen separating spectators from the judge, lawyers, and
defendants. Appeals twice stopped the case in its tracks. Meanwhile, the prosecution teams fought every battle, seemingly
blinded by its perceived need for convictions. And the result?
Five of the six defendants went free, four with acquittals and
one on probation. No one was convicted of murder except
Johnny, whose conviction was twice overturned. Ultimately,
just one person was convicted of a serious crime. And the
seventh (and only white) defendant never spent a day in jail.

But for the six defendants of color, their lengthy pre-trial
incarcerations, coupled with the repeated and routine denials
of parole based on the presumption of guilt on their unproven
pending charges – charges that they would never be convicted
of – were the facts of their lives. Even after his conviction was

overturned the second time and despite the support of dozens of prison employees, Johnny Spain was denied parole by the prison system, and obtained release only by order of a court after twenty-one years in prison. Justice was not served.

As I look at things today, nearly a half-century after I met the San Quentin Six, it seems that this pattern repeats itself more often than it changes. From Trayvon Martin's death in 2012 and George Zimmerman's subsequent acquittal, through many other deaths with no one held responsible until, finally, Derek Chauvin's conviction for murdering George Floyd in mid-2021, the arc of justice has done little bending.

2

Every Case is the San Quentin 6 Case – Practicing Law with David Mayer

People of the State of California v. Otis Barrow

People of the State of California v. Tuan Tran, et al.

The San Quentin Six case taught me many things, but none more important than the following principle, which would affect the rest of my lawyering: In taking a case, a lawyer should do every-thing possible – everything within human reason – to prevail. I learned many other things as well that have affected both my life as a lawyer and also my development as a human being. But first and foremost: Leave no stone unturned on behalf of your client.

My added bonus was practicing law with David Ross Mayer, an extraordinary experience. David was brilliantly intuitive, so we had few of the hard-and-fast usual rules that they teach you in law school Trial Practice courses. At the same time, though, he was exceptionally well-prepared. And in the interests of his client, he never backed down from a fight. As our practice together developed, we soon came upon several guiding principles, some of which became "office policy" that stood us in good stead.

And I was learning some life lessons. First that racial animus and resulting bias went well beyond the Six case, and second, that the animus was by no means limited to Black people. Growing up in an environment where I was taught to treat all people fairly no matter their race, religion, or background, I still needed to internalize the lesson that this perspective was definitely not the prevailing one either in our justice system or in our nation.

My first days as a lawyer

David Mayer impressed me from the start. I think it began with our prison visits. When we got to San Quentin to visit Johnny Spain, we usually tried to get to the prison by 9:00 a.m. to make sure we got an early start, because of the delays we were subjected to by the staff. I remember several times when our visits were delayed for so long that it seemed we wouldn't get them at all. Round about 11:00 a.m. or so, David would start making phone calls from the pay phone in the visiting room. He'd start with the "watch commander," the lieutenant or captain in charge of prison administration that day. He seemed to know all their first names and used them in addressing them – something that undoubtedly ticked them off. Yet it almost always brought results. Once we were delayed so long and put off by every prison official David could find that he called Director of Prisons Raymond Procunier in Sacramento. Incredibly, David got him on the phone. "Ray," he said, "we've been out here since 9:15 this morning waiting to see Johnny Spain and we're still waiting at 2:15. We're not leaving until we see him, so why don't you make it happen?" Johnny showed up ten minutes later.

I think the prison officials were a bit afraid of David. But I was in awe. I knew – and I think they sensed – that his always friendly manner belied a will of steel. It is often said that great trial lawyers must have a "killer instinct." David certainly had that, but the best part was that the other side almost never knew it until the end. He killed 'em with kindness. He once told me that his ideal scenario was to "slip the knife in between their ribs and *twist* it without them ever knowing what happened." Cold blooded? Perhaps. But both descriptive and effective.

When it came to our law practice, David and I applied the same principles we'd learned in the San Quentin Six case. That meant litigating each case as if it were the most serious and important case ever. In a way, David and I had both "grown up" in that case: I because that was all I knew, and David because he'd learned that it was the most effective way to fight. So when, after a year and a half of practicing together, we were retained by the father of a young man named Tuan Tran to represent his son on a shooting case that occurred in a crowded parking lot, we applied those principles by subpoenaing every local kid who was there at the time.

But before telling that story, let me back up to early 1974, when Judge Stoll threw out the San Quentin Six indictment. I was fortunate to spend my entire last semester doing criminal cases under the supervision of the Marin County Public Defender's Office. I was equally fortunate to be given several serious cases to work on: an arson and two assaults with a deadly weapon, one involving a shooting. Some of the senior PDs simply had no patience for supervision. Prepping my hearing questions to cross-examine the alleged shooting victim, I went to my supervising PD for help. He asked me where the "Vic" had been wounded. I told him in the calf. "Plead your guy out to poor marksmanship," said the deputy, and went back to his own work.

I greatly admired Frank Cox, the deputy PD on the Six case. He was friendly, but as he was always overworked, he had little spare time. Fortunately, I got plenty of help from two young public defenders, Gaile O'Connor and Glenn Becker. Gaile mentored me through the arson case and helped when I was freaked out about the shooting case. Glenn became a lifelong friend, and several years later we tried a case together that's described in a later chapter of this volume.

So, when in February 1975, a whole six weeks after my bar admission, Judge David Baty appointed me as counsel on a felony burglary case, I figured I was ready. When I went to trial in April, though, it was an extremely scary experience. I knew all the things that I'd learned. But I had little idea about all the things I *didn't* know, like how to get discovery of the prosecutor's file early in the case, and how to get the best possible instructions to the jury – vitally important issues. I was very lucky that the jury hung 9-3 to convict. The DA reduced the charges to a minor misdemeanor with no jail time; my client pled guilty and was happy.

As for David, the fact that he was intuitive by no means meant that he was foolhardy. Just the opposite. He was excellent at "making a record," another vital trial lawyer skill. In our first couple of years, we represented many clients trying to get paroled under a sentencing law that gave them an "indeterminate" sentence, which could be, for example, from one to fourteen years. His method to convince parole boards to release our clients – and sometimes convince courts on *habeas corpus* petitions when the boards refused – was to methodically show that when the board denied parole and advised the prisoner to do X Program one year and Y Program the next, and the client had done each one successfully, there was no longer a basis for keeping him in custody. In effect, we succeeded by using the prison's own regulations against them.

David taught me how to do the same thing with cops in criminal cases. A typical example was a simple series of questions about the importance of officer's police report: "Officer, if there was anything important that occurred, you would write it down in your report, right?" ("Of course.") And then: "Can you show me in the report where you say Mr. Jones had a knife?" The cop couldn't, of course, because it wasn't there. I knew from law school to avoid the deadly open-ended question "Why didn't you write it down?" But by using the officer's own best tool against him (back then, the cops were almost all men), we gained a lot of credibility at the expense of the police.

Despite his strong will, he also had a cautious side. In June of that first year, I was put in charge of a reckless driving case. My client, Reza, was riding a motorcycle up the main artery between San Rafael, the county seat, and the next town. He made a U-turn from a left turn lane without the left-turn signal turning green, likely because his bike wasn't heavy enough to trip the sensor plate under the pavement. Then he sped up to ninety-plus miles per hour on the way back. A patrol car behind him gave chase. When Reza got back to San Rafael and hit some traffic, he slowed down considerably. But the policeman busted him for driving recklessly at over ninety miles per hour.

The DA offered a deal that called for five days in jail, which Reza and I both thought was unfair, especially because drunk drivers, even if very drunk, didn't go to jail on a first offense. Of course, they were mostly white, and Reza was Middle Eastern. But I was convinced that Reza would be found not guilty because when he hit traffic, he *slowed down* and thus wasn't "reckless." David was not so sure and urged caution. He emphasized that my affirmative story might be pretty good, but what were all the *negatives* out there? This was based on an essential tenet that I had not yet learned: The strengths of your case are not nearly as important as the weaknesses. Don't try cases from strength. Rather, figure out the hundred things that can go wrong and try to eliminate all of them.

I listened, but we went to trial anyway, in front of an all-white jury, and we won. Perhaps I was lucky.

By the time we had been practicing together for a year, David and I developed some basic principles. One that I was particularly proud of, being a complete newbie, was that if eight lawyers said X and Y strategy would never work and David and I agreed that it would, we always voted for our way. One person could screw up and screw up badly. But if we two agreed after a thorough review, we'd assume the consensus was wrong and our own conclusion was right.

We made another important principle into our "office policy," after the Marin DA made its own rule: that if the defendant did not take the plea-bargaining deal offered before the preliminary (probable cause) hearing, the DA would make the plea deal steeper in terms of time incarcerated and probation conditions. This was manifestly unfair in our opinion. Our clients had a right to test the prosecution's evidence and shouldn't be penalized for seeing that they had at least probable cause. So, we came up with our Mayer & Zitrin "policy" and sent a letter to the DA's office articulating it: If a plea deal got worse after the preliminary hearing, we would refuse to accept it and go to trial. We couldn't really enforce this, of course, because we had an ethical obligation to act in the best interests of our clients. But it seemed like the right position to take with the DA.

As it happened, right after we advised the DA of this principle, we had a burglary case in which the defendant, Darren Marcello, and his younger brother, an underage kid whose case was in juvenile court, were accused of burglarizing a house and stealing a stereo. Before the preliminary hearing, the DA offered Darren a pretty sweet deal – plead to a felony that could be reduced to a misdemeanor after probation and spend only ninety days in jail. Darren turned the deal down. In the felony court department, the deal had escalated considerably: plead guilty to a felony sentence and then suspending the prison sentence only on condition of doing a year of county jail time. By imposing the prison sentence first, Darren would forever have the felony on his record. But the price of crim-law poker having gone up, we turned the deal down and headed for trial, with David in charge and me as back-up.

We had the seeming misfortune of getting Robert Millard, one of the county's most conservative old-line Republican judges, for trial. But as the evidence came in, it was obvious that Darren's younger brother was the one who broke into the home. David argued that Darren had gone into the home only to retrieve his younger brother's leather jacket that the kid had left inside. Still, the jury came back with a guilty verdict. The case was set for sentencing while Darren remained free on bail.

At sentencing, the District Attorney argued for hard state prison time. David argued instead that Darren had barely committed a crime. Judge Millard looked down at Darren, then at the DA, and ruled that he was exercising his discretion to reduce the conviction right then to a misdemeanor, and he put Darren on probation with *no* jail time. We got a conviction but won the case – *and* the point that we would not accept the DA's new policy about plea bargains getting worse after the preliminary hearing. They never tried to apply that rule to us again.

Darren Marcello caught a big break. But he was a white kid, not so different from the majority of kids in Marin County, maybe including Judge Millard's sons. In contrast, Gary James, the defendant in my first trial, was a black kid, and even worse in the eyes of the DA, he and his co-defendant had driven up to beautiful Sausalito from the largely poor black community of East Palo Alto. I remember vividly a meeting I had with the deputy DA assigned to that case a few weeks before trial. We were in the corridor in front of his office when he asked, "Why do you want to defend this guy?" "Our problem up here," he continued, "is these people who don't belong here coming in from outside and committing crimes right in front of us." Until then, I hadn't really understood that the racism I saw in the San Quentin Six case was systemic, and that it was applied with equal force to "these people" invading our nice white county. It was pretty damn disgusting.

Otis Barrow and "furtive gestures."

But by then, this strong systemic bias should have been obvious to me after Otis Barrow's arrest. Otis was a former client of David's who lived in a rundown motel in San Rafael known for widespread drug use. He called us after being arrested by a highway patrolman driving south on Interstate 5 in Willows, about 140 miles north of San Francisco. Willows really was in the middle of nowhere: the county seat of Glenn County, a town of 6,000 souls in a county of 22,000 people spread over 1,300 square miles. After Otis was pulled over and searched, the CHP officer found a balloon of heroin in his pants pocket. Back then, it was common to see small quantities of heroin bought and sold wrapped in small balloons. And back then, simple possession of even a small quantity of heroin could result in a prison sentence.

When we read the police report, it was obvious to us that the cop had absolutely no reason to search Otis. All he could point to was a vague "furtive gesture" that Otis supposedly made looking at the cop when his squad car passed Otis's Datsun. "Furtive gestures" has long been one of the police community's favorite go-to phrases, and even today, it has vitality in many states as a reason police use to stop someone, particularly while driving. To us, it was short for "I didn't really see anything, but he looked at me funny," or, perhaps more accurately, "'this Black guy looked at me funny."

It's true that there are both made-up furtive gestures and real furtive gestures, like someone suddenly throwing out an object from a car window. In those instances, these gestures might – just *might* – be probable cause to stop someone *if* accompanied by other significant information. But alone? Fortunately, in 1970, our state Supreme Court had spoken and said "no."

The case had the complicated name of *People v. Superior Court (Kiefer)*. Mr. Kiefer was stopped for speeding and immediately pulled his car over to the side of the road. Mrs. Kiefer, in the passenger seat, appeared to look at the officer, then turned, put her arm over the back of the seat, then bent forward, then straightened. And did nothing else. The officer had no real information to believe a crime may have been committed. Still, the officer searched the car and found a small quantity of personal-use marijuana, a drug-possession felony at that time. In evaluating the case, first the *Kiefer* court reminded us that searching a car after a traffic stop violated the Constitution. Then, the justices did a thorough review of what it termed the "many" – this was then a common police claim – "furtive gesture cases." Here's what the court concluded in throwing out the case:

> An innocent gesture can often be mistaken for a guilty movement.... It is because of this danger that the law requires more than a mere "furtive gesture" to constitute probable cause to search.... Police reliance on so-called "furtive movements" has on occasion been little short of a subterfuge.... In order to conduct a search on the basis of mere suspicion or intuition, guilty significance

has been claimed for gestures or surrounding circumstances that were equally or more likely to be wholly innocent.

The justices then gave examples of some innocent but arguably furtive gestures: reaching for a driver's license or registration; rolling down a window; turning down the radio; applying the parking brake.

Even though it was a few days before I was formally sworn in as a member of the bar, David and I decided that I would conduct the hearing on our motion to suppress evidence, which if we won would exclude the heroin balloon from evidence and result in Otis's case being dismissed. I had done other motions to suppress while a student, and was still permitted to appear under my still-active student certification so long as David was present and Otis agreed. Based on the law, I felt pretty confident when I prepared to argue the motion.

The court hearing in Glenn County was the only time in my legal career that I appeared in a "justice court." By December 1974, when I argued Otis's motion, justice courts were becoming anachronistic relics, though they still dotted the landscape in many rural counties, in order to bring a measure of justice closer to those for whom the regular municipal and superior courts were a long distance away. Non-lawyers had presided over many of these courts until a state Supreme Court decision earlier in 1974 ruled that non-lawyers could not hear cases that could result in someone being jailed. Within a few years, these courts had completely disappeared.

I had one memory from childhood about what a justice court might be like. When I was about nine my father was cited for running a traffic light in Poughkeepsie, New York, a bucolic Hudson Valley town. Dad decided to contest the ticket right then and there because the light was entirely obscured by a large maple tree. We found our way to the court of the "Justice of the Peace," which turned out to be a beautiful old mansion. We entered the home and were directed to the justice's parlor, where he sat and heard traffic violation cases. The justice soon took up Dad's case, quickly dismissing it when he heard which light and which tree. An elderly but powerful dowager lived in the house with the overhanging tree and none of the city's elders could convince her to cut it back.

My childhood image was not far off. With Otis's presence excused, David and I drove up together from our office, and reached the court address several minutes before the scheduled hearing time. The sign marking the Glenn County Justice Court was in front of another private house in a residential section of town. The sign directed us around the side, where a small entryway led to a parlor containing a big rectangular table, with the justice at one end and enough room for some chairs at the foot of the table, where a certified court reporter sat. On the near side of the table sat the deputy District Attorney and the arresting officer. We were directed to the far side of the table.

The hearing was brief and straightforward. Using the garden-variety skills I'd already been taught, I asked the officer about how he prepared his police reports, how he did them with care, checked them over before submitting them, and put in those reports everything that he felt was important about the case. I asked him if he had reread the report before the hearing, and whether it appeared to be as accurate today as it was when he wrote it. I then quoted the report's language back to him – "As my vehicle passed Suspect's vehicle, Suspect turned his head and looked at me, then quickly turned his head to the right before he resumed looking forward. RO ["reporting officer" in police talk] noticed that his furtive glances appeared to be suspicious. Accordingly, RO activated the vehicle's lighting equipment and effected a stop of the subject vehicle." That was it; that was the entire reason for the stop. When the justice asked the DA whether he had any further questions, the DA said he did not.

Then another interesting event took place that, once again, I never experienced again in a courtroom. The justice said, "Let's go into chambers." By then, I had spent plenty of occasions going into a judge's chambers to negotiate a plea or discuss ground rules for an upcoming hearing. But I was unprepared for this judge's chambers. The court reporter got up and left the room, and the judge asked the cop to wait outside, then opened the drawer in front of him, pulled out a pipe, and lit it. We were now in chambers!

After a puff or two, the judge made it clear that the officer had no reason to stop Otis. He told the DA he would grant our motion unless the DA was prepared to dismiss the case right then. That way, the blemish of the "bad stop" that losing the motion would bring would not appear on the DA's or CHP officer's records. Here, David spoke for the first time: "With prejudice, Your Honor." That phrase was super-important, because a DA could dismiss a case "without prejudice," which reserved the right to refile the charges if new information came along – a very loose standard. This dismissal had to be *with* prejudice to the DA filing again. The DA agreed.

Two things that I didn't think about at all at the time have struck me in hindsight. I was just glad at the time that an honorable judge was going to follow the law. The first issue I didn't focus on was that by allowing the DA to dismiss, he was letting the DA's office that had filed an unsustainable charge, and the CHP officer himself, off the hook for clear violations of Otis's rights. This kind of "permission" served to perpetuate the inequality of the legal system. Here, the transgressions of the cop and DA did not seem huge, but they nevertheless led to the arrest, charging, and temporary incarceration of a man – an African American man who seemed "out of place" in a white county – that was completely unjustified. A few years later, as I become conversant with the ethics of being a lawyer through my reading and teaching, I appreciated that my duty on that day was to Otis, not to fixing the behavior of law enforcement personnel or to the Black community. This dichotomy – this choice between client and society – is, sadly, too often irreconcilable in the practice of law.

The second issue I didn't think about enough until much later: the analogy between this Northern California justice court and the hundreds of justice courts that dotted rural counties in the South where for generations Black people like Otis could be pulled over for no reason at all, not even a "furtive gesture," and be jailed or, on occasion, even lose their lives. I thought about my friends in Columbus, Georgia, whose grandmother bought a beachfront home at American Beach on Amelia Island, Florida. American Beach was a haven for Black businessmen and their families during the Jim Crow thirties, forties, and fifties. Although it became less of a mecca after a hurricane destroyed many homes in 1964, just as segregation was ending at Florida's public beaches, many families, my friends included, kept their old houses.

When visiting my friends' home some years ago, I asked how "back in the day," a large Black family could caravan in two cars for 280 miles from Columbus to Amelia Island, clear across southern Georgia, and not get stopped by the police. The answer was that they simply didn't stop. Sometimes they could make it on a tank of gas, and if they needed gas, they'd refill just enough in the biggest, most well-lit town on the largest highway. But they never stopped to use the bathroom. Bottom line? "We were blessed."

Shootout at the 7-Eleven

Tuan Tran was the son of Vietnamese immigrants who fled to the US. The family ran a 7-Eleven store in San Rafael, the Marin County seat. On the weekends, kids from the area would hang out in the 7-Eleven's parking lot, often yelling racial epithets at the family and tagging the building's walls with ethnic slurs.

One day at an Asian-American church picnic in San Francisco, Tuan mentioned his family's dilemma to an acquaintance. Unbeknownst to Tuan, his acquaintance was a powerful member of a San Francisco Chinese gang. The next Saturday night, two black sedans filled with kids from San Francisco showed up in the parking lot with guns and Bruce Lee-style nunchucks. Shots were fired, and one of the local white kids was wounded. Tuan was charged with attempted murder as an "aider and abettor." On Monday morning, we were contacted by Tuan's parents. Mr. Tran was an obviously well-educated man who told us he had a doctorate in economics and had been a senior economist in the South Vietnamese government. While owning a 7-Eleven store was hardly the same thing, he and his wife provided well enough for Tuan and Tuan's sister. He wanted no stone left unturned in defending his son. So, applying the San Quentin Six case principles, we filed every conceivable motion, investigated every possible lead, and subpoenaed every local kid mentioned in the police report to the preliminary hearing, planning to call each to the stand.

One of my jobs was to draw to-scale maps of the 7-Eleven parking lot to use as exhibits to show all the local kids we had subpoenaed to the "prelim." We photocopied the maps and transferred them on to clear plastic overlays. At the hearing, after the DA called police witnesses and two of the white youths to verify the shots, we started our "affirmative defense." With David and I alternating witnesses, we first called one kid and then another, handed them the maps, and asked them to put initials and numbers where everyone was located, and when. For each witness, we used three maps. The first one: Where were you and all your friends when the two black sedans arrived? The second: Where were you and everyone else when the fisticuffs started between the white and the Asian kids? The third: Where were you and everyone when you heard the shots, and from what location did the shots come from?

This incurred the wrath of the deputy DA, who argued that we were unethically hijacking a hearing whose sole purpose was just to show "probable cause," and turning it into a circus. By day's end, we had only gotten through three or so witnesses when it came to the end of the court day. We had twelve to go. Fortunately, the judge – our favorite, David Baty – seemed to be enjoying himself, and the law then permitted our calling as many affirmative witnesses as we wanted. So, he recessed the case and set another hearing date a week later. Since Tuan was out of custody, this was fine with us. We could take all the time we needed. We picked the case up the next week with the fourth subpoenaed witness. Again, we converted three different maps to overlays, each marking a point in time.

We remembered our evidentiary procedure, of course, and it actually served us well as we moved on to Witnesses 5 and 6. The smooth, sing-song-y introduction of a piece of evidence has a kind of semi-hypnotic rhythm to it:

"Your Honor, I'm showing this piece of paper to opposing counsel…. May I have this piece of paper marked as defendant's Exhibit X for identification?" Get the little ID sticker from the clerk. "Your Honor, may I approach the witness?" "Mr. Witness, are you familiar with the 7-Eleven on Foxhead Avenue? / Would you look at this piece of paper? / Does it appear to look like a map the 7-Eleven store and the parking lot out in front?" Then, having "authenticated" the "piece of paper" as a map, "Mr. Witness, please show me where you were when you saw those black sedans enter the parking lot." "Would you please put your initials by where you were?" To the best of your recollection, where was Freddie Smith at that time? / Would you please put his initials where you believe he was?" Then "Joey Jones," "Jimmy Green," etc., etc. After each set of maps was completed: "Your Honor, we move that this map with Mr. Witness's notations be admitted into evidence as Defendant's next in order." And on to the next one.

After six witnesses, Judge Baty asked us to have a conference in chambers. "Let's look at these overlays," he insisted over the DA's objections. What the maps showed was a bunch of scribbles worthy of a two-year-old. Each set of maps from a witness contradicted the others in almost every detail. Based on the maps, no one could tell what actually happened in that parking lot, much less prove it at a trial. After four full days of preliminary hearing and half of our witnesses yet to go, the prosecution's case had fallen apart.

"Why don't you put it over six months to dismissal?" suggested the judge. In English, that meant that the DA's office would continue the case on its own motion, and if Tuan stayed out of trouble for another six months, the DA would dismiss the case. After consulting his superior, the deputy DA came back and said that would be okay. Six months later, all charges were dismissed against Tuan Tran, and his record remains clean to this day. Had we turned the case into a bit of a circus? Guilty as charged, but it worked to exonerate an innocent client.

EPILOGUE

The Tran family ran the 7-Eleven for another seven years, until Tuan's father passed his CPA exam and got a well-paying job in downtown San Francisco, Tuan went off to college and wound up with a master's degree in computer science and began a successful career. We never heard from Darren, Reza, or Otis again.

For me, this series of cases underscored that no one is immune from the justice system. But they also dramatically underscored the disparate treatment of our four clients. While there was no way to prove this, I was convinced that both Otis and Reza were treated more harshly than if they had been white. And the one guy who got a break was a white kid who was clearly guilty of burglary despite his secondary role.

As for Tuan, he should never have been charged in the first place. Chinese gangs were well-known to the police, and most of the larger police departments in the Bay Area had gang task forces focused on these groups. There was absolutely no evidence that Tuan had asked his gang member acquaintance to do anything for him, or even that the acquaintance was a gang member. The irony was that the gang members who showed up at the 7-Eleven that Saturday night did more to end the racist taunts directed at the Tran family than any government entity could. In no way do I condone behavior that involves shooting a weapon. But after that Saturday night at the 7-Eleven, there were no more racist incidents in that parking lot.

3

Always Listen to Your Mother

People of the State of California v. Elvin Drummond

Sometimes life brings you challenges you just don't expect. One of the most challenging is a truly innocent client. For me, this client came towards the end of my third year of practice in the form of Elvin Drummond. When a client is truly not guilty of the charges, the pressure on the lawyer rises exponentially. When the case is a murder case, the pressure multiplies several more times; the client's life is in your hands. When the case is your third jury trial and both the forensic and eyewitness testimony is dead set against you, the case is an unrelenting pressure-cooker and the task before you seems insurmountable. For me, as a thirty-year-old lawyer, my fear of losing this case was matched only by my hubris in taking it on.

We take a murder case

In 1976, my friend Bill Balin joined a group of idealistic young lawyers who had created a mini-non-profit called the Criminal Legal Aid Collective. The idea behind "CLAC" was for lawyers to work collaboratively with law students and lay people, men and women, Black, white, and brown, to represent indigent criminal defendants *pro bono*. Teams were created with an eye toward avoiding elitism while also providing enough people power to spread the workload: motions, full-on investigations, and thorough trial preparation that a single appointed counsel could not manage alone. Most of the lawyers had "day jobs," either as legal aid attorneys or doing general civil work. The founder, Lee Stimmel, was in a civil law practice with his father.

Some months later, I joined the group. I had been doing primarily criminal work from the beginning of my practice but hadn't had a jury trial in two years. Part of my desire to work with CLAC was altruistic, to be sure, but I knew that while I now had a good foundation as a criminal defense lawyer with some serious cases – a cop shooting, armed robberies – under my belt, I needed to gain more experience doing jury trials. CLAC might offer both that experience and the chance to give some people a better and more thorough defense.

In the fall of 1977, CLAC got by far its most serious case: a murder. Elvin Drummond was accused of killing James Molson by stabbing him six times in the chest in an alley in the Western Addition just a quarter of a mile west of City Hall. Elvin admitted that he stabbed Molson, but he said that it was entirely in self-defense after Molson had pulled a knife and lunged at him. Elvin came to us through Paul Persons, then a law student volunteering at Legal Aid. Elvin had gone to Legal Aid to get court orders to visit his daughter Shaleen, because his ex-girlfriend, Leona Maxwell, wouldn't let Elvin visit the little girl. Elvin told Paul that Leona was on drugs, and that shortly after Shaleen was born, she had taken up with a guy named "Bo," who had threatened Elvin several times.

Paul arranged for a court ordered series of visits, and armed with the court order, Elvin was able to visit Shaleen.

One day, Paul got a collect call from Elvin from the jail. Elvin told Paul he'd been charged with murdering "Bo" and that the court had already held a probable-cause preliminary hearing in which Leona testified that Elvin had stabbed Molson in cold blood. Elvin said his lawyer had sat there and basically done nothing, barely asking Leona a question. At the next CLAC meeting, we discussed whether we could take the case. Our most experienced lawyer was Phil Martin, who had almost eight years of doing criminal defense work. But Phil was too overwhelmed with his own caseload to take on a murder. He promised that if I agreed to be the lead attorney, he'd back me up and help guide me. I was promised the biggest, most diverse team that CLAC had put together – six people who would all share in the work. I agreed to do it.

I can't remember now exactly why we all believed that Elvin was not guilty, but we did. One reason was that we trusted Paul Persons' judgment. Paul was perhaps our most respected member. He fit the stereotype of the gentle giant, a bear of a man with a reddish beard and a warmth and kindness that always showed in his eyes, with the sole exception of when he was on the basketball court, when he turned into a demon. Another reason may have been Elvin's lack of any serious record. He had one misdemeanor conviction for resisting arrest, but for a Black man in San Francisco's Western Addition in the 1970s, that was like no record at all. We knew that the percentage of adult African American males in the City with no rap sheet at all was very small. Besides, at twenty-four,

Elvin had held a steady job as a security guard for the Municipal Railway system until he'd recently been laid off after job cuts. Finally, we knew that Molson had been to prison twice and had a history of arrests and convictions for violent crimes. All this lent credence to Elvin's story of self-defense.

Phil and I went up to County Jail #2 on the seventh floor of the Hall of Justice to interview Elvin before we made a final decision on whether to take the case. We both found the soft-spoken Elvin to be entirely believable and hoped that we were reading things objectively, because the hard evidence in the case was bad, just short of overwhelming. There was only one witness, Leona Maxwell, who stated unequivocally at the preliminary hearing that Elvin had stabbed Molson without provocation.

Perhaps even worse was the coroner's report. Unlike Leona, the Coroner's Office was supposed to be neutral. But the report in this case was damning: Molson had six stab wounds, all in the same area of the chest, all at approximately the same 45 degree angle to the horizontal, all at about the same depth into Molson's body. The similarity of the wounds caused the coroner to conclude that most likely, Elvin had either held Molson up against the wall of a building or stabbed Molson while he was on the ground. That didn't leave a lot of room for self-defense. Nor did the fact that Molson had a cut on his wrist. Cuts are often found on the fingers and hands of stabbing victims. They're called "defensive wounds" because they're generally caused when the victim extends a hand outward in an effort at self-protection. The wrist was not the most typical place for a defensive wound, but it was close enough to his hands to be a problem.

Today, with a court order or enough money, the defense might be able to get another medical examiner to do a second opinion. Back then, there was no opportunity for this; we neither had the money nor a court willing to order such an examination at state expense. Besides, the reality was that the wounds *were* similar in location, angle, and size. No truthful autopsy report was going to change that.

Instead, David Mayer and I spent a fair amount of time during my first weeks on the case acting out Elvin and Molson in the alley. Elvin had told both me and Paul that as he got out of his car to go pick up Shaleen from Leona, Bo approached him with his knife out. Elvin had been threatened by Molson twice before, once when Molson fired a shot through the door to Elvin's apartment, and another time when Molson swung at Elvin with a knife and then turned and cut the tires on Elvin's car. Elvin said that this time, he thought he was going to die. He quickly got out the knife he kept in a holster on his belt, ducked down low, and stabbed Molson quickly as he lunged, which Elvin demonstrated with a series of quick backhand motions. With Elvin, short and stocky at 5'8" and Molson a tall and lanky 6'2", we came to believe that Elvin's story made sense, and that a lunging attacker could well be stabbed six times in a brief second or so. Think Frazier-Ali, with Frazier staying low and delivering jabs to Ali's body.

This was all just theory, of course, and without more wouldn't give us much of a chance at trial even with the high standard of "proof beyond a reasonable doubt." We did have two helpful facts in our favor, though. Molson's toxicology report showed small amounts of cocaine and heroin in his system. Much more significant was that when Elvin was booked into the jail, he had a cut on his left index finger – a cut totally consistent with a defensive wound.

While I worked on the case with Phil and David's advice and assistance, two of the non-lawyers on the team, both women, one white and one Black, scoured the neighborhood just west of City Hall for potential witnesses. They found two witnesses to previous altercations between Leona and Elvin who could prove useful at trial. The police reports mentioned only one witness to the homicide other than Leona, an Aubrey Franklin. Franklin's statement to police was that he came into the alley just as Molson began to fall, and while he did not see the stabbing, he did see Elvin with a knife. He also saw Elvin searching Molson's clothing after the stabbing and saw Elvin dragging Molson's body towards Elvin's car. Seemingly not key evidence, but he was at the scene. So, our two "investigators" went out to meet him and conduct a more thorough interview. And they returned with something extremely important: Aubrey Franklin was certain that when Molson fell, he and Elvin were standing *in the middle of the street*.

The coroner's report had concluded that Elvin had held Molson up against a wall or stabbed him while on the ground. But Franklin was sure Molson was not stabbed when on the ground *and* was nowhere near a wall. Aubrey Franklin had just become our most important defense witness, even though we thought the prosecution would do us the favor of calling him to the stand themselves during their case. Armed with this information, I made an appointment for a second interview with the medical examiner. By the time we were done, the doctor agreed that it was at least possible that Molson was standing face-to-face with Elvin without necessarily being up against a wall.

Prepping Elvin, and The Letter

Because we entered the case after the preliminary hearing and Elvin remained in custody, the court had already set a trial date in mid-November. We needed to fashion and polish our defense quickly. We knew that the best thing we had going for us was the requirement of proof beyond a reasonable doubt – *if* we could get a jury to truly apply that high standard. We also knew that Molson had indeed had a knife, because after Elvin moved his body towards his car, it was lying on the ground where the body had been, along with a pack of cigarettes and some sunglasses. And we could explain Elvin's effort to get Molson into his car as a desire to get him to the hospital in those days before cellphones. Beyond that, we had Elvin's arguably defensive wound and, most importantly, Aubrey Franklin's testimony. But Aubrey's testimony was not straightforward, as it would have been if he had seen "Bo" pull a knife and advance on Elvin. Rather, we'd have to add 2+2+2 in front of the jury to show why it was so important that Franklin saw Molson fall in the middle of the street and that Elvin didn't stab him on the ground.

Aubrey Franklin's narrative convinced me to a virtual certainty that Elvin was not guilty. I was extremely afraid of the consequences of Elvin's being convicted due to the strong evidence we faced. At the same time, though, I felt that if I could not win this case, I ought to give up practicing law altogether. After all, no lawyer should allow an innocent client to go to prison. In hindsight, of course, this was more of my young self's hubris. It was a tough case, as any self-defense case would be. But at that time, I saw my winning as a necessity to continuing in my profession.

So, David pretty much took over all my other cases, and I started visiting Elvin in the jail several times a week, mostly because I was so afraid of losing.

In one of those visits, about a month before trial, Elvin showed me a letter he had just received from Leona. The two-page letter was handwritten on purple paper and was accompanied by a picture of Leona reclining on a couch. The letter began "Dearest Elvin, Hi Darling" and repeatedly expressed Leona's love for him. Elvin, who still loved her and was not a sophisticated man, wanted to believe that Leona really meant it. But the letter was an obvious and inartful attempt to convince Elvin that Leona loved him and wanted him back in order to get from him what little he still had.

The first page was bad ("Baby, I'm at a stage where I've been so depressed lately, I don't want to beg anyone for anything, so that's why I'm asking you to sign your unemployment checks to me and Shaleen….") But that was a mere warm-up for page two. "Elvin, Shaleen and I **love** you and no matter what, believe me we will wait for you, no matter how long…. Baby, I'm going to make a home for **you**, baby, so when you come out, you can come home to *US*. ♥" And, "I hope your furnish (sic) is still in your house, because I want everything that belong to you, that included the car, which I already have, the furnish, unemployment checks, all this belongs to **US**, baby."

I had to explain patiently to Elvin the true intent of the letter, which he saw, sadly, readily enough. Looked at objectively, the whole letter was something written by a poor Black woman from public housing with little education and a disabling drug habit. But I had little chance to philosophize about that because I realized that Elvin had just gotten us a great piece of evidence. Leona was the only eyewitness to the stabbing, and if her testimony was believed, Elvin would be convicted of first-degree murder. I thought I'd be able to do a decent job of questioning her motives and credibility, and this letter, I thought, would do a lot of that job for me. I explained this to Elvin and asked him for the letter.

We certainly faced some tough evidentiary issues, but the case itself involved a relatively small array of witnesses: cops, the medical examiner, and Leona Maxwell for the prosecution, and Aubrey Franklin for us – unless – we could always hope – the DA's office called him themselves. That left only one more main witness: Elvin Drummond. Elvin was not only unsophisticated, but very soft-spoken – a true introvert. His schooling was typical of someone born into poverty in a Black area of San Francisco in the 1950s: a series of public schools that did a poor job teaching the kids who needed help the most, especially students of color. I knew my work was cut out for me in preparing his testimony.

By prepping his testimony, it's important to note, I don't mean creating some fiction. Far from it. Not only would that be highly unethical, but frankly, the truth speaks volumes. It was just a matter of presentation. Under the Constitution, it's the client's absolute right to testify in a criminal case. And as between lawyer and client, this is a decision controlled by the client; a lawyer is ethically prohibited from preventing a client from testifying. Many defendants want to testify. Still, it is the exception rather than the rule when an accused testifies, at least once the lawyer is done doing some convincing. Each murder case I had eventually wound up going to trial, and in only two did my client testify. It's true, of course, that courts throughout the country admonish juries that if a criminal defendant does not testify, that should not be held against the accused in any way. But the reality is that juries *always* want to hear from the defendant, and are a bit put off when they don't. Nevertheless, testifying in one's own defense can seem self-serving and defensive, and can easily fall apart in so many ways.

So it was that after going over Elvin's testimony for days and writing out a complete direct examination, on each of the last eight days before the first day of trial, I was at the jail going through the entire direct examination and the points that Elvin should expect on cross-examination. For this to work, it was vital that Elvin trust me, and fortunately that part was easy. He was so pleased that we had taken his case and given it the attention it deserved – which his court-appointed lawyer did not do – that his trust in us was strong.

Each evening after dinner with my wife and eighteen-month-old son, I set out for the Hall of Justice, a twelve-minute drive away. Each night I sat with Elvin, we went through his testimony from beginning to end, and I fired some cross-exam questions at him. It all came together really well except for one part of the exam – the most crucial part – that just didn't sound right. When we got to the moment where Bo came at him with a knife and I asked, "What happened next?" (no leading questions are allowed on direct examination), Elvin would answer "I got out mines." For some reason, Elvin couldn't muster saying that he feared for his life. In addition, the street expression "mines" was not going to play well in front of what would likely to be a mostly white and Asian jury. Even the idea that it was common in Elvin's community for almost every man to carry a knife holstered on a belt in those days was something I'd have to carefully explain.

We worked on this short passage every night for over a week. Finally, on the weekend before trial, we turned a corner. The answer to "What happened next?" became "I was afraid for my life" (at last). And then? "I quick reached for my knife." And then? "I was ducked down and stabbed him quick as I could after he came after me." Great. Ready for trial.

The trial begins

There have been few things in my life scarier than sitting in Department 22 of the San Francisco Hall of Justice for the Monday morning trial call. The pit in my stomach was huge. I wondered where I had gotten the chutzpah to take on such a serious case with so little experience. And, of course, that anticipatory anxiety is always the worst – just sitting there waiting for something to happen. Peggy Holder, the long-time Master Calendar Clerk, read the calendar through in stentorian tones before returning to the list to assign trial departments. "Judge

Holder," as we called her, ran a tight ship and, back then, at my first San Francisco trial call, seemed cold and intimidating. Later, I learned that she was just someone who did her job well and with great precision. She'd respect and get along with you fine so long as you did the same and followed the rules.

I was assigned out to trial at City Hall, Department 19, the Honorable Francis L. McCarty presiding. Back then, the Hall of Justice didn't have enough courtrooms for felony trials, which had a statutory time limit within which to begin trial. So, it was not unusual for cases, especially the most serious like murder, to be sent out to City Hall. Murder cases at City Hall created a bizarre confluence. City Hall is a legendary building, noted for its ornate Beaux-Arts beauty, its huge dome (taller than the Capitol in Washington), and a magnificent rotunda featuring the "Grand Staircase"; it's been the site of thousands of wedding pictures with its magnificent north and south light courts and its ornate early-century oaken doors. Oddly concealed behind some of those doors were tiny holding cells where in-custody defendants were kept before trial.

Judge Fran McCarty, then sixty-nine, was also legendary. A San Francisco old-school politician, he'd served several terms on the city's Board of Supervisors in the 1950's, including a term as board president. But his most famous accomplishment was as the architect of the Giants move to San Francisco. As chair of a City baseball commission, he not only succeeded in getting the Giants to move, but also to get voters to approve a bond measure to build a new ballpark, Candlestick Park. The pictures in his chambers showed off his Giants relationships: McCarty and Willie Mays; McCarty and manager Alvin Dark;

McCarty, Giants owner Horace Stoneham and Governor Edmund G. "Pat" Brown at the Candlestick groundbreaking ceremony.

Fran McCarty had the reputation for being strict but fair, not a bad profile for a judge. One of my CLAC teammates, law student John Weinstein, had agreed to sit with me through the whole trial, partly to take notes, but more importantly for me, to make sure that I ate something for lunch and didn't pass out from fright in the courtroom. McCarty called us and Deputy District Attorney Douglas Munson into chambers to lay the ground rules. That was the first time I knew Doug Munson was on the case. I thought maybe I'd caught a break, as my former opposing counsel, known to us as "Bojangles" because he wore taps on his shoes, was known as a curmudgeonly guy who was always super-prepared. In contrast, Munson was both dapper and kind. But any thought of him not being prepared was quickly disabused by his thorough and accurate opening statement. The veteran of dozens of murder trials, his ramp-up time was a small fraction of mine.

Before opening statements, which are used to just summarize the evidence and *not* (supposedly) to argue the case – we had to select a jury. At that time, years before I was taught how to conduct a proper jury *voir dire* by the extraordinary Cathy Bennett, I was flying by the seat of my pants. The only saving grace was the presence of a half-dozen CLAC members in the audience, including my "second," Phil, who got to chime in with their impressions during our recesses.

Given my hyper-anxious state, I remember only two things from that *voir dire*. One was that just as Judge McCarty said "Mr. Zitrin, you may begin your *voir dire*," a potential juror raised his hand and when the judge acknowledged him, said "Your Honor, I think Mr. Zitrin thinks his client is guilty." I didn't know how to react, but my friends in the courtroom told me I turned to them with an expression that said, "What the fuck do I do now?" Fortunately, the judge knew what to do. He immediately excused the juror.

The second was that I took a liking to a well-dressed, single, middle-aged man who worked as a social worker. He said he was a Republican, and I sensed, at a time when few gay men were out, especially in venues like jury selection, that he was gay. Not that any of that – except "Republican" – offered much in the way of clues. But I liked his forthright, practical manner, and so did a couple of our team members. Others argued, though, that "Republican" was strike one and two, if not strike three. After all, even then, San Francisco was about 70% Democratic and on the progressive end at that. But "Republican" did not mean what it does today, and ultimately, with the support of at least some of our team, I went with my gut and kept him on the jury. We knew the decision could be particularly important because, as a well-dressed, well-educated professional – and as a white male – he made an excellent candidate to be jury foreperson.

The testimony begins

The testimony came in pretty much as we expected. We had done so much preparation that there was little we didn't know and not much we hadn't planned a rebuttal strategy for.

The first witness called by Doug Munson was the reporting officer who came to the scene of the homicide. He wasn't an important witness other than to set the scene: Where the body was, where Elvin, Leona and the baby were, and so on. But even with this ordinary witness, we scored some important points. First, I did something that had no real importance in terms of guilt or innocence, but that I felt was important to make a point. The officer placed the knife, cigarette pack, and sunglasses in the wrong place on the pavement. Knowing that the crime-scene photo had those items elsewhere, I asked the cop whether in fact they were actually "over there…" and then, showing the witness the photo, he had to admit that he was mistaken. In other words, I was right and he was wrong. Which was my way of getting the jury to believe that I knew the evidence better than anyone else.

The officer had written in his police report that Elvin had immediately said, "I'm the one who stabbed him," and did not resist arrest. He also wrote that he noticed a cut on Elvin's finger. He faithfully testified to these uncontroversial but helpful facts on cross-examination. But the officer also testified that at some later point Elvin told him, "Bo shot at me," and handed the officer a bullet. On cross-examination, I was able to clarify that Elvin said, "I thought he was gonna shoot me." Molson did in fact have a loaded gun, but not on his person or under his body. It was on the front seat of his car. Elvin's statement that he was "shot at" could be explained, but I had to hope that the jury would be patient, follow the judge's instructions, and wait for our defense case before jumping to conclusions.

Next came the deputy medical examiner. For this witness, it was a matter of minimizing his conclusions and making sure he admitted that there were possibilities other than those conclusions – in other words, enough for "reasonable doubt." It went as well as we could hope. The doctor maintained that given the similarity in the depth, angle, and proximity of the wounds, they were most consistent with Molson being held against something. But he acknowledged that he could only say with certainty that Molson was stationary, with slight movement at most. During my cross-examination, he agreed that just a small amount of force would be needed to stab the chest wall, that the six wounds "probably" happened very quickly and could have happened as fast as an arm could move. That gave us some things to work with.

Aubrey and Leona

After some other brief police and medical witnesses, we assumed Doug Munson would end with his one eyewitness, Leona. But before calling her he surprised us by calling Aubrey Franklin, whom we considered "our" witness and a key to our defense. I was never sure why Munson made that decision. I suspected, though, that with one shaky eyewitness, he felt that Aubrey would mostly corroborate Leona's testimony. And to a certain extent he did. He testified that he saw Molson stand with both hands at his head, and then fall to the ground. He saw no knife in Molson's hands, but he did see Elvin's knife. And he saw cigarettes and sunglasses fall out of Molson's pockets as he fell.

But thanks to our investigators, we knew Aubrey's full account far better than the DA. On cross, Aubrey readily acknowledged that as he fell, Molson was in the middle of the street, with nothing holding him up. He was certain that Elvin never stabbed Molson after he fell. While Elvin tried to drag Molson to his car, apparently to go for help, Aubrey could see both of Elvin's hands, and he had dropped his knife. And one more strong point in our favor: As Elvin moved Molson, Aubrey saw a knife fall from the folds of Molson's clothing. The blade was visible and it had blood on it. Munson tried to dissuade Aubrey on this last point on re-direct examination, but Aubrey was certain: the knife blade was bloody.

That left one prosecution witness for the next morning: Leona Maxwell. On direct examination by Munson, she testified just as she had at preliminary hearing: Elvin killed Bo in cold blood. She didn't see a knife in Bo's hands. As soon as he approached, Elvin started stabbing over and over. Pretty straightforward. Then it was my turn.

The night before, I'd gotten in a heated discussion with my more experienced "second chair" Phil Martin. I wanted to ask Leona if Elvin continued to stab Bo after he fell. I felt we had Aubrey's clear testimony that Elvin never did that. I *knew* Leona was lying – or, rather, I thought I knew – and I figured that she'd go for this extra stabbing, which she had never testified to before, if given the opportunity. And if she said "no," it didn't hurt. Phil argued strongly against this, pointing out the dangers of the idea, because if Leona was believed by the jury, it would just make Elvin seem more violent. But I figured that if they believed Leona, Elvin was a dead duck anyway.

So, I took the risk and asked her, and she rose to the bait. Yes, he stabbed Bo over and over again while they were on the ground. Now, Leona not only directly contradicted Aubrey, but she had Elvin inflicting twelve or fifteen stab wounds, not six in rapid succession.

Then, I had what was for me the most exciting, almost "Perry-Mason-like" moment: Leona's letter.

There are strict rules about how evidence is brought before the court, shown to a witness, and then placed into evidence. In some courtrooms, the rules must be strictly followed in an almost ritualistic dance. A few judges, like the Honorable Walter F. Calcagno, the judge who presided over several of my cases and, more famously, the trial of Dan White, killer of Harvey Milk and George Moscone, insisted on the ritual. So, when I taught trial-practice seminars in law school, I always made sure my students were taught the ritual:

Pull out a document, don't call it what it is, "a letter," but just reference "a piece of paper." (Calling it a letter would be testifying about it.) Show the document to opposing counsel while saying for the transcribed record, "I am showing the document to opposing counsel." Then ask the clerk to mark the document "for identification" as your side's exhibit "next in order." Then, identifying it by its exhibit number, ask the judge whether you may "approach the witness" to show her "Exhibit X." Once granted permission, hand the witness the piece of paper and say, "I'm handing Exhibit X to the witness." Only then are you ready to ask her, "Do you recognize Exhibit X?" If she says "yes," ask her what it is, and when you're done examining the witness about it say, "I move Exhibit X into evidence," so that the jury may consider it.

Judge McCarty and Judge Calcagno were good friends. In fact, McCarty's daughter Sharon married Calcagno's son Walter, Jr. But their approaches to the introduction of evidence were somewhat different. McCarty knew the rules of evidence but was quite a bit more relaxed, and he didn't require literal adherence to the ritual. Besides, he knew – as his friend Judge Calcagno did – that there were exceptions to the ritual. One of the most important is that a lawyer *doesn't have to* show a document to a witness to ask her to testify about it. A lawyer is free to simply ask, "Was there such a document?" Many judges, for reasons I never fully grasped, didn't understand this rather basic tenet, one of the rules of cross-examination. Too often, judges would insist that I "show the witness the document," when that's the last thing I wanted to do.

In addition to teaching my trial-practice students the evidence ritual, I also explained why they might not want to use it. Cross-examination is still one place where a lawyer is relatively free to use wit and verbal skill rather than programmed methodology. By holding up the letter in my hand and asking Leona whether she wrote a letter on purple paper to Elvin, I not only increased the dramatic effect, I also gave Leona the opportunity to either adopt that she wrote the letter or deny it. If she had denied it, I could have proven it by going through "the ritual" and showing it to her. Instead, she admitted it. Once that happens, it's virtually impossible for a witness to deny what's in it, and Leona did not. And, in this way, the document itself was not (yet) before the court, just her oral *testimony* about it. Because it was all questions and answers, I had the advantage of looking down at the letter and asking questions about my favorite sections without having to read the whole letter or marking it for identification or even showing it to the DA. Only after Leona had admitted to everything in the letter that I wanted to highlight did I mark it and introduce it in evidence. And Doug Munson, an honorable attorney, just sat there without trying, as many would have, to disrupt the proceedings.

The defense case

Elvin's testimony began our case, and I learned just how much the daily sessions in the jail paid off. He was as good a witness as I'd seen. He described how Bo "attacked me," and that he was "afraid for my life." Before returning to the details of that day, I asked Elvin for some background. He described how, while he and Leona were living together, she would often get violent; how Leona had attacked him with a knife, and that he had called the police and given them the knife she used; how Leona had told him he'd never see Shaleen again before leaving with the baby; how she and Bo had come to his apartment, and that Leona scratched him while Bo beat him about the face; how on another occasion, Bo had cut up Elvin's car tires, then came to Elvin's front door and fired a shot through the door. And how Elvin found the bullet – the one he gave to the police after stabbing Bo. He explained that when he told the cop Bo had shot at him, he had meant that incident, a month before the stabbing.

Then we returned to the day of the stabbing. Elvin had come for his court-ordered visit. Bo was there and told Elvin, "Stay away or I'll blow you away," and repeated that when Elvin didn't leave immediately. Then, as Elvin retreated towards his car, Bo followed him, pulled out a knife and attacked. Elvin held up one hand to ward off Bo – his left, the one with the cut finger – and with his right, reached for the knife on his belt and stabbed Bo until he stopped moving forward: "I thought I was gonna die." He searched Bo's clothing looking for the gun he thought Bo also had – the gun that was on the front seat of Bo's car. He moved Bo's body in an attempt to get Bo into his car to take him to the hospital.

Cross-examination was pretty straightforward and did no damage to Elvin's testimony. Because, of course, he was simply speaking the truth:

"You didn't run when Bo came towards you?"

"No."

"Why?"

"I wanted to talk to Leona and see my daughter."

Our other witnesses were four neighbors, two who had witnessed the incident when Leona used a knife and who verified that the police had come, and two who heard the gunshot into Elvin's door, which supported Elvin's testimony. But the strangest moment in the trial happened during this testimony. When the first of these four witnesses mentioned that he had also seen Bo's brothers around Elvin's apartment, two big, tall, burly, bearded men in the audience started yelling at the witness.

Judge McCarty immediately stopped the testimony and asked the two to approach the ornate oak railing – literally "the bar" that separated the "well" of the courtroom from the audience. With an educated guess about who these people were, I saw an opportunity, and asked the judge whether he would ask them to state their names for the record. Back then, there were microphones in the courtroom so that jurors could be interviewed from their seats. With the jury still sitting in the courtroom, the judge asked the bailiff to turn on the mikes and, in turn, Bo Molson's two brothers announced their presence: "Joe Molson," said the first. "Willie Molson," stated the second. The fact that these two scary-looking guys were Bo's brothers was not going to hurt our case.

When we finished the testimony of our corroborating witnesses, Doug Munson, now more than a little unhappy, called the two brothers to testify that they did not, in fact, hang around Elvin's apartment or help Leona remove Elvin's belongings from his place. But the damage had been done. Things really could not have gone better for us from the beginning of trial till the close of testimony. All that was left now was argument, jury instructions, and the verdict.

My mother Charlotte intervenes

It so happens that two seminal events in my work life were occurring on consecutive days. My closing argument was scheduled on the day after the last class of my first semester teaching legal ethics. Not only that, but my mother was in town to visit us and to see her grandson. I must tell you a bit about her.

Charlotte Marker Zitrin, MD, was my touchstone. More than anything else, it was her support and confidence in me that enabled me to grow from an introverted and anxiety-ridden child to a confident and (somewhat) fearless adult. As a physician, she was a pioneer. Not only was she one of a handful of women in her medical school class, but within a year of her graduation, she was writing published papers on childhood tuberculosis. She had two successful medical careers, first as a pediatrician and then as a psychiatrist, which required an entirely new three-year residency in her late forties.

But on a personal level, she too was shy and anxious – and indeed remained that way her whole life. She just didn't let those qualities stand in her way. Because she didn't seek the limelight, she let my father stand in the spotlight's glow. They were both extraordinarily successful, but he gained a fair measure of fame, something she never sought and didn't want for herself. My father was brilliant – worldly, exceptionally well-read, a wordsmith, and a perfectionist. On practical matters, though, my mother was the voice to listen to. Perfection? "Don't look for poifect; poifect you can't find," she'd say, imitating her best friend's mother's Yiddish accent.

On Thursday morning, accompanied by the entire six-member CLAC team and my mother, and feeling butterflies bigger than elephants, I went off to deliver my first argument in a murder case. I hit all the high points. Reasonable doubt. That Leona lied, and why. That the coroner's suppositions were wrong, and why. Aubrey's uncontested testimony. Reasonable doubt. Molson's history of violence against Elvin. Leona's history of violence. The letter on purple paper. More reasonable doubt.

At lunchtime, Judge McCarty called a recess when I was all but finished. We all marched off to have lunch at the same place we ate at every day during the trial. Trial lawyers are often as superstitious as baseball players. The five other team members, including Phil Martin, my "second," were all telling me how eloquent and brilliant I'd been. The only one with doubts was my biggest supporter, my mom.

"Rich," she said, and repeated until the others quieted down. "*Rich*," she urged sharply, "you have to ask the jury, 'Is Elvin Drummond the kind of man who would take the law into his own hands?'" She said it again, with emphasis. She knew that the homicide had taken place when Elvin went to pick up his daughter for a court-ordered visit, and that Elvin had worked through the legal system to get those visits. And that when Leona used a knife on him, he called the police and gave them the knife. And when Molson fired a bullet, he kept the bullet and gave that to the police. And that he didn't resist arrest and immediately said that he had stabbed Molson.

But mom knew that this question had an extremely important double entendre – that Elvin would not take a knife into his own hands except in self-defense. It was brilliant, and the first thing I out of my mouth that afternoon: "Members of the jury, is Elvin Drummond the kind of person *who would take the law into his own hands?*" I saw six jurors shake their heads, "no."

EPILOGUE

The arguments took up the whole day on Thursday. Mom flew home to New York on Friday morning, and I trooped back to court to listen to Judge McCarty reading the long and complicated instructions to the jury that all murder trials feature. The jury reached its verdict quickly, by the end of the day: "Not guilty," said the foreman, the Republican social worker we'd believed in. Elvin heard it clearly, but he was *sure* he heard the word "innocent!"

Nothing was holding Elvin in jail except the time it took to process him out. But he had nowhere to go. His old apartment was now unsafe, and all of his possessions had been taken. So, I went down to Hall of Justice with John Weinstein, who had sat through every minute of the trial, to pick up Elvin from the jail. We took him back to my house, where my wife set him up with a room while I drove John home. By then, we had discussed with Elvin what to do next. He was afraid to stay in the City, and frankly, after witnessing the Molson brothers' anger, we were afraid for him too.

John was from Portland and had a lot of good close contacts up there who could help Elvin get a job. Elvin now had no car, because for some reason beyond our comprehension, the police had released the car to Leona, though she had no claim to it. So, we bought Elvin a bus ticket and gave him a couple hundred dollars and a bunch of good people to contact, especially two of John's aunts. On Sunday, Elvin came out with me to play basketball at my favorite pick-up game. The next day, Elvin was on his way to Portland. A couple of months later, after taking the police department and tow company to Small Claims Court, I got Elvin a couple of thousand dollars for allowing Leona to take his car.

Elvin did well in Portland for a while. But the reality of being born into Elvin's life makes success difficult in the best circumstances, and harder still when you're uprooted to a strange town where you know no one. Elvin had grown up in the Western Addition, then a largely Black community. Before he left for Portland, hard as it may be for privileged people to understand, Elvin had never seen the ocean, three miles to the west of where he lived, and had been across the Bay Bridge to Oakland just once in his life. Moving from the small world that surrounded him to another big city without friends or much of an education, Elvin barely had half a chance at living a peaceful, happy life.

A few years ago, from out of the blue, I got a message at my office from a Shaleen Drummond. I returned the call at once and had a very nice conversation with Elvin's daughter. She and her family were doing well in Louisiana. She was in touch with her dad, and they loved each other. But Elvin was living life on the margins, sad but perhaps not surprising. He'd been incarcerated in Texas and gone down some other slippery slopes. To my regret, I'm not sure where he is today, or whether he's still alive.

My mom, blessed with a far different background and life experience, lived long enough to meet her great-granddaughter Lauren Charlotte, named for her. Two months later, she called me in the morning with some advice about my kids, as she often did. That night, in apparently perfect health, she died in her sleep at ninety-five.

As for me and my colleagues, though we tried our best to represent our client, Elvin, not just his case, we could only do so much. I was reminded that Elvin was dealt a rough hand. And, as I tried to tell all my criminal clients, "I will never be able to get you back to even," to the day before he was arrested.

4

The "Gershwin Brothers"

People of the State of California v. George Burrell & Ira Moon

In the practice of criminal law, a "dead-bang loser" is a case that looks absolutely unwinnable. "Dead-bang" cases come along all too frequently. But sometimes, these cases have a very small window – a pinprick of opportunity—that if carefully followed can lead to a hole in the prosecution's case. And once in a great while, poking that pinprick of a hole can enlarge it until the prosecution's whole case evaporates like air rushing out of a balloon. That's what happened in the Gershwin Brothers' case.

The incident

George Burrell and Ira Moon (thus "the Gershwin Brothers," after the famed Tin Pan Alley songwriting team of George and Ira Gershwin) were arrested in the interior of a warehouse on 16th Street in San Francisco at about 5:30 in the morning on New Year's Day. When the cops stormed into the warehouse after being alerted by a silent alarm, they found my future client, George, wearing gloves, with a flashlight in his back pocket and sheetrock dust in his hair. There was a pickaxe leaning against the wall next to Ira, and gouges dug out of the sheetrock next to a wall safe.

George and Ira were both booked and charged with burglary. They were kept in custody as state prison parolees on no-bail parole holds. Deputy Public Defender Marco LaMacchia was assigned to represent Ira. Since the public defender's office had a policy of never representing multiple clients in a case due to a possible conflict of interest, I was appointed from the "conflicts panel," a list of pre-qualified stand-by lawyers for cases with more than one defendant, to represent George. By then, with the Drummond murder trial and a couple of other felony trials under my belt, I was eligible for all felony court appointments. They didn't pay much, to put it mildly, but they allowed me to do the work I wanted to do and were a big improvement over the family law cases and the very occasional drug case that paid the bills.

The client interview and the police report

In the afternoon after appearing with George at his arraignment – when the charges against him were read – I headed up to the jail to interview him. George was neither terribly forthcoming nor particularly interested in talking. His reticence came as no surprise. He was familiar with the system. After all, as a Black ex-con, why should he trust his appointed counsel? He didn't know me; I was some white guy thrust upon him by the court system. I was *part of* that system.

George did tell me this much: He and Ira were friends. They'd been walking back from a late New Year's Eve party in the Bayview District. They were heading west on 16th Street along the route of the 22 Fillmore bus, hoping to catch one to get back home to the Western Addition. At that hour no bus came along, so they kept on walking. Back then, that part of 16th Street, near where it passed under the Central Freeway, was filled with warehouses and small distribution businesses. Ira spotted a broken window in the door to one of those warehouses, stuck his head inside and then back out and said to George, "C'mon, let's check it out." Which they did. They found themselves in the interior of a warehouse housing a lot of water heaters. Then, before you know it, the police showed up and they were arrested.

Many clients, like George, are perfectly likeable people. It's just that their backgrounds and experiences often are largely foreign to those of their lawyers – or at least lawyers like me, who grew up in an upper-middle-class town, the son of two physicians. Many had never known a lawyer until they were assigned one in a criminal case. Life generally dealt them a pretty bad hand. When I and most of my fellow lawyers inevitably made youthful mistakes, we usually got second and third chances. For guys like George and Ira, the world offered few first chances.

It's understandable that with very little time to build trust, our clients are not likely to tell us the whole truth, or even much of it. I once had a client who was a sociopath—or at least I thought so, though I'm no shrink. I followed him through his juvenile days into young adulthood up until he was sent off, finally and inevitably, to state prison. One time I asked him to simply and for just this once tell me the truth. And here's how he answered: "Do you want the truth, or do you want the whole truth? [Pause.] Or do you want to know what really happened?"

It's a reality that in many cases, the client's version of the "truth" may ultimately not be as important as what the police say in their reports. We worked with the tools at hand, and those tools were often the cops' police reports. In the ordinary felony case, absent some good reason to cast doubt on those reports – like when police contradict each other or themselves, or where video was available – the reports and later testimony were likely to be accepted by judges and most juries as gospel – whether they were true or not. Marco and I would have to read those reports and see how our clients' accounts could fit in.

In George and Ira's case, the police report was simple and straightforward. The interior warehouse belonged to a water-heater distributor. There were many water heaters scattered around the storage area, a mezzanine with offices for the company's sales force, and a wall safe near the entrance. The police concluded that George and Ira were working on getting into the safe and arrested them both. The report didn't leave us with much to investigate. Besides, in public defender or court-appointed cases, we would be lucky to get $300 for an investigator, which even back then didn't go very far.

Marco, not yet thirty, was the junior member of our team. This was one of his first felony assignments, but despite his unkempt Italian afro and slight build—he was so thin it seemed as if a client raising his voice could blow him over—he was a good young defense counsel. When Marco and I each concluded our client interviews, we compared notes. I learned that Ira had been no more forthcoming than George had been.

Searching for a defense at the preliminary hearing

When representing suspected felons, especially ex-felons on parole like George and Ira, lawyers have to be extra careful about judging our clients. Even if you know they "did it" – committed the crime or at least did *something* illegal – your role is to be their mouthpiece, no less, and most of the time, no more. These clients are not interested in hearing you preach to them. They don't want to hear about how to be better citizens. They don't want to hear about how they can stop using dope. They want to hear how you're going to get them off. And our job was to search for a way – perhaps a pinprick hole – to make that happen. None of this is meant to be critical of our clients. In fact, they're right, because under the American system of criminal justice, even if they "did it," "did it" does not mean "guilty" until the jury comes back and says so.

Over fifty years ago, Byron "Whizzer" White, star football player turned United States Supreme Court justice, put it this way:

"Defense counsel has no obligation to ascertain or present the truth. He must be and is interested in preventing the conviction of the innocent, but we also insist that he defend his client whether he is innocent or guilty. If he can confuse a witness, even a truthful one, or make him appear at a disadvantage, unsure or indecisive, that will be his normal course. Our interest in not convicting the innocent permits counsel to put the State to its proof, to put the State's case in the worst possible light, regardless of what he thinks or knows to be the truth. We countenance or require conduct of the most honorable defense counsel which in many instances has little, if any, relation to the search for truth."

When I had a case like George and Ira's, it always gave me comfort to think of this strong statement from a rather conservative Supreme Court justice.

Because George and Ira were in custody, under California law, the preliminary hearing was held only a few weeks after the initial arrest and arraignment. A felony preliminary hearing is mostly for the prosecution to show "probable cause" to hold the defendants to answer at trial. Probable cause is at the other extreme from "proof beyond a reasonable doubt." All the DA needs to show is that's there's a reasonable possibility that the defendants are guilty, and that's not much. The DA puts on some but usually not all of the evidence – in the form of documents and live testimony – because all of the evidence is almost never needed to move the case forward to trial.

But by the end of this preliminary hearing, I thought we had a pretty good shot at winning the case. Now hubris is a very dangerous thing for a lawyer, more so for a young lawyer, and especially for a young criminal defense lawyer, where wins are few and in the vast majority of cases you don't have much evidence on your side. But I was coming off a string of trial successes and feeling my oats. Besides, the DA had inadvertently given me a clue to what I thought might be a pretty darn good defense.

Nothing had been taken from the warehouse proper or from the safe, which was never opened. But the DA had called a couple of salespeople who worked on the mezzanine floor of the warehouse to testify that the building had been locked up securely for the holiday. When it was our turn to cross-examine, I asked whether they personally had anything missing. To my surprise, both said that in fact, they had: They had had small cardboard piggy banks in the shape of water heaters that were a gift from a water-heater manufacturer. Both the witnesses used the piggy banks to store loose coins. But when they got back to their offices after the new year, one cardboard piggy bank was empty, torn open on a desk, and the other one had disappeared.

Over the many years that I taught trial practice courses in law school, one of the first and most important lessons was that good lawyers try cases not from strengths, but from *weaknesses*, especially in criminal cases. If you have a case with a winning strategy, it's unlikely to do much good unless you have answers to all the strengths of the prosecution's case. Still, as soon as this prelim was over, I told my co-counsel Marco I thought we might win this case. He looked at me incredulously: "What are you talking about? They were caught red-handed!" "Yes," I replied, "but they *had no money*. According to the jail property report, your guy had nothing, and my guy had three cents in his back pocket. If they had taken the money from the piggy banks, where was it?" In my view, there was at least a good possibility that someone came in first, broke the window, set off the silent alarm, took the piggy bank money and split when he couldn't get in the safe. "And then our guys come along and just wander in."

"Intent at the time of entry"

Here is the key to this defense: In most states, including California, burglary is a crime committed when there is "specific intent" to commit a crime *at the time of entry*. That is, in order to be found guilty of felony burglary instead of attempted grand theft, or trespass, only a misdemeanor, George and Ira needed to have formed the specific intent to steal or commit a felony when they first went into the building. This was a lesson I'd learned from my first trial just four months after becoming a lawyer. I was very lucky to get a hung jury because, despite my own ignorance, three jurors realized that the state had not proven what the judge told them was necessary: intent upon entry.

Now, a few years wiser (though still a bit willing to grasp at what might seem like a straw), I knew that the fact that George and Ira didn't have the coins from the piggy banks strongly suggested that someone else had been in the warehouse first. That would make our guys' story – a simple "C'mon, check it out," sparked by curiosity – consistent with a simple trespass or attempted grand theft, but *not* a burglary.

When we gathered for the settlement conference—what we call our plea-bargaining session—neither the judge nor the supervising DA could believe that our clients were going to turn down the three to four years in prison they were offered. They were looking at the case as a slam dunk. "You gotta be kidding!" the DA told us. "We're giving you a break by knocking some time off the sentence. They're busted inside the warehouse. They're obviously in the midst of going at the safe. You're nuts!"

With a losing case, the DA's deal would have been a pretty reasonable one – not great, but reasonable. But by this time, I had not only convinced myself that we could win (as I've noted, a potentially dangerous thing), but Marco as well. We both had a case of "trial fever": the feeling lawyers sometimes get when preparing a losing case for trial and finding themselves convinced that they might just win it. And our clients weren't much interested in pleading out to time in the joint anyway. They'd been there and done that. Plus, there was another point in our favor: This DA obviously did not have a clue about our defense. Typically, but mistakenly in this case, they had only charged burglary and the "lesser included offense" of trespass. They did *not* charge attempted grand theft for trying to break into the safe – a felony that didn't require an "intent to steal" when the "Gershwins" entered the warehouse. The absence of a theft charge would be very important at trial. We turned the deal down.

The Honorable G. Vagelis Kostos, Judge Presiding

On the day of trial, we were assigned to the Hon. G. Vagelis Kostos. It would be the only case I ever tried in front of Judge Kostos, whom I – like many other defense lawyers – had always tried hard to avoid. Kostos was an old-timer, a hulking, lumbering figure with a shock of white hair who could look both inscrutable and intimidating from the bench. The son of an immigrant who had sold apples on Ocean Beach after emigrating from Greece, Kostos was considered the worst judge in the criminal division: very prosecution friendly, with little if any curiosity about the life experiences of the defendants who appeared before him, and, frankly, no expert on the law. When he moved from Probate Court to a criminal department, the probate lawyers, who for years had had to put up with his sloppiness and ignorance of the sometimes-technical nuances of trust and estates law, were overjoyed.

I remember once sitting in Department 22, the Hall of Justice's coordinating master calendar court, where felony cases were assigned out to trial by "Judge" Holder, listening to seventeen lawyers in a row ask to be sworn to declare under penalty of perjury that Judge Kostos could not be fair, in the words of the statute, to "my client or the interests of my client." The California statute allows any litigant one such peremptory challenge to a judge, or what we more colloquially called a "bounce," a "bump," or a "ding." Kostos was "dinged" repeatedly and consistently.

However, our clients' parole holds, which lasted only ninety days, were over, and they didn't want to wait for what could be weeks to get another open courtroom. Marco and I looked at the available judges coming up and figured they were no prizes themselves. We gulped, kept our mouths shut, and were assigned out to Kostos.

The "Dude Dunnit" defense

The point in a case like this – indeed, in most criminal cases – is to show that while the defendants may have been in a compromised situation, someone else had – or at least *possibly* had – committed the crime: here burglary, or entry with the intent to steal. Our argument was that because our clients had none of the coins from the piggy banks, this proved that someone else, alone or with others, had gone in first, brought in the pickaxe and the gloves, set off the silent alarm, and split with the money from the piggy banks, perhaps when they heard police sirens. We didn't actually have to *prove* this, of course, but only raise a reasonable doubt that this alternative to our clients' guilt was a reasonable possibility.

The testimony at trial came in even better than I'd expected. The DA showed that our guys had been inside when the alarm went off and had been found with incriminating evidence – the pickaxe and gloves, sheetrock dust in the hair – all stuff we couldn't really quarrel with. Between preliminary hearing and trial, our investigator had gone out and interviewed more salespeople who worked on the mezzanine. Four of them reported that their water-heater piggy banks had been emptied. We called all four as witnesses, and they trooped into court one at a time to testify that each had lost the money from those cardboard banks. By the time we got to the third witness, the jury was nodding along when the witnesses testified to losing their coins.

Then we called the sheriff's deputies who inventoried the defendants' possessions when they were booked into the jail.

They affirmed that there was no money on Ira and three cents in George's back pocket. And the police officer who testified gave us a piece of new testimony about the piggy banks: One had been found torn to shreds in the alley between the warehouse and the next building. This was a valuable piece of evidence in our favor, particularly because two of the salespeople had testified that the cardboard piggy banks themselves were missing. Things were looking good for the idea that "some other dude dunnit."

The red Corvette

In retrospect, maybe it was gilding the lily to introduce one more piece of information for the jury to think about, but from their first interviews our clients had told us one and only one thing about what happened at the warehouse: They distinctly remembered seeing a red Corvette parked in front of the warehouse as they approached the building, and watched it drive away. From our interviews with the salespeople, we knew that a couple of them had seen a red Corvette occasionally parked in front of the warehouse. When they testified, we asked them about having seen the red Corvette. The judge scowled at us.

After some discussion with his client, Marco told me that Ira wanted to testify. "Great," I thought. I was happy to keep George off the stand. A jury always wants to hear the accused testify, but the reality is that testimony can often hurt a criminal defendant. Since most defendants are neither particularly skilled at words nor totally innocent, stories often get mixed up, vigorous cross-examination can expose lies or half-truths, and simple direct examinations can become nightmares. Besides, Marco was limited in what he could allow Ira to say: Since "did it" does not equate with "guilty," criminal defense lawyers are given great leeway to cast doubts on the facts. But they can't knowingly allow their clients to lie; that would be suborning perjury, a clear violation of lawyer ethics.

So having Ira testify was a plus for George. As far as the jury was concerned, Ira would be speaking for both clients, satisfying the jury's desires. But only Ira would be on the spot. And if Ira said something incriminating, it could only be held against him, not George.

Ira testified that he saw the broken window, told George he was going to stick his head in and take a look-see, and after he did, he poked his head back outside and said, "Hey, George, come on over here and check this out." All consistent with no intent, especially as to George. But Ira also testified that he and George saw a red Corvette pulling away from the front of the building.

When the judge heard this, he was livid, and immediately called us up to the bench. "What are you doing?!" he railed. "You're trying to show that *someone else did this!*" Marco and I looked at each other in amazement. Only then did we fully appreciate why Kostos was always bounced off cases by criminal defense lawyers – because proving that "someone else did it" was an essential and rather routine part of our job. Not *proving* it, exactly, but raising a *reasonable doubt* as to whether it was our guys and not someone else who broke into the warehouse and set off the alarm. Kostos had struck at the heart of what defenses lawyers try to do.

Rendered speechless, we had no instant reply to Kostos's bizarre accusation. The judge told us that we had better use the lunch break to clean up our act. As soon as we got out of the courtroom, Marco turned to me and asked, "What do we do now?" I had absolutely no idea.

We decided to seek out Tom Bruyneel, then the public defender's Chief Trial Counsel, who was always willing to share his wisdom with his stable of young deputies. Tom was considered San Francisco's best defense lawyer, a "true believer" and role model always generous with both his time and his advice. We began searching for him during the lunch hour, keeping in mind our 1:30 p.m. deadline. We finally tracked him down in the grungy cafeteria in the Hall of Justice basement.

We asked Tom whether we were missing something about our duty to the court, to which he replied, "Of course not!" Still worried, we asked what we should do about Kostos's objection to our defense. We were surprised by his answer: "Don't worry, he'll probably forget about it over lunch—and if he doesn't," Tom added, "just don't back down. You have the law on your side."

But over lunch Kostos had indeed forgotten about the Corvette. When we got back into court, we were able to finish up the testimony without further incident.

Closing argument and cherry pie

The main argument a criminal defense lawyer has on his or her side is the vitally important concept of reasonable doubt. I had already begun to "steal" from Tom Bruyneel's own renowned closing argument to explain this key principle. Here's a consolidated snippet of part of what Tom used to say:

"Ladies and gentlemen of the jury, when he was a young man, William Penn was convicted of sedition in England. The jury wanted to find him not guilty, but the judge objected and sent the jury back and ordered them to find Penn guilty. And so Penn came to America and founded the state of Pennsylvania. And when this country was founded, we decided that no king, no judge, no Star Chamber could take away the liberty of one of its citizens.

"It's as if we decided to treat the members of our community like members of our own family. If someone came to your door and said, 'Your Mary hit my daughter,' or 'Your Sam stole my son's bike,' would you say, 'OK, I'll deal with him'? Or would you say, 'Before I take action against my own child, prove it to me! Show me proof that makes me as certain as I possibly can be, and then, and only then, will I deal with him.'

"And so now, [Mr./Ms. DA] is coming knocking on your door saying...."

When I was trying criminal cases, perhaps the most well-known example used by DAs to counteract reasonable doubt and demonstrate the power of circumstantial evidence – the one that instructors taught at "DA College" – was the story of "Johnny and the Cherry Pie." And that's just what the DA in George and Ira's trial used. I was overjoyed as she launched into the narrative. In this particular case, the story was definitely not going to help her. Here's the essence of what she said:

"Sometimes we use 'circumstantial evidence' to prove our case. 'Circumstantial evidence' is evidence from which you have to draw an inference – a conclusion – before you can decide its meaning. The judge will instruct you that this kind of evidence is every bit as valid as any other evidence. Now the defense lawyers are going to get up here and argue about 'reasonable doubt.' And often when they do, they attack this circumstantial evidence because you have to draw an inference.

"But use your common sense! Drawing a conclusion is easy to do most of the time. Let me give you an example. Mom bakes a cherry pie and leaves it on the kitchen table to cool. An hour later she comes back and sees the empty pie pan on the table – no pie, only some crumbs. She goes to Johnny's room and sees that all over his mouth and hands is sticky red goo that smells like cherries.

"Mom didn't see who ate the cherry pie, but she has circumstantial evidence – very strong circumstantial evidence – that Johnny ate the cherry pie. The cherry pie is gone, and Johnny has cherry goo all over his face and hands. That, members of the jury, is circumstantial evidence for which there's no reasonable doubt."

One of the problems with trial institutes, seminars, and DA colleges is that they focus on general principles and generic examples, often not tailored to the facts of a particular case. Tailoring is what the DA had failed to do here. I got up to make my closing argument in a case I was now almost certain we were going to win.

I went through the evidence with the jury, emphasizing that the judge would instruct them that one cannot be guilty of burglary unless the person had the intent to steal *at the time of entry.* And I reminded them that Ira had testified that he put his head in the broken window and called to my client, George, "Hey c'mon and check this out." Spontaneous, spur-of-the-moment, certainly not showing anyone's intent – especially George's.

But then I got to our best evidence: that the money from the piggy banks was nowhere to be found on our clients. And that's where "Johnny and the Cherry Pie" helped prove reasonable doubt, as I explained:

"Deputy DA Lew talked about circumstantial evidence and Johnny and the cherry pie. That's an interesting illustration, and in her example, there would be little doubt that Johnny ate the cherry pie. But let's see how that story applies to the facts of our case. When the police came and looked at George and Ira, they didn't find any pieces of cherry pie; there were only three pennies in George's back pocket. And where was the pie tin? Not on the kitchen table, not even inside the warehouse. It was outside in the alley in the form of a torn-open piggy bank, while George and Ira were still inside.

"The obvious explanation: Someone else threw the piggy bank away out in the alley. It couldn't have been George or Ira, since they were busted inside the warehouse. That's not just a reasonable doubt, it's strong proof that George and Ira had nothing to do with stealing that money – or that they ever planned to break into the warehouse to steal anything."

In other words, "some other dude dunnit."

Marco and I suggested that our clients might be guilty of trespass – they had no right to be in the warehouse – but that's all. And since trespass was punishable by ninety days and they had already been in custody about a hundred, we knew they would get out of jail immediately.

"My father sold apples on Ocean Beach"

In short order, our clients were acquitted of burglary and convicted of trespass. They planned to return to the jail and get their release papers that evening. Because they could only be sentenced to credit for time served, the judge pronounced sentence right after the verdict. During a break in the proceedings to dismiss and thank the jury, I took the two defendants aside to warn them about laughing during Judge Kostos's sentencing remarks.

Any good lawyer working in close quarters with the same judges and opposing counsel is obliged to learn their habits and quirks. I had heard that one of Kostos's favorite things to do was to deliver the "My Father Sold Apples" speech to defendants at sentencing, usually before incarcerating them for years. The short version of the speech went something like this:

"*Before I sentence you, I want you to know that there is still hope for you. When my father came to this country, he worked for many years selling apples from a pushcart on Ocean Beach so he could build a better life for his family. And I, his son, was able to go to law school and become a judge. And this could happen to you, if you use your time in prison to think about these things and come out a better man. Learn the lesson my father taught me."*

I'm sure that the judge was completely sincere in giving the lessons of this speech. But he and our two defendants came from different planets. And unlike most defendants being sentenced, our clients were getting out of jail that evening. Judge Kostos may have been sincere, but he had never made any effort to learn about how George and Ira, and other defendants of color experienced their lives growing up as products of their upbringing. Kostas's failure to appreciate this made the disconnect between judge and defendants almost complete. So, before his speech, all Marco and I could do was to them to *please* not snicker during the speech, but to sit there quietly and respectfully.

They did well. Well, they did ok.

EPILOGUE

During the Gershwin Brothers case, Marco and I speculated many times about what had actually happened, often an important component of testing a defense. One thing seemed clear to us: George and Ira had not taken the money from the cardboard piggy banks. But what *had* happened? Our clients had told us little. Was our "dude dunnit" story the truth – had someone else broke in, brought the pickaxe and gloves, ripped off the piggy banks, heard a noise or otherwise got frightened, and took off down the alley throwing the remaining piggy bank down as he fled?

Was it possible that the red Corvette was not just a red herring, and that when it pulled away as George and Ira walked down the street, it contained a thief, or even an inside man trying to steal from his own company?

Or did George and Ira have a confederate? An accomplice who fled when he heard noises or police sirens, who had the money from the piggy banks, and who had left the pair holding the bag – and literally holding the gloves and pickaxe?

Marco, newer to the game than I, really wanted to know. Ira would tell him nothing. He asked whether I'd go to see George to ask him before he was released from custody. But by this time, after five years in practice and ten felony trials, I had become a little jaded, and I had learned from experience that whatever George told me even after the trial might not have much relationship to the truth. So, I told Marco I wasn't interested, that the only thing that mattered is what happened in the courtroom, and since we'd never know what actually happened, it didn't make any difference. We were not supposed to be Sherlock Holmes. Our clients were out of custody and out of our lives. Our job was to get our clients off, and that job was finished.

5

Back to Back to Back

People of the State of California v. Arnold, Arnold and Jones

People of the State of California v. Leonard Sanders & Willie James

People of the State of California v. Gypsy Harris & Ralph Bradley

After five-plus years of practice, I was firmly ensconced in the roster of court-appointed lawyers in San Francisco, assigned to represent defendants when there was more than one in the case, which gave the Public Defender a conflict of interest. I was also working as a "special" deputy public defender in Marin County north of SF, picking up overflow cases as they needed. As a result, there were times when I was going out to trial back-to-back. Among those trials was the "Gershwins'" burglary case. But before it came Satch Arnold, and right after, in rapid succession, Leonard Sanford and Gypsy Harris, among others. Each of these cases was difficult in its own way. Collectively, they had much to teach me, about advising my clients while still respecting their individual autonomy, and as a reminder of the painful lessons of our less than even-handed justice system.

SATCH

Rather incredibly, after my first trial, a hung jury, I had won acquittals in my next five criminal trials. The next trial up was that of Samuel "Satch" Arnold in Marin County, another dead-bang case. Sometimes, as with the "Gershwins," these cases do have small pinprick windows that can lead to acquittals. But usually, they do not. This one seemed like it did not. It was a robbery followed by a hot-pursuit chase ending in Satch, his wife Irma, and his co-defendant Harold Jones being arrested.

Caught red-handed

I met Samuel Arnold in the Marin County Jail just after I had been appointed to represent him by Judge David Baty, my favorite judge. The first thing Arnold told me is that everyone called him "Satch." The second was that he had been to the joint twice, and was on a parole hold, which meant no bail was possible. The third thing I learned was that his crimes were all drug-related because he was a heroin user. The fourth thing he told me was that I should never use the term "junkie." He made it clear that he was not a junkie, but a "dope fiend." I didn't necessarily understand the difference, but I certainly respected using whatever term he preferred.

The final thing he told me was that he knew he didn't have much of a case, but he was very concerned about his wife, Irma, who was driving the getaway car. Irma had a clean record, and Satch felt that it was his fault that she was involved in the case at all. He said he understood the seriousness of the case, since Harold Jones had a gun and shot it off during the altercation that followed the botched robbery. And that could mean prison time not only for him but for Irma, despite her having no prior convictions.

The likelihood of conviction in this case looked exceptionally high. Satch and Harold had gone into the Circle Market in San Rafael – a large convenience store right near a freeway entrance – with Harold holding a gun and Satch going behind the counter to clean out the cash drawer. As they moved to leave, the owner ran out of the store and Harold fired a shot in the air, then went over and kicked him a couple of times hard between the legs. The store owner doubled over in pain as Satch and Harold jumped into the car and Irma sped off, hopping onto the freeway.

Unfortunately for them, the owner must have alerted the police because within thirty seconds on the freeway, the three could hear sirens behind them. Apparently, the cops also had a description of their Buick because they zeroed in on it right away. The result was a hot-pursuit chase like the ones we see on television cop shows.

This chase ended when, heading south and approaching the Golden Gate Bridge, where a tollbooth would stop them, Irma, turned off at Tiburon Boulevard, a four-lane divided road heading east to the Tiburon peninsula. By this time, four squad cars were closing in. Eventually, the three decided to ditch their car and run up a forested hill on the south side of the road. The cops did the same, and just like on most of those TV shows, the police eventually caught up with Satch and his companions, lying on the ground exhausted. In their immediate vicinity was a bag of money and a .38 caliber pistol. Bad facts for Satch, bad facts for all three. They were all charged with armed robbery and aggravated assault, including Irma, who as the driver of the car, qualified as an aider and abettor. Harold had engaged in almost all of the violent activity, but under the law, Satch and Irma were equally guilty of robbery.

Conflicting interests and appointed co-counsel

As in San Francisco, the policy of the Marin County Public Defender – and almost every public defender's office – was to never represent more than one defendant in any one case. Even if two people seem perfectly aligned – say, twin brothers and best friends with the same history, background, rap sheet, and culpability – there can always be something that drives a wedge between them. If nothing else, the prosecution might agree to take a deal from one to testify against each other. For that reason, when people's freedom is at stake, public defenders have long maintained that they should never represent more than one person in the same case. And the state – both DAs and judges – long ago acceded to this legitimate ethical principle. After all, *each individual* deserves someone who is loyal only to that one person. That's really what the phrase "conflict of interest" is all about. In fact, it would be much better understood if both lawyers and lay people thought of its inverse – loyalty.

The public defender gets word of the case the moment it's filed, so usually the deputy assigned gets to pick which person to represent. Frank Cox tended to pick the toughest defendant.

But John Burks was not star defender Frank – far from it – so it wasn't surprising that he picked Irma, the lightweight who "just" drove the getaway car. The most serious case, Harold Jones's, went to Vern Smith, whom I knew because he had been the DA's pleadings drafter in the San Quentin Six case. I didn't know him well – I'd probably exchanged all of ten words with him – but I knew he was smart, because his replies to our motions were almost always spot on. I was worried, though, about how thorough and vigorous a defense lawyer he'd be.

I needn't have been concerned. Vern made it clear from the beginning that despite the daunting odds, he'd defend Harold to the absolute best of his ability. And he did. Not only that, he and I shared a legal secret that almost no other lawyer knew about – one that might just help. It was called the "Doctrine of the Election of Acts and Facts."

"The Election of Acts and Facts"

For well over a century, California has had an unusual aggravated assault statute, Penal Code section 245. Commonly called a "245" (California criminal lawyers love statute numbers) or an "ADW" for assault with a deadly weapon, it actually encompasses two separate crimes merged into one section of the law. One is the ADW, an assault with a firearm or other deadly weapon. But the other kind of assault is one committed "by any means of force likely to produce great bodily injury." No deadly weapon – in fact, no weapon at all – need be involved. Beating someone to a pulp would be this kind of 245.

There are other differences that make the ADW assault both easier to prove and more serious in consequences. Because an assault usually means just the *threat* of bodily harm, waving a pistol around, even without firing it, is an ADW. And use of a gun, even if not fired, enhances the sentence by adding extra time on to the punishment. But the physical beating kind of assault requires a subjective finding of great force, and thus is harder to prove. And the sentence doesn't get enhanced.

But when a defendant is charged with a 245 and the facts support both an ADW and a beating, there's a danger that there won't be a unanimous jury on either one of the two possible events. Six jurors may vote to convict because a gun was waved (with six others disagreeing), while six jurors could vote to convict because of the beating (with the others disagreeing). Thus, twelve jurors could agree on something, but not the same something.

To fix this problem, a case way back in 1900 came up with the doctrine of "the election of acts and facts," very rarely used but on the books since then – and still good law. Here's the idea: When there's a charge of aggravated assault, the DA may choose to elect which "acts and facts" prove the assault charged. Vern Smith and I came to know this legal "secret" during the San Quentin Six case. There, among the many motions I wrote was one demanding that for each assault charge in the indictment, where different allegations could have been used to prove the same charge, the DA should be forced to elect which fact pattern would be used for each charge.

Vern, researching it back then from the other side, realized that the DA should acquiesce to our demand. He did that because he had done his homework and discovered, as we already had, that if the DA *does not* elect a specific act, the assault that the DA must prove is *the first "acts and facts"* on which evidence is presented at trial. In Satch's case, we figured, correctly as it turned out, that the deputy DA assigned our case had never heard of this doctrine. Unlike the Six case, the last thing we wanted to do was to have her elect which assault to prove; she would have certainly chosen the gun. So, we did not make a motion for her to elect. Instead, Vern and I plotted how we could get evidence of the kicks to the groin in front of the jury before the gun got mentioned. Not only would that cut the maximum sentence, but it would permit an argument that the kicks were not so bad as to amount to aggravated assault.

Even assuming we could get the kicks in evidence before the gun, it didn't help us on the robbery charge, or on the extra time Vern's client was looking at for his personal use of a firearm. But it's true in law cases, as in life, that "you can only do what you can do." And we did what we could. When the jury came back after deliberations, all three defendants were convicted of robbery, and Harold with personal use of a gun. Fortuitously, while the jury convicted Harold of the assault charge, they were hung on that charge as to both Satch and Irma, probably because they couldn't agree whether they had aided and abetted Harold when he kicked the store owner violently in the groin.

An unusual sentencing hearing

During our several visits in the usual three weeks between conviction and sentencing, Satch begged me to argue for a lesser sentence for his wife instead of arguing about his own sentence. With a clean record, Irma had been released pending trial – a good sign. Getting probation, maybe with a stay in the county jail first – a far cry from state prison – seemed at least a possibility.

At first, I wasn't sure how this sat with me. After all, Satch, not Irma, was my client. Satch likely was right about the outcome: He was going off to the joint anyway, and his wife was represented by a "WV6," what we called a bad defense lawyer—short for Walking Violation of the Sixth Amendment's right to counsel. But could I ethically argue for Irma's probation because I could make a stronger pitch than her own questionably competent lawyer? If I argued for her, it meant abandoning any chance of reducing Satch's sentence. Was that hanging him out to dry?

By then, I'd had several semesters teaching legal ethics under my belt. One of my favorite exercises to discuss with my class was the one I called "Should the lawyer be the client's savior or mouthpiece?" In class, students began by coming down strongly on the side of doing what *they* felt was in the client's best interests. I ultimately disagreed. I felt that the client had the right to decide. After all, as David and I used to say to each other, "We don't do the time." It was easier to say that in my ethics class than to practice it in court in a real case. Still, Satch was an adult, and he made his desires clear. In the final analysis, I believed that not only should I argue for Irma but that I must. My client had given me a clear directive; my job was to execute it.

At sentencing, I stood up and said that I would submit Mr. Arnold's sentence on the probation report, which of course recommended the inevitable state prison sentence. And then I launched into a defense of Irma. Her lawyer had already given a rather inept argument, and hearing a plea for probation coming from someone other than her own lawyer got the judge's attention. After some deliberation, the judge suspended Irma's sentence on condition she have three years' probation and serve nine months in jail. That made Irma eligible for work furlough, where she could work during the day and return to custody at night.

Irma quickly got a furlough-eligible job waitressing in San Rafael and eventually moved to a halfway house. A couple of years later, I heard she had successfully made it off probation. That almost made me feel that the case was a success.

LEONARD

Sometimes, going to trial can really work to your client's detriment – even winning a trial. The sad story of Leonard Sanford demonstrates that unfortunate lesson. Like Satch, Leonard was arrested with his co-defendant right at the scene of the alleged crime. Things didn't work out as planned.

Leonard Sanford was busted with his friend Willie James on a sunny Saturday afternoon as Willie was moving items that were not his from a garage that was not his into an old sedan that was. It seemed that Willie was doing all the work. Leonard was just sitting in the driver's seat of the car. Still, of course, they were both arrested.

At arraignment in San Francisco's dingy Hall of Justice, I was appointed to represent Leonard, while a friend, Norman Frederick, was appointed for Willie. The first and in some ways the most important issue in this case was whether I could get Leonard released from custody pending trial. An ex-con and drug addict, Leonard definitely had his life on the upswing: He had a job he'd held for a while that paid pretty well, a wife and son he loved, and a drug-maintenance program keeping him clean and sober. He really seemed like he was putting it together. For poor, largely minority, defendants, staying out of custody was often the key issue in their cases, especially for those like Leonard who seemed to be turning things around. Remaining in custody greatly increased the pressure on them to plead guilty, and to accept more jail, probation, and even prison time, regardless of what crimes they were actually guilty of, or even if they were not guilty at all.

Happily, due to a good "score" from the San Francisco Release Project, I had a lot of ammunition to argue for Leonard's release, most significantly so he could continue his job. The judge let him go. When we met afterwards in my office, Leonard told me that Willie was an old friend from the joint. The two decided to drive out to the ocean in Willie's sedan, and Willie asked Leonard to drive. On their way, Willie spied a garage with the door open, and some nice-looking equipment just inside the garage. He asked Leonard to pull over and got out to take a look. Leonard told me he just sat in the car while Willie threw some stuff in the trunk.

Unfortunately for them both, that's when a police cruiser drove by on routine patrol. What the officers saw was an open garage door and two Black guys in a white and Asian neighborhood putting goods in a car. They drew what to them seemed like an obvious conclusion. Without any idea if Willie and Leonard had a right to be in that garage, the cops detained them and held them for questioning. A short time later, a couple drove up and pulled into the driveway. It turned out they had gone to the store and forgotten to close the garage. And yes, the goods in the car belonged to them.

Leonard and Willie were both charged with burglary. Once again, either because of sloppiness or a disinclination to have to prove that the items taken were worth more than $500, grand theft was not charged. But in terms of guilt or innocence, this case wasn't looking much better than Satch's. The pre-trial settlement conference was held just two days after Satch's trial ended. Leonard's trial was set for the following Monday, and I figured a plea deal was very likely. I had tried to keep my client's best interests in mind. Sometimes that meant fighting to avoid a felony burglary charge. Here, though, it meant allowing Leonard to keep his job and thus his new-found stability by getting into the work furlough program in the jail. I thought I could get that deal if he pled to a felony, and with several felonies on his record already, his real issue was being able to keep that job.

The DA was willing to accept Leonard's burglary plea with no formal sentence imposed if he served nine months in jail.

That would make him eligible for work furlough and his drug treatment program, and, with no sentence formally imposed, it could reduce his felony conviction to a misdemeanor if he completed probation. Given Leonard's circumstances, it was the deal he needed.

But the DA's office had a strict policy of only offering "package deals." That meant that if Willie didn't plead guilty, Leonard's deal was off the table, and he'd have to go to trial. The package deal had always seemed to me to be an unethical policy of the DA's office. It seemed like an excuse to try to extract more guilty pleas. After all, why shouldn't each defendant be treated as an individual? Although many DA's offices never had this policy and many others have abandoned it, to this day there's nothing in the prosecutors' code of ethics that strictly prevents it. So, when Willie was offered a deal of state prison time, he refused to plead guilty, and off we went to trial. Leonard called his boss at work and got himself his maximum remaining sick days – four. Not a lot of wiggle room for what we thought could be a six- or seven-day trial.

We go to trial

Before we began picking a jury, I took pains to make it clear to our trial judge that Leonard wanted the deal he'd been offered. It wasn't often when I was happy with a plea bargain, but this one would let Leonard continue his recovery. Besides, under the circumstances I thought a conviction was very likely. First and most simply, we had bad facts. And second, Leonard, though a soft-spoken and sweet individual, was 6'5", 230 pounds, and Black. So, I wanted it on the record that we were essentially forced out to trial. In addition to trying to preserve the deal, I told the trial judge that we would not be calling Leonard to the stand, and in fact that I would not call any witnesses at all, only cross-examine the witnesses who were called in order to provide competent representation, and then do a closing argument to the case to the best of my ability. None of that guaranteed anything, but my hope was that after a conviction, Leonard's cooperation would get him the same deal as before trial.

Before telling the judge all this, I had a detailed conversation with Leonard, who readily consented. I also had a bit of an ethical debate – with myself. Was it ethical for me to do less than my utmost to get Leonard off? It was a brief debate. First, I really didn't have witnesses and would likely have wanted to keep Leonard off the stand anyway. But second and more importantly, as I'd learned representing Satch, my goal was not necessarily to win, but to act in what my client and I both believed was in his best interests.

The trial got off to a quick start. By lunch on the second day, the owner of the house and garage testified that the items in Willie's car belonged to him and his wife, and a police officer testified that he saw Willie at the opening of the garage grabbing stuff and moving it towards the car, and that "contraband" was found in the trunk. That was the prosecution's case. When we broke for lunch on Day Two, I figured we could rest without witnesses, argue the case, have a verdict by Day Three, and send Leonard back to work pending sentencing.

That is, until Norman joined me at The Lineup, a bar and restaurant around the corner from the "Hall" where many of the lawyers ate lunch during trial. "Willie's insisting on testifying," he told me. I asked what Willie was going to say, and Norman confessed that he had no idea. Still, we both knew that whether a criminal defendant testified was a matter the lawyer could advise the client about, but the decision rested solely with the client. I didn't think Willie had the verbal skills or cunning to bear up under even a reasonably rigorous cross-examination, and I agreed with Norman that Willie was unlikely to help his case. But my main thought was, "There goes our three-day trial and Leonard's chance to get back to work quickly."

In any trial, lawyers are entitled to make an opening statement. Unlike argument, opening statements are supposed to stick to the facts: "Members of the jury, the evidence will show…." The lawyer for the plaintiff or prosecution, going first, must make an opening statement right after jury selection. But the defense can decide to defer statements until the start of the defense. Both Norman and I had deferred our opening statements, the most common course. And without putting in any evidence, I wasn't going to make a statement at all. But now Norman had a problem. "What am I going to say in opening statement?" he asked me. I suggested that he stand up and tell the jury, "Rather than hearing about his testimony from me, I'm just going to call Mr. James to the stand and let you hear it directly from him." That's what he said, and the jury seemed relieved that they'd avoid one more lawyer speech.

With Norman not knowing what Willie was going to say, his examination was filled with questions like "What happened next?" and "And then?" Willie testified to the story we had both heard: He and Leonard were driving out to Ocean Beach when they saw an open garage. Willie asked Leonard to stop and got out to examine the items lying in the driveway near the garage door. He found a few interesting things and picked them up, opened his trunk and put them in. He went back to the garage and was picking up something else when the squad car pulled up. Nothing mentioned about physically going into the garage. So far.

Cross-examination was far lengthier than it should have been, with a prosecutor not yet adept at cutting to the chase. Still, after asking Willie several times in several different ways, the DA was able to get this statement about going into the garage: "I guess my foot might have crossed over the threshold." In a moment of lost self-control, Norman put his head in his hands.

Testimony wrapped up and arguments took place on Day Four. I made the best argument I could. Leonard, the alleged "aider and abettor," never got out of the car, even to open the trunk. He had no active participation. Besides, if Willie didn't actually go into the garage, the case wasn't a burglary. And if he did go in but didn't have any intent to steal when he entered, it *still* wasn't a burglary. And of course, reasonable doubt, reasonable doubt, and reasonable doubt. The judge gave his instructions to the jury and sent them home.

On Friday, Day Five, the jury began its deliberations. Now very worried about the trial's length, I urged Leonard to call his boss to come up with some reason why he'd missed two extra days. I was hoping that if we wrapped things up with a verdict that day and Leonard remained released prior to sentencing, he might be able to keep that job.

It was not to be. At the end of the day, the foreman reported that the jury was still working but hadn't yet reached a decision. The judge ordered them to return Monday morning. And so, they did, and they worked all through the day Monday and came back for more on Tuesday, Day Seven. At this point, I was sitting in the crummy little basement cafeteria of the Hall of Justice thinking that Leonard had lost that job when a bailiff came down to find me. "They've come to a verdict on Sanford," he told me. "Sanford?" I thought. "Why not James?" He was much more obviously guilty than Leonard was.

Norman and I and Leonard, waiting in the hallway with his family, trooped back into Department 26, and the jury was called in to read its partial verdict. We stood, as protocol required, as the jury members entered and took their seats, and as the foreman handed the verdict form to the clerk. "People of the State of California versus Leonard Sanford," she read, "we the jury find Leonard Sanford 'not guilty.'" Frankly, I was shocked by the result, and so was Leonard.

We had won the case. But in the larger sense, we had lost the man. Seven days in, Leonard had probably lost his job. Well on his way to recovery, and without the support of the work-furlough social workers that a plea deal or even a conviction would have provided, sustaining recovery and finding other work was likely to be extremely difficult. Leonard was happy with the acquittal, but you could see the palpable concern on the face of his wife. We all hugged, and Leonard left the building a free man.

Two days later, Willie's trial hung 8-4 to convict. He eventually pled guilty to the same deal he turned down before trial.

As for Leonard, the next time I saw him, he was in County Jail #1 on the sixth floor of the Hall of Justice, busted for robbery with use of a gun. Leonard had indeed lost his job and slipped back into drug use. At his request, I was appointed again to represent him. After reading the police reports, I knew he was in a heap of trouble this time.

The complaint against him and his co-defendants charged three different robberies, only the most recent of which involved Leonard. A Lesbian couple, who also were partners in crime, was accused of robbing three elderly women in their apartments. In the third incident described in the police reports, the couple took along a large Black man with a sawed-off shotgun. They invaded the woman's apartment, stole jewelry and cash, and when they heard sirens from the street, they went out the back door and through the tradesman's entrance, then hopped across some backyard fences in an effort to get away. Meanwhile, to focus police attention away from themselves, they instructed Leonard to go out the front door, which he obediently did, holding the shotgun in his hands with the elderly tenant in tow, right into the waiting arms of ten police officers.

Up in the jail, I asked Leonard what the hell he was doing with a shotgun. He told me the women gave it to him and promised him $500 for the job. He needed it for dope. And when they told him to go out the front door, he didn't think about not complying.

The women were quickly caught and went off to prison after cutting a deal to resolve all three robberies. That left Leonard, whose trial was set for the first week of January. With overwhelming evidence against him, the best I could do was to argue for less prison time. We drew Judge William Mullins for the settlement conference. A tough old member of the Irish political crowd, Mullins was nonetheless a man with a heart. At the conference, I told him the whole sad story of Leonard's last case, and the bad luck he had by being acquitted and not getting work furlough. The DA had recommended ten years, and Mullins had almost settled on eight, when I pleaded with him one more time. Mullins, noting it was the last court day before Christmas, knocked another year off the sentence, telling us it was his Christmas present to Leonard. I never heard from Leonard again.

GYPSY

Sometimes clients are simply afraid to go to trial no matter what. Even if they're completely innocent. In what was the opposite of Leonard Sanders' situation, I had to push my client not to plead guilty to something she didn't do.

I was appointed to represent Gypsy Harris on a robbery charge about a month before Satch Arnold's robbery case went to trial. Because her co-defendant, Ralph Bradley, was in custody, the evidentiary preliminary hearing was heard about ten days before Satch's trial started. Gypsy was out of custody despite facing the same charges as Ralph, who remained in jail because he had a felony record. While Gypsy had a long record of "B cases," she had an equally long record of always appearing in court. And showing up in court was the most important factor in determining whether to release someone before trial.

When Dashiell Hammett, Raymond Chandler, and others in the Golden Era of detective fiction back in the 1930s described "cheap hookers," they called them "B-girls," after section 647(b) of the California Penal Code, the statute prohibiting prostitution. Professionally, Gypsy was a B-girl. Ethnically, she was mostly what we then called "American Indian." Like too many indigenous tribespeople brought up in poverty, Gypsy got involved with alcohol by age fifteen; by age seventeen, she was hooked on hard drugs. She drifted for some years before settling in San Francisco's Tenderloin District. Notorious both then and now, the Tenderloin was the part of town filled with cheap "SROs," or single-room-occupancy hotels, liquor stores on every corner, and a high concentration of prostitutes trolling the streets. Today, it's the center of San Francisco's homeless population. Then and now, a good number of seniors on fixed income live there, though they venture out at their peril.

When I sat down with Gypsy in my office, she freely told me about her history, and then about what happened on the day she was charged with robbery. She wasn't at all afraid of lawyers. Rather she was candid as always. She knew that when you get busted, lawyers help you get the best deal possible. They were part of her cost of doing business.

She told me that Lionel Wright, who she knew from the neighborhood, came up to her one afternoon on her corner – Leavenworth and Eddy – and said he'd pay her for sex. They went up to her room in a nearby SRO hotel, but he didn't have any money, so when her friend – she wouldn't acknowledge him as a pimp – Ralph Bradley showed up, she and Ralph threw Lionel out, with Lionel a little worse for wear.

Apparently, Lionel went to the police and claimed that after Gypsy had solicited him for sex on the street, Ralph and Gypsy had beaten him up and stolen $100 from him. If true, that would be robbery "by force or fear," to quote the language of the criminal statute. Gypsy was especially outraged at the solicitation part of the story: "I didn't do nothing! I never solicilated him! He tried to solicilate me!" It was not hard to believe her story. Robbery was not in her repertoire, and well beyond her rap-sheet profile.

After laying out the story a couple of times, Gypsy asked me what kind of time she'd have to do when she pled guilty. Not "if" but "when." Whenever she got busted on a "B" case she would plead guilty, do a little time, clean up a bit, and go back on the streets. Gypsy was clearly afraid to plead not guilty – something she had never done. She was slow to appreciate that now she was charged with robbery – a crime with way higher stakes, and one she swore she didn't commit. I told her that first we'd have to go to a preliminary hearing to let the DA present evidence. Even that scared her. She thought she should be pleading guilty by now. Fortunately, I was able to convince her that at least for the moment, she had to play out the hand.

Department 19

The current San Francisco Hall of Justice wasn't opened until 1961, and yet by the late 1970s, it felt fifty years old. A set of concrete boxes housing courts on the first three floors, jails on the sixth and seventh, the police department's Central Station in the lobby, and, at that time, the DA's office, the Public Defender, and the police department's detective bureaus filling the rest of the space, it was dingy, dark, and dirty, and remains so today. It never had any of the elegance of the old Hall of Justice on Kearney Street in Chinatown. Perhaps that's why the opening shot of *Ironside*, starring Raymond Burr as the City's chief of detectives, used the old Hall, which had already been torn down, for its opening montage.

Eventually, the jail was rebuilt and modernized. But back at the time of Gypsy's case, by overwhelming consensus the worst place in the building was Department 19. Back then, California courts were separated into "municipal" and "superior" courts, municipal courts handling misdemeanors and felony preliminary hearings. Unlike the other courts on the first three floors, Department 19 was located on the sixth floor. Foreshortened, containing only enough space for the judge, bailiff, clerk and two counsel tables, plus two narrow rows of seats behind counsel, it had no space for either an audience or a prospective jury panel. It's location on the sixth floor was to have its holding cell connected directly into the sixth-floor jail. Unsuitable for jury trials, the courtroom was used almost exclusively as a felony prelim department.

But first, every morning, the "drunk tank" calendar was called at 8:30 a.m. Penal Code section 647(f), or "drunk in public," is a misdemeanor that carried a sentence of six months but, in reality, was a revolving door to get the falling-down drunk safely off the streets. Those picked up the night before were placed in the holding cell after breakfast and paraded in in groups in front of the judge. If they'd sobered up sufficiently to walk out, their cases were dismissed, and they left custody immediately. By the time the prelim calendar started at 9:30 a.m., the place reeked of alcohol.

Department 19 was a place where idiosyncratic lawyering and judging ruled the day. The judges assigned to that department for six-month to one-year stints felt like they were in purgatory. Judge Frank Smith in particular used to struggle with getting through more than an hour of testimony before a recess. He could make it from about 9:45 to 10:55 until he'd look at his court reporter, and then at the clock as it moved toward 11, then look back at the reporter, and say "I can see that Madame Reporter is tired. We will take a ten-minute break" - which always ran an extra five minutes. Once I made a bet with Bob Lincoln, a young deputy public defender, who told me he was certain Smith would look at the clock first, and then the reporter. I said no way: reporter, then clock, and then back to the reporter. We each put a quarter down on counsel table to seal our bet. When Smith looked first at the reporter and then the clock, Bob slid his quarter over in my direction. Just another day in Department 19.

But serious stuff took place there too. Once I had a robbery preliminary hearing set there where a single eyewitness identification was the only evidence. Eyewitness IDs are notoriously inaccurate, particularly if they are cross-racial, "white on Black" especially. I was representing a young Black guy who was out of custody. I asked him to bring a bunch of friends who looked like him up to Department 19 on the day of the prelim, so I could get a fair shot at testing the witness' ability to identify him. Having *one* Black guy in the courtroom sitting right next to his lawyer was way too big of a hint. When Judge Sam Yee took the bench, he looked out into a sea of Black faces, then screamed, "Are you trying to intimidate me with all these black people?" and threatened to hold me in contempt. Fortunately, the witness didn't show up, the moment passed without further confrontation, and I escaped without being rolled up into custody.

Mark saves the day

Gypsy's preliminary hearing was set in Department 19 with that same judge, Sam Yee, presiding. Because the alleged victim, Lionel Wright, was a public defender client on a couple of minor cases, Ralph Bradley also had a court-appointed lawyer, a guy named Mark Rosenbush, who was still in his twenties and less experienced than me at the time. Fortunately, it turned out Mark was a terrific lawyer and found a great defense at the hearing.

As for me, I woke up with 102-degree fever. But with in-custody prelims, the show must go on. I was there physically but not near my best mentally. Mark had the "heavy," the ex-con with the felony record, so he was taking the lead anyway. He had two witnesses to tackle, Lionel Wright and his wife Melba. The rule in most courts, including in California, is that witnesses in the case are excluded from the courtroom until they testify. The theory is a solid one; if witnesses on the same "side" got to listen to each other's testimony, there would be too much temptation to conform their testimony to be consistent. So, when Lionel testified first about what happened, his wife Melba had to wait outside in the hallway.

The DA took Lionel through his version of events: Gypsy solicited him on a street corner; after he got to Gypsy's room, Ralph came in and beat him up and took his $100. Mark conducted a very brief cross-examination with one key question: What form was that $100 in? "Five twenties," said Lionel. Melba Wright, waiting outside the courtroom, was called next. She said that when Lionel came back to their apartment, he had a black eye and other bruises and abrasions. Mark asked Melba how come Lionel, who had no job and was on public assistance, had as much as 100 dollars on him. Melba said that she had given him that $100 that morning. Mark's next question was "What kind of bills did you give him?" "One nice crisp $100 bill," replied Melba. And there was our defense. I barely had to say a word. Despite this inconsistency and without giving it much if any thought, Judge Yee held both defendants to answer to felony charges in the Superior Court.

Mark and I weren't really surprised by this inconsistency. The whole case had felt bogus to us from the beginning. And Gypsy was no $100-a-throw call girl, but a fifteen-buck street prostitute. We both went to talk to the deputy DA in the three weeks between preliminary hearing and Superior Court arraignment, pointing out the obvious and asking him to dismiss the case. No dice. They'd gotten them "held over" – sent to the Superior Court for trial – and with Ralph's record, they wanted to get their hooks on him. Even with probation, Ralph would be a captive, be put on "supervised probation," meaning having a probation officer to report to and making him subject to probation revocation for any slight misdeed. And the cops, who were familiar with him, would have him in their sights. We got nowhere.

Finally, I chased down the DA for a conversation without Mark present. There was an urgency to this private audience that I of course did not share with the DA: Gypsy was now ready to plead guilty despite being entirely innocent. In her world, that was what you did, and she didn't fully appreciate the consequences, nor the differences between a robbery charge and a B case. Her current probations were "unsupervised," which meant that she was relatively unfettered. But even a plea to a felony with "straight probation" would dig those police hooks into her just like for Ralph. I urged the deputy as strongly as I could to drop Gypsy's case. No dice. None of my pleading helped soften the DA.

Heading to trial

Gypsy and Ralph both were arraigned, and a trial date and settlement conference set. It seemed to me that my job now became to convince Gypsy that *this* time, she couldn't just plead guilty, because the sentence could be state prison and at best she'd be stuck with supervised probation, where any transgression could mean state prison or months in jail. She was still reluctant, so with some trepidation, I decided to push hard, knowing that Gypsy didn't commit this crime, but worrying the entire time whether I was forcing her to make what could be a dangerous decision. Because innocent or guilty, robbery defendants can always lose at a jury trial, and losing often means state prison.

Here I faced the opposite situation from Leonard's case, where we both badly wanted a deal that would have gotten him on work furlough where he could continue his job and his recovery. But every case is different. In fact, Gypsy's case presented me with a more difficult ethical dilemma. In both Satch and Leonard's cases, I was doing something that they each strongly wanted while respecting their autonomy as clients. Autonomy was their right. As David and I often told each other, "We don't do the time." But in Gypsy's case, I felt like I was overriding her will. Ignorant or not of the circumstances, not really appreciating the great defense we had, she was nevertheless convinced that she had to plead guilty. And ultimately, it was completely her call.

At the settlement conference, held the week after Leonard was acquitted, the DA offered Gypsy a plea to a felony second-degree robbery, with supervised probation and no time in jail. A great deal in most circumstances, but one I could not abide in this case. Gypsy and I left the courtroom to discuss it. I pushed to have her wait until the day of trial, telling her the deal would still be available on that day, when judges made one last effort to clear the calendars. That was true, at least most of the time.

Gypsy finally agreed to wait the extra week. When the case was called for trial on a Monday morning in Department 22, the department deputy DA stood up and dismissed the case. A fair result, but only after a power-play of brinksmanship to extract a pound of flesh from an innocent person. At least I felt that pressuring Gypsy had been justified.

EPILOGUE

I never had any further contact with Gypsy. But a few months after her case I read something in Herb Caen's column in the *San Francisco Chronicle* that told me she was alive and well and back plying her trade. Back then, everyone read Herb Caen, and hundreds of folks used to send him little tidbits to print in his column. This one read: "Seen written in lipstick on a newspaper vending box at Leavenworth and Eddy: 'Trixie, if I'm not here or on Jones, I'm upstairs with a trick. Wait for me. Gypsy.'"

As for me, these three cases left their mark in several ways. First, they reaffirmed my belief that lawyers should respect their clients' decisions about their cases. Second, Gypsy's case reaffirmed that once in a while, in unusual situations, there's an exception to that rule; that it's okay for the lawyer to push the client really hard so long as ultimately, the lawyer will do what an unpersuaded client wants.

Pushing Gypsy to stay the course felt right to me. But some years before Gypsy's case, I had a juvenile client with significant mental health issues who had shot a small caliber gun at someone. He told me he wanted the juvenile court to send him to the Youth Authority, the most serious possible disposition. I tried to dissuade him, arguing that help from social workers and a good program of mental health treatment was a far better way to go. He said he didn't want anyone "shrinking my head." I pushed harder, trying to scare him straight. He told me he had "lots of friends in YA." I couldn't budge him as I did Gypsy. So, I went into court and argued to the judge for what he wanted – "send him to YA." The judge did, but on a trial basis with judicial review after 120 days. By that time, my client had seen quite enough and wanted the treatment alternative that he'd refused earlier. Fortunately, the Youth Authority report agreed, recommending home confinement with a treatment program, and the judge granted his request.

Finally, all these cases reinforced how capricious the legal system can be. And a capricious system is not one well designed to consistently mete out justice. In Satch's case, the arbitrary nature of the assault charges did not make much difference, because which event came into evidence first didn't affect his conviction for robbery. But in another fact situation, the "election of acts and facts" – or the prosecution's failure to elect – could mean the difference between "guilty" and "not guilty."

The effect of the system was more serious for Leonard and Gypsy. For Leonard, the DA's refusal to allow him to plead guilty and maintain his job and drug maintenance program was a real tragedy. The trial itself – the ultimate constitutional protection in a criminal case – was actually his undoing when coupled with his surprising acquittal. It left Leonard on an island with no job, no drug help, and ultimately no hope. Gypsy was more fortunate, but had I not come close to overriding her will, Gypsy would have wound up in the cycle of supervised probation that all too often leads to imprisonment.

As I look back from today's vantagepoint, I see how our justice system has improved in some ways: many judges and some prosecutors now oppose strict "three strikes" laws and mandatory minimum sentences; fewer states are using the death penalty; many more prosecutors are now on board correcting wrongful convictions; and fewer DAs require the kind of "package deals" that doomed Leonard. But in many ways, the system has become more repressive and regressive.

The number of people incarcerated in prison today has increased dramatically – several times the number of incarcerated back in the 1980s. Court decisions eroding the constitutional rights of criminal defendants have also increased dramatically, including limits on Fourth Amendment protections against unlawful searches and seizures and the Sixth Amendment's right to absolutely confidential counsel. And many states have passed "victims' bill of rights" legislation that could more accurately be described as bills to limit the rights previously enjoyed by criminal defendants. Meanwhile, the disparity between those with money and poor, mostly Black and brown people, does not seem to have improved much, if at all.

6

The Oldest Client Goes to Trial

Annette Friel v. Paroni Markets, Inc.

Should a lawyer take a ninety-eight-year-old woman through a jury trial? Can someone that old tolerate that stress? For a lawyer used to trying criminal cases, where you do pretty much anything and everything you can think of, the answer in the case of Annette Friel was "Sure, why not?" Age, in our world, is not an issue. But there's a caveat: Is the lawyer's "why not" is driven by ego, money, or "winning" rather than the best interests of the client? Still, with the insurance defense counsel making an offer we had to refuse – less than half of her medical expenses – Annette Friel and I not only went to trial to the shock of our opponent, but we did so with excellent results.

Mrs. Friel was ninety-six years old when she became my client after slipping and falling in Paroni's Supermarket on 24th Street near her home in Noe Valley in San Francisco. One day a couple of months after that fall, Francis Grady, Mrs. Friel's younger sister, walked into our office at the other end of Noe Valley and asked to see a lawyer. My partner and mentor, David, was the only one in the office at that moment. He met with Mrs. Grady and signed her up – or, rather, signed up her sister – to a contingency fee contract for the "slip-and-fall" case. To this day, Mrs. Grady brought in the only "walk-in" case I've ever had.

David soon regretted his decision to represent Mrs. Friel. He was a criminal defense lawyer through and through and didn't want to deal with having to learn how to do a civil jury trial, with all its differences: pre-trial discovery, burden of proof, having to show each element of that proof, and more. So, he talked me into taking the case, promising some help from my sister, then our junior partner.

We went to interview Mrs. Friel in her home a half-dozen blocks away. She was small and slight, with a pleasant face and a beautiful high-pitched voice that sounded almost as if she were singing. When she had an occasional sad thought, as when she remembered the death of her husband "right here on this couch," she had the habit of smacking her lips together three times and shaking her head, her false teeth jiggling as she did so. But by and large, Mrs. Friel was a constant ray of sunshine to everyone who met her. It was impossible to dislike her.

The scene

Mrs. Friel often went grocery shopping with her downstairs tenant, Devin Holcomb. On the night of her fall, she and Devin had gone to Paroni's in the early evening. They were by the meat display when Mrs. Friel realized she needed to use the bathroom. There was a flight of stairs behind a door next to the meat display. A butcher was usually stationed there so he could cut meats to order in the cutting room upstairs.

But on this evening, no one was there. So, Mrs. Friel and her escort mounted the stairs and found themselves in the meat-cutting room. Mrs. Friel soon slipped on the meat and fat debris on the floor, fell, and broke her knee. When we later visited the supermarket in the company of the junior lawyer on the defense team, the floor of the meat-cutting room was completely covered in scraps of meat and fat. You didn't have to be in your nineties to slip and fall on that stuff.

I asked the young lawyer whether I could take a few pictures, and to my surprise she said yes. I have no idea why. She could have simply refused. Lawyers are ordinarily focused on the vigorous (most lawyers use the word "zealous," a word I've come to avoid) representation of their clients, protecting them at almost all costs. We were not in court or a deposition and were having an otherwise pleasant conversation about nothing in particular, which might have accounted for why this lawyer simply let her guard down. Clearly, the floor of the meat-cutting room was a big point in our favor, and the pictures I took fit the cliché: They were worth a thousand words.

Depositions and the "known trespasser" rule

By this time, I'd tried well over a dozen criminal cases, but not a single civil jury trial. Perhaps because we were criminal defense lawyers who didn't know any better, and perhaps because we figured that we had to make sure who in the market saw what, when, and where, we set the depositions of every single Paroni employee who was working that evening. I was hoping to find someone who had told Mrs. Friel that it was okay to go up to the bathroom. But even more important, I wanted to make certain that no one told her *not* to go up those stairs.

Joe McManus, the defense lawyer, thought we were complete idiots, totally unskilled at this kind of work, wasting our time and over-prepping the case by setting the depositions of seventeen market employees. Except we weren't. I was just following the same script I'd learned to follow ever since my very first cases with David: Do everything that has to be done to pin down the evidence so it can't wiggle into something else later. The fact that no one saw Mrs. Friel go up to the bathroom or told her not to go was a crucial fact. The only way to make sure no one told her not to go up those stairs was to take a brief deposition of everyone working in the store that evening.

The dozen Paroni supermarkets around San Francisco all had the same clear policy: "No customers allowed in the bathrooms." That meant that legally, Mrs. Friel was a trespasser, someone who did not have the right to be where she was, ninety-six years old or not. But under the law, it made no difference whether she has the store's permission to go to the bathroom, either through the big double doors on the west side of the store, then up a wide stairway and down a clean concrete corridor past the market's offices, or up the narrower stairs next to the meat display on the east wall. When it came to "premises liability," a 1968 case called *Rowland v. Christian* had done away with the traditional common law distinctions between "invitees" (those with permission to be where they are), "licensees" (those who have permission for certain limited purposes), and "trespassers."

Essentially, the California Supreme Court had decided that someone could be liable for a dangerous premises condition regardless of whether the injured party had a legal right to be there. In this sense, trespassers were not criminals. They might just be people who wandered off from where they were supposed to be. After *Rowland*, the issue was whether the owner of the premises *knew* there were likely to be such trespassers. If so, when it came to liability, trespassers were no different than those who were invited to be there.

This was the essence of our claim in Mrs. Friel's case. During the depositions, several store employees acknowledged that they knew customers sometimes used the bathrooms. The manager on duty the night of Mrs. Friel's accident told us that she estimated that three people a day used the bathrooms. When I asked her whether she knew which path those people took to get the second floor, she said she didn't know. Three people a day? Over the years, that's a lot of trespassers.

"General damages"

In personal injury cases, money for "general damages," commonly called "pain and suffering," is added to "special" damages – hospital bills, doctor's visits, medicines, etc. A serious injury may not only be permanently painful but may prevent a person – especially people in the prime of life – not just from working, but from riding a horse, jogging in the park, or simply getting around easily without assistance.

Depending on how serious these issues are, general damages in such cases can be huge.

But with an elderly person – particularly very elderly – long-ago retired and not particularly mobile anyway, garnering significant sums for general damages is much more difficult. I asked some plaintiffs' lawyer friends how they dealt with this issue. Most relied on a general pitch they called the "golden years" argument – that folks should live out the rest of their years in peace, comfort, and contentment. That pitch didn't sound so great to me. I wanted to know what Mrs. Friel used to do before she broke her knee that she couldn't do now. But Mrs. F was not one to complain. Her most constant refrain, in her lilting, musical voice, was "Oh, I'm okay!" or "Oh, that's just fine!"

Still, there must have been something Mrs. Friel used to do that was beyond her abilities after the accident. Since she lived only a few blocks from my home, I took to stopping by on my walk home from work to chat with her. In one of our many conversations, she told me that she used to like to walk down the stairs from her second-floor flat, go outside, and pick the grass out from the cracks in the sidewalk. People would walk by and say hello, and she'd greet them in turn. Over a period of weeks, she spoke fondly of this several times, and it was obviously something that had given her great joy.

She also used to visit her neighbor across the street, a woman more housebound than herself. My sister and I visited the neighbor, and found ourselves ushered into a museum. Miss Julia, who was Mrs. Friel's age, lived in a one-floor Victorian cottage that her father had built for her years before the

Great Earthquake – when her mother was pregnant, awaiting her arrival. In a city known for its Victorians, this wasn't just another one; this house was the same as when it was originally built: all the original woodwork, leaded glass, built-in cabinets, ornate doors separating front and back parlors, and Victorian light fixtures that by then were extremely rare. This had been Miss Julia's home her whole life, a little jewel on the edge of Noe Valley. But now, after her fall, it had become too difficult for Mrs. Friel to visit. Miss Julia, almost as sweet and kind as Mrs. Friel, invited us back for tea. To spend another hour in that beautiful place with our gracious hostess made our second trip a real pleasure.

Mrs. Friel's visits with Miss Julia, and her daily ritual of weeding the sidewalk cracks were, I thought, much more affecting than some vague reference to Mrs. Friel's "golden years." My personal injury lawyer friends were singularly unimpressed, which worried me since they, not I, were the experts. But my gut told me they were missing the point. Put plainly, these were the things that Mrs. Friel had loved to do, that had given her the most amount of pleasure. Her daily trip outside was something important and real *to her*. And that made it a big deal.

We try to settle the case

Everyone involved on both sides of the case was familiar with *Rowland v. Christian.* But the insurance company lawyers were less familiar with the fact that a crazy criminal defense lawyer didn't know any better than to go to trial with a ninety-eight-year-old client. Fortunately, Mrs. Friel remained game for what she saw as an adventure, so I never had to evaluate the conundrum of whether I was pushing her out of her comfort zone just so I could chalk up a win and make some money.

Mrs. Friel had run up $22,000 in medical and hospital bills, but the Paroni lawyers only offered $5,000 to settle. Our starting demand – a soft one – was over $100,000. After he had spoken to both sides privately, the judge emerged from chambers to inform me and defense counsel that he couldn't even get our demands into consecutive numbers of figures: We were at six figures, they at four.

In other words, no settlement.

"I never thought I would wind up like this: a cripple!"

With the depositions of all the store personnel done, I felt increasingly confident about our case. But Mrs. Friel never complained. Good lawyers don't want whiny complainers as their clients in injury cases, but a little expression of regret, pain, or disappointment wouldn't hurt, and I could get none of this from Mrs. Friel. Then, about a week before trial, having tried just about everything I could think of to get her to talk about how much more difficult her life had become, I asked a question on another subject.

Mrs. Friel had a bathtub-shower combination. That meant that in order to get into the shower, Mrs. Friel had to step over the lip of the bathtub. She had mentioned that doing this was a bit difficult. One of the first things I wanted her to do if we won the case was a re-design of that shower so she could just walk straight in. And so, about a week before trial, I asked her "How has it been for you having to step over the lip of the bathtub to take a shower?" To my surprise, she shook her head from side to side and smacked her lips together three times, as she always did when remembering something upsetting. And then she said, "I never thought I would wind up like this: a cripple!"

Eureka! I had managed, completely fortuitously, to unlock her suffering, and in a way that would undoubtedly garner great sympathy with the jury. It was the first and only time Mrs. Friel ever complained about anything.

Mrs. Friel's memory was not the greatest, so I determined to come back to her house almost every day until trial to chat, working up to ask her that same key question. And every time I asked her the question about the lip of the bathtub, sure enough, she shook her head, smacked her lips three times, and in her kind, high-pitched voice told me, "I never thought I would wind up like this: a cripple!" Great, I thought. Now we've got something that really shows her pain to the jury. The dollars will roll in at trial.

Trial

Because of her age, Mrs. Friel was entitled to "preference" for getting a courtroom — a courtesy given to the elderly or people nearing death, so that they can have their day in court before passing on. It was my first trip to Department 1, a huge courtroom with everyone, men and women alike, dressed in navy blue suits, and a nervous hum reverberating around the room. For a guy unused to this scene, it was one of the scariest places I'd ever been in. Besides, I was the only lawyer dressed in brown sports coat and slacks, convinced by what I'd read that that would make me more accessible to the jurors I was about to select, particularly given my six-foot-three stature and full beard. Despite my being confident about not wearing the "lawyer uniform," the fact that I stood out just made Department 1 all that more daunting.

The presiding judge assigned us out to a commissioner, Frank Drulette, who worked as a sitting trial judge when the lawyers for the parties stipulated, or agreed, that he could have the same judicial authority as a duly sworn judge. I had done my homework on which judges, both good and bad, were likely to be available to us, but hadn't counted on a commissioner, whom I knew nothing about. I tried to check him out in the few minutes between the assignment and the case file being moved to his courtroom. We could always refuse to stipulate and get another courtroom.

I couldn't find any courtroom scuttlebutt about Drulette, so I decided that I didn't want the risk of the unknown, and I told a deputy clerk that we wouldn't stipulate to have Drulette hear our case. When the "PJ" heard this, he turned to the clerk and in a stage whisper with clear lip movements designed for me to unmistakably read, said, "Too bad, then; they won't get a courtroom." The law might require giving our nonagenarian preference, but the presiding judge ruled the courtroom, and in his courtroom, he *was* the law. We took the commissioner.

I had enlisted my friend and fellow lawyer, John Weinstein, to sit with me during the trial as he had done for Elvin

Drummond. More importantly, he'd pick up Mrs. Friel, get her in her wheelchair, and get her down to court before the proceedings started. The first day, John took her on a tour around San Francisco's City Hall, where she marveled at the Great Staircase, the marble floors, stained oak doors, and huge gilt-edged dome. City Hall remains a spectacular building, and no one ever enjoyed a tour of it more than Mrs. Friel. As we were picking the jury, with the rear of the courtroom full of prospective jurors, she leaned over to me and John and said in a clear, lilting voice filled with wonder: "Imagine! All these people, here just for me!" I forgot all about wondering whether I had pushed Mrs. Friel to trial. She was clearly relishing the experience.

With a couple of minor glitches, the trial went beautifully. No one had seen Mrs. Friel and Devin going to the bathroom, and no one had told her not to go. We called the manager of the market who was on duty that day, who repeated that there were two ways to get up to the bathroom – one up a wide set of stairs and past the market's offices on the second floor, and the other through the meat-cutting room. She repeated her estimate that three customers a day used the bathroom, and that she had no idea which of the two paths they took. And that night, instead of two butchers on duty – one on the floor by the meats and a second in the meat-cutting room – there was only one, who was often upstairs. These were crucial facts, all in our favor.

When it was Mrs. Friel's turn to take the stand, she was, needless to say, a big hit with the jury. How could anyone dislike her? She told the jury how she missed her visits with "Miss Julia" and especially, as she'd told us many times, that she enjoyed going outside to pick the grass out from between the cracks in the sidewalk, chatting with her neighbors as they passed by. She didn't remember where she fell, saying it was inside the meat-cutting room when, actually, based on Devin's testimony and where the market's employees found her, she fell after she had gone through the door from the butcher room to the upstairs hallway. My opposing counsel, McManus, a friendly old-school insurance-defense lawyer who'd tried scores of jury trials, seemed to make a big deal about her mistake in location on cross-examination, but I couldn't figure out why: We *knew* where Mrs. Friel fell. What could it matter that this ninety-eight-year-old didn't recall it accurately?

The only part of the trial that didn't go as planned was when I asked Mrs. Friel the magic question:

> Zitrin: *"Mrs. Friel, how has it been for you having to step over the lip of the bathtub to take a shower?"*
> The Witness (happily and without hesitation): *"Oh, fine!"*

Which proves it's almost impossible to prep a ninety-eight-year-old witness.

The doctor gets into a snit

In almost all personal injury cases, the insurance company hires a doctor to examine the plaintiff. These exams are commonly called "IMEs," or independent medical examinations, but they're not independent, because the doctor is hired by the insurance company, and naturally will tend to lean towards minimizing the injury suffered by the plaintiff. The doctor in this case, Stuart Garner, had a reputation as a straight shooter, and so he was. As a personal-injury-trial virgin, I decided to attend the IME, which due to my client's age and immobility took place in her home. It turned out that being present was a good decision. In those days, most lawyers didn't often attend IMEs, but after my first time, I never, ever missed one. There are all kinds of things that can happen between your client and the other side's doctor that could both hurt and help you. And you'll never know if you're not there.

When Dr. Garner got on the stand, he hedged about the permanence of the damage to Mrs. Friel's knee. I felt Garner was quibbling, and made the mistake of taking him on, trying to point to a variation between his written report and his current live testimony. This was a mistake for two reasons. First, the issue we were battling about was of minor importance at most. Mrs. Friel was ninety-eight, and her knee, logically, would never be the same. Also, Garner was an experienced expert witness and, frankly, a likeable guy. I'd always made a big effort to be the most likeable professional in the courtroom, which could give me a big advantage. But I was definitely getting "out-likeabled" by Garner, who knew his business. I ended his examination before I did too much damage to myself. He left the witness stand in a bit of a snit.

And then Mrs. Friel stepped up – or, more literally leaned forward. Here, I must explain the positioning of the parties in the courtroom. In a criminal trial, as I've mentioned, the DA sits closest to the jury, while the defendant and his or her lawyer are stuck on the other side of the room, next to the bailiff, the court calendar, and the water cooler. But for my first time in front of a jury, *we* were the plaintiff! So, we sat next to the jury. And, because the jury can best examine the witness' demeanor and easily hear the witness' testimony if the witness is nearby, the witness box is also on the jury side of the courtroom.

So it was that as Dr. Garner walked off the stand in a huff, he walked right by Mrs. Friel, who held out her left hand from her wheelchair and said in that sweet, mellifluous voice, "Oh, Dr. Garner, how nice it is to see you again!" And the doctor could do nothing other than smile, take her hand, and return the greeting.

Mrs. Friel had saved the day. The doctor's annoyance and my overaggressive cross-examination were forgotten.

Argument

Argument is always one of the most fun parts of a trial, and – as my mother had taught me in Elvin's murder case – a place where the words you choose can be extremely important. I had been especially looking forward to this argument because for the first time in front of a jury, I'd have two arguments instead of just one. Just as the District Attorney has a rebuttal argument after the first round in a criminal case, in civil cases the plaintiff also gets a rebuttal argument. The theory is that because the plaintiff has the burden of proving the case, the plaintiff's lawyer should get the last word.

This makes sense in a criminal case, in which the proof must be shown beyond a reasonable doubt. But in almost all civil cases, the plaintiff must only prove the case by "a preponderance of the evidence," which simply means tilting the balance of proof even a little bit in your favor. Still, I was given this precious gift, and relished the idea of using it to the greatest possible advantage. I saved up some of my best ammunition, as I had seen DAs do against me, for my second turn to speak.

My first argument was simple and straightforward. Mrs. Friel and Devin saw the door to the stairs, there was no butcher at the meat counter, no one there to stop them from going through the door, and no warning sign on the door (we had pictures). Mrs. Friel went through a room full of meat and fat debris on the floor (more pictures), fell, and broke her leg. Then a brief reminder that the judge would instruct the jurors that it didn't matter whether Mrs. Friel had the right to be there or not, so long as the store knew that people might use those stairs to get to the bathroom. And finally, some simple math: Since three people a day used the bathroom (over 900 a year), and according to the manager no one knew how they got up there, that and "no public bathrooms" signs throughout the store meant that either path to the bathroom was an equally likely route – 450 people through the double doors, and 450 through that dangerous meat-cutting room. Sure, I knew – and the jury most likely would assume – that the clear majority of people probably went to the bathroom through the double doors to the offices. But even if a tenth of those people took the door next to the meat counter, that would still have added up to ten people a month using the more dangerous route upstairs, clearly something the store should have been aware of.

Joe McManus knew by this time that he had miscalculated by not offering us more money. He was an experienced trial lawyer and understood well that we had presented a pretty seamless case with an almost perfect plaintiff. But lawyers don't just give up in the middle of trial, so he stood up and did his best. "What could we have done?" he said, and then repeated it again. "What are we supposed to do to prevent this kind of thing?" This was exactly the argument I'd hoped he'd give.

The night before, I'd gone into my seven-year-old son's stash of fruit-scented marking pens and made some signs to show the jury the next day: "Danger, Do Not Enter, Meat Cutting Room" in raspberry red, and "Stop! Do Not Use This Door!" in blueberry blue. That morning, I'd stopped at the hardware store just across from the supermarket and bought a hook-and-eyelet that could be screwed into a door to latch it closed when no butcher was on duty. I was ready for rebuttal.

"Members of the jury, Mr. McManus just asked you, 'What could we have done?' Well, let me tell you: They could have made a sign like this one I made last night, and taped it to the door." (I added something about my son's scented marker collection to gild the lily just a bit before moving on.) *"They could have bought a latch for the door like I did this morning at the hardware store right across the street from the market! Do you know what this latch cost? Sixty-nine cents! The butcher could have used this to lock the door when he went upstairs. But they did nothing!"*

The jury was totally with me.

I don't think there's such a thing as trying a perfect case, and I certainly did not meet that standard here. One of the things working in my favor was that, while I had done many civil court trials, I had never had a civil jury trial, and having a jury is just flat out different and much harder. So, I prepared like crazy to avoid looking like an idiot. Fear, sadly, remained one of my best motivators as a trial lawyer.

But I made plenty of mistakes in this case, the last being my telling the jury that I'd purchased the door latch for less than a buck from a store right across the street from the market. I saw this as a cool factoid. But by bringing in information not in evidence in the case – that I'd bought the door latch right across the street – I knew I'd breached my ethical duty. Mentioning it unnecessarily and gratuitously meant I was actually testifying in argument about something the jury had never heard, clearly inappropriate. This was my first experience having the last word in argument, and I just couldn't help myself. For a few weeks after the trial, I was paranoid that McManus would raise this impropriety in a motion for a new trial. Could I have screwed up this great case by letting my ego get the best of me at a crucial moment? Looked at with years of hindsight, I see it as a trivial transgression, not material enough to affect the verdict. But at the time it loomed large. Fortunately, McManus made no motion, and I learned my lesson at the cost of only a few hours' sleep.

The Aftermath

The jury deliberated for quite a while, long enough for me to get a little worried. It turned out, though, that they were adding up what the verdict should be by specifically including the cost of renovating the bathtub, so that Mrs. Friel would have a flat surface to walk into the shower. They awarded her $181,000, far more than the $78,000 that had been our final demand, and greatly in excess of the $15,000 the insurance company offered on the day of trial. Commissioner Drulette granted "remittitur," which he was entitled to do sitting as "the 13th juror," and knocked the verdict down to $140,000. But even that number was so high for a case of this type that we accepted it gladly.

EPILOGUE

Mrs. Friel retained her sunny disposition for the rest of her days. We celebrated her 100th birthday with her in her home. John Weinstein, who had been part of the more dramatic aftermath of Elvin's case, brought his infant son, and we took a picture of her holding baby Aaron. She died peacefully in her sleep at 103.

As for the door to the butcher room at the Paroni Market, when I visited the market from time to time during family shopping trips over the next fifteen years, I noticed that no one had ever put either a warning sign or a latch on the door at the meat counter. The dangerous condition existed until the market closed many years later.

As always, there were lessons to be learned from this case. The most important for me as a trial lawyer was the reminder to never let my ego get in the way of my client's case, especially by doing something flashy, as I'd done by presenting the factoid about where I'd bought that door latch. But there were other lessons as well, including the re-affirmation of what David had always taught – that in trying cases, there should be

Mrs. Friel and baby Aaron Weinstein

few boundaries other than the wishes of the client. Mrs. Friel's age was never a boundary, just an issue to overcome.

One helpful lesson I filed away for future work was that I'd been grossly underestimated because of my criminal law background. Back then, civil trial lawyers tended to look down their noses at criminal defense lawyers, assuming that they knew next to nothing about the "real world" of civil trial work. Many also felt that criminal work was filled with "bottom feeders" hanging out with bail-bonds agencies across the street from the criminal courts. They had a much healthier respect for former deputy district attorneys, whom they saw as skilled, well-trained, and disciplined. Personally, though, I found civil trials significantly easier than even the simplest criminal case.

It's true that then, as now, some criminal defense attorneys were bottom feeders, though they had no monopoly on sleaze in the profession. But civil litigators' negative impressions of defense lawyers could not have been more wrong. Almost all the best trial lawyers I know cut their teeth on criminal defense. Equally adept in their knowledge of the law and their comfort in the courtroom, they make split-second decisions that can be the difference between winning and losing. With the facts usually aligned against them, these lawyers often live by their wits, more inventive and imaginative than any civil litigator. As for DAs, they were usually reasonably well-trained. But with the facts generally on their side, most relied on a more mechanical, formulaic approach, like the deputy in the Gershwins' case, without thinking to do much heavy lifting.

Finally, I was struck by the fact that this trial seemed to be just a moment in time that came and went, with nothing really changed as a result. Mrs. Friel never got her bathtub fixed. Indeed, with a nice home to live in and enough pension money to be comfortable, she didn't need the money we'd won for any other reason. As for Paroni's, they never did latch the door to the cutting room at night, as if the case had never happened. The case had occurred, but it had changed almost nothing.

7

Kenny Krazy

People v. Simon Stanley

Murder cases are tough enough without the client bearing an "a/k/a" moniker that appears right on the face of the murder complaint, where a jury can't possibly miss it. Not a good start. That's without considering the six eyewitnesses to felony murder. And murder during the commission of a felony was murder in the first degree. Given the bad facts and the flaky but truthful witnesses, this case was no picnic. It was hardly helped by the outlaw image of my client, a member of the punk-rock scene, perceived by most as a venue of vitriol and violence.

Simon and the punk-rock SRO

Ever since the Barbary Coast days, San Francisco has had a proliferation of small, inexpensive lodgings called single room occupancy hotels, or "SRO's," like the one Gypsy Harris lived in. In the 1930s, the City became known to some as "Hotel City," when 90,000 of its 600,000 residents were living in SROs, almost as many as in regular apartments. An SRO hotel room was generally an 8'x10' cubicle with a bathroom and tub or shower down the hall. In the 1850s these hotels, all cheap and many both shoddy and seedy, were home to gold prospectors, the peddlers who sold them goods, dock workers, and a few "ladies of the night."

Later, SROs became home to migrant workers, day laborers, and immigrants who swept the streets, washed dishes, scrubbed laundry, and had to work way too hard and too long in order to make a better life for their families. Over time, SROs became populated by Chinese immigrants, Blacks from Texas and Louisiana, Central Americans from Guatemala, El Salvador, and Mexico, and also Filipinos, Koreans, and others from the Pacific Rim. Many of the hotels were located in Chinatown, the largely Black Fillmore District and Western Addition, and the largely Latino Mission District. And many of the rooms didn't house just a single person, but three or four family members.

The run-down Tenderloin east of City Hall and the environs of Sixth Street just south of Market Street, then known as Skid Row, both had big SRO clusters. San Francisco has long attracted counter-culture people of almost every stripe: street musicians, beat generation poets, struggling artists, actors who drove cabs while seeking fame and fortune, and others who just came for the lifestyle. And many came for the drugs, so prevalent in San Francisco since before the Summer of Love. They too gravitated to these hotels, especially those in the Tenderloin and Skid Row. By 1974, the year the Grateful Dead recorded the album "From the Mars Hotel," named for an SRO on Fourth Street off Market where Jack Kerouac had often bunked down, the number of SROs in the City was still over 600, and the number of residents was still over 5% of the

City's population. Today, over 500 SROs remain, still a big component of the City's housing.

In 1979 and 1980, Simon Stanley lived in one of those SROs, along with a bunch of his self-styled Punk Rock friends, like Magdalene Momma and David Delinquent. Almost all of this crowd was known by their *noms de punk.*

When he was arrested on murder charges, Simon Stanley's first problem was his own *nom de punk* – "Kenny Krazy." It appeared there right in the charging document – *People v. Simon Stanley, a/k/a Kenny Krazy.* His second problem was that he'd fled the jurisdiction when he heard that the police had come to the SRO with an arrest warrant. He wasn't caught until thirteen months later. And California law says that flight may be used at a trial as evidence of guilt.

His third problem, and by far his biggest, was that when they were interviewed by the police after Renato Franco's death, six among his crowd of friends talked freely to the cops. Despite their counterculture looks and demeanor, when it came to interviews with police, they acted as most typical scared white teenagers and twenty-somethings would have: They gave full statements. The take-away: They heard "Kenny" say that he was going to go down the hall to Franco's room to take his leather jacket. He came back wearing the jacket and carrying a bloody Swiss army knife in his hand.

When I first met Simon, it was in a holding cell in the security corridor just outside the courtroom where his first appearance, arraignment, was about to take place. This meeting was fairly typical for a court appointment. The Public Defender's Office had a conflict of interest because it was representing one of the punk-rocker witnesses on minor misdemeanor charges. I happened to be the "conflicts attorney" assigned to the courts that day, and since I was one of a smaller panel of lawyers also qualified to take murder cases, I "caught" the case.

Shortly after a perfunctory arraignment – entering a plea of not guilty and setting an evidentiary preliminary hearing – I visited Simon in the jail. He was surprisingly matter-of-fact for someone accused of murder who had just been busted after a year on the run. When I asked what he wanted me to call him, he said, to my mild surprise, "Simon." He also told me – why I wasn't sure – that he was gay and that he was the only gay punk-rocker he knew.

As for what happened, he acknowledged that he had stabbed Renato but insisted that it was self-defense. He was ambivalent about the leather jacket, admitting that he took it but claiming he didn't intend to steal it and only took it after Renato was stabbed. He added that he and everyone else on that floor was afraid of Renato, who was known for his bad temper and crazy conduct. As an example, Simon told me that Renato had recently smeared his feces on the doors of several people whom he didn't like.

If the prosecution could prove that Simon intended to steal Renato's jacket, it didn't matter if Simon intended to kill Renato. Under the felony murder rule, a homicide during the commission of a felony makes an intent to kill unnecessary, and going into Renato's room to steal his jacket would be a felony. Smearing shit on doors, disgusting though that may have been, was no excuse for any kind of violent retaliation. I'd have to look elsewhere for a defense.

Eggs

Ever since Elvin's case, I always wanted someone sitting with me at trial. Most often it was a law student. If nothing else, given my continual state of high anxiety, a second would make sure that I ate something for lunch, even if it was just a grilled cheese sandwich from the ratty basement cafeteria, known to regulars as "The House of Toast." For Simon, I borrowed Len Mastromonaco, then in his last year of law school, from one of the lawyers who shared space in our building. Len's inducement was the rare opportunity to see the inside of a murder case from soup to nuts.

We didn't have much to work with – a coroner's report and six similar witness statements, each with a consistent recitation of the events surrounding Franco's death. There was one strange reference in the coroner's report. While I couldn't imagine what it had to do with Franco's death, particularly when considering the scene – a sleazy, dirty SRO hotel, I was ready for some straw-grasping. So, I told Len I wanted to focus on why the coroner said there were coagulated eggs under Renato Franco's body. I asked him to buy a half dozen raw eggs at the corner store. He returned, clearly puzzled by what I had in mind. I told him we were going to throw the eggs against the baseboard of our bathroom and find out how long it took them to coagulate on the linoleum floor. Len asked the logical question: "Why?" I told him the truth: I had no idea, but we had to do something, and the eggs were the only thing out of the ordinary that we had so far. "But how can that do us any good?" Len wanted to know. Good question. Again, I had no idea, but if nothing else it would inject a bit of smoke into an otherwise crystal-clear case.

So, we set about throwing eggs against the baseboard, with Len duly recording on a yellow legal pad the amount of time each egg took to coagulate. He'd be the one to testify about the eggs at trial – assuming we could figure out how our experiment was relevant and get it into evidence.

Preliminary hearing and a better defense

The preliminary hearing took place before then Municipal Court judge Maxine Mackler Chesney, one of the smartest and fairest judges I've known. Many of the best judges start in the DA's office, and Judge Chesney was one of them. There are plenty of win-at-all-costs, marginally ethical DAs. But I have long felt that honest and honorable DAs often make great judges. These DAs bring objectivity, practicality, and compassion to their work. Translating those principles to a judgeship is a natural progression. Maxine Chesney had all these qualities. After a meteoric career as a San Francisco deputy DA, moving swiftly from trial attorney to senior attorney, head trial attorney, and finally Assistant Chief Deputy in just ten years, at age thirty-seven she was appointed to the Municipal Court. After a few years, she was elevated to the Superior Court and was soon appointed to the federal district court for the Northern District of California, where, after twenty-five years, she still sits with distinction as a senior judge.

Back then, in August 1981, she was beginning her third year in Municipal Court, ably presiding over our preliminary hearing. Nothing surprising in terms of testimony happened at the hearing. The DA called four out of the six eyewitnesses, which seemed like a bit of overkill to me but actually gave me the opportunity to see which of the punkers were credible and which were not. But the reality was that despite their looks and dope-fiend demeanor, each gave relatively cogent and unshakable stories. They were all pretty good witnesses.

The star witness was a skinny, small, blond kid who looked sixteen but said he was nineteen, called "David Delinquent." His real name is lost to posterity. "Mr. Delinquent" was more important than the others because he and Magdalene Momma had followed "Kenny" down the hall to Franco's room and could see and hear some of what happened through the partially opened door. Given his previous sworn statements, David's testimony was less surprising for what he said than how he said it:

THE DA: *Now, David, tell me what you heard Kenny say when you were all in Kenny's room.*

DAVID DELINQUENT: *He said "I'm gonna get my knife and take that asshole's fuckin' jacket!"*

DA: *What happened then?*

DD: *He walked down the hall and me and Magda followed him down.*

DA: *Could you see inside Renato's room?*

DD: *A little, the corner of the room.*

DA: *Could you hear them?*

DD: *Yeah, they were yelling at each other but I couldn't hear all the words. They were talking about the jacket. I heard Renato say "Fuck you, fuck you!"*

DA: *Then what happened?*

DD: *Then Kenny came out wearing the fucking jacket!*

It was then that the judge leaned over to the witness box and stopped the proceedings.

JUDGE CHESNEY: *Mr. Delinquent, let me explain. If you are testifying about what you heard Mr. Simon say or what Mr. Franco said, and they used a four-letter word, you may use it, because that's what you are testifying actually happened. But if you are just talking and answering a question without quoting someone, please remember that that language does not belong in the courtroom. Do you understand the difference?*

DAVID DELINQUENT: *Yes, Your Honor. I understand.*

THE DA: *OK. Now David, after Kenny came out of Renato's room with the jacket on, what happened next?*

DD: *He was holding a fucking knife!*

JUDGE CHESNEY: *Mr. Delinquent! Remember, you can't use that language in this way.*

DD *(chagrined)*: *Oh, right, Your Honor, I fuckin' forgot.*

JUDGE CHESNEY *(laughing)*: *OK, I think it's time for a ten-minute break.*

One helpful bit of testimony did come up in my cross-examination of David. He made it clear that all of the punk-rockers, everyone on their floor, and most of the people in the building were afraid of Renato Franco because of his frequently outrageous and violent behavior. After Simon was held to answer to the charges, to be arraigned again in the Superior Court in three weeks, I had an idea of a possible defense – not a complete defense, but one that could possibly result in something less than first-degree murder.

After the hearing, I used my small investigation budget to send my best investigator to talk with Simon's friends at the SRO and find out more about Renato Franco. Each of them described a different incident demonstrating Franco's violent temper, and a couple of the punkers thought that he had been "5150'd" at least once. The code "5150" refers to the section of law that allows the police to hold someone for an involuntary psychiatric commitment and evaluation because the person is a danger to themselves or others – a danger that more than one of Simon's friends had faced.

Maybe I couldn't show much mitigation for Simon's actions in stabbing Franco, but perhaps, if I showed that *Franco* was crazy-violent at times, I could at least raise the possibility that the homicide was something less than first-degree murder. This was a longshot but better than nothing – and probably better than the 'egg defense,' which really didn't exist. I called on my dad's old friend, one of the country's leading forensic psychiatrists, Joseph Satten, MD, who had helped me out in the San Quentin Six case. I asked him, "Is it possible for you to give an opinion on someone's propensity for violence based only on that person's medical records without examining him?"

When Dr. Satten answered in the affirmative, I set about subpoenaing all the hospitals in town that had psych wards where 5150 patients were taken for evaluation. I developed a reasonably thick file on Franco and handed it over to Dr. S.

To make it clear, Franco's violent propensity could well provide a defense to first degree murder if Simon and Franco had had an altercation, or if I could raise doubt about Simon having formed the intent to kill. But it did not, strictly speaking, create a defense to first-degree *felony* murder, because the felony part of that charge meant that if Simon intended to take Franco's jacket, it was not necessary for the DA to prove intent or the "malice aforethought" usually required for first-degree murder. Still, I thought that it was at least possible that if a jury was convinced that Franco was a really dangerous guy, it could raise some doubt about whether some kind of altercation intervened before Simon took the jacket, and it could create antipathy for Franco and maybe a pinch of helpful sympathy for Simon.

A couple of weeks before trial, when Dr. Satten had reviewed all Renato Franco's medical records, we met to discuss his opinions. He was prepared to testify that based on the records showing Franco's medical history, and reports of Franco's long and unstable history of violence, Franco's profile was that of an inherently dangerous person. We got to work preparing how to present that testimony, but at my request, our preparation and note-taking was entirely oral, to prevent any chance of providing a memorandum or other documentation that the DA might be able to subpoena, and in that way find out what we were up to.

The Trial Judge and DA

We went out to trial in early October. The deputy District Attorney was one of the office's most skilled: Hugh Anthony Levine, trained in Frank Hogan's famed Manhattan DA's office, long considered among the best prosecutorial offices in the country. He'd moved to the West Coast and was immediately put on the homicide team. The judge had far less experience. J. Anthony Kline, also originally from New York, had been the then-young Governor Jerry Brown's legal-affairs secretary, an important position that involved giving the governor the last word on whether to sign law-related legislation and whom to appoint to the bench. Eventually, Brown appointed "Tony" Kline to the trial bench, where he remained for only about a year, during which he handled only two murder trials. Shortly before leaving office, Governor Brown elevated Kline to the appellate court, where he became an excellent appellate judge who remained on active duty for thirty-eight years before finally retiring at age eighty.

Back then, though, Judge Kline was a rookie, with less trial experience, and much less murder trial experience, than the lawyers in the case. This showed from the first day of pre-trial motions when we got to the issue of peremptory challenges to the jury. These challenges are ones that each side can make without giving a reason or a cause, except that a challenge may not be based on race. In tough cases, the defense always wants more challenges, and the DA just wants to get on with the trial. At that time, death penalty murder cases in California allowed up to twenty-six peremptory challenges, while other cases allowed ten. This case was not a death-penalty case but was a murder, so I argued that we should have twenty-six challenges. Back then, the issue of whether "regular" murders should get twenty-six challenges a side was not entirely clear, though the probable answer was "no." In a shrewd move, however, Levine agreed to the additional challenges. The number of challenges had nothing whatever to do with the evidence or the strength of the prosecution's case. And the last thing Levine wanted was to take a chance that some appellate court might decide in Simon's favor and reverse a conviction based on something that had so little to do with the actual evidence.

Kline was uncertain but dubious. He told us he'd let us know his ruling the next morning. Both Levine and I suspected that he had gone down the judges' corridor to discuss the issue with Judge Claude Perasso, then considered the criminal court's judicial guru. The next morning, Kline agreed to the extra challenges, erring on the side of a avoiding any possible appeal of the issue.

A second issue that Kline had to decide didn't appear to require Perasso's involvement. Yom Kippur, the holiest day of the Jewish year, was going to occur on the fourth day of trial. Levine and I, both being Jewish, did not want to be in court that day, but at that time, it was not a court holiday and there was no formal basis to take the day off. Kline, too, is Jewish, and was brought up in the Five Towns area of southwestern Long Island in a largely Jewish community. But on this issue too, he sought the advice of Claude Perasso, his more experienced but decidedly non-Jewish, Catholic-school-educated colleague. Kline did finally agree to close the court that day.

The final issues I raised more directly affected the possible evidence in the case: a motion to suppress any reference to "Kenny Krazy" (denied immediately) or to Simon having nipple rings – not so unusual today, but in 1981 something the jury could think was a sign of self-inflicted pain and perhaps violence. I argued, naturally, that they were irrelevant to the case, which indeed they were. Again, Kline deliberated overnight, and again came down on our side, on the fallback, catchall grounds often used by judges that, to paraphrase California Evidence Code Section 352, "the probative value was outweighed by the prejudicial effect."

Off to trial: the prosecution's case, "David Delinquent" and Len the law student

We picked a jury without having to use any of those extra challenges. Hugh Levine then began his prosecution with two police officers who responded to the scene, and the coroner, who reported that Franco died from a stab wound through his aorta that was consistent with stabbing by a Swiss Army knife. My questions were limited to eggs. I asked the cops whether they had noticed the coagulated eggs under and around Franco's body, and what if any conclusions they drew (not much of anything). I asked the coroner why he put it in his report. He said in order to be absolutely complete, and he assured the jury that he drew no egg-related conclusions. Then came Magdalena Momma and Crashout, two of Simon's friends, who testified that they heard "Kenny" say he was going to go down the hallway and take Renato's leather jacket. "Magda" also testified that she was with David Delinquent outside Renato's room and heard an argument, though she couldn't understand what was said.

Levine's last, and star, witness was David Delinquent, whose testimony paralleled his preliminary hearing testimony, although he managed to limit the four-letter words to what he heard at the scene. My cross-examination focused on Renato Franco being a dangerous dude, and David obliged with a couple of stories as examples. Trying to impeach him by questioning what he heard and saw down at Franco's room seemed to be simply reinforcing bad testimony, so I left it alone.

We had only three defense witnesses – Simon, Len, my law student, on the science of egg coagulation, and Joe Satten, the psychiatrist I hoped might possibly help by painting a negative picture of the violent Renato. I had planned to put Simon on the stand first, for two reasons: First, juries always want to hear from the defendant to get his version of the truth. Second, I wanted a little distance between him and the jury's deliberations, and I wanted to finish with the person I thought was my strongest witness, Dr. Satten. But something happened that convinced me to change that plan on a moment's notice.

First thing on the morning of David's testimony, we'd prevailed with Judge Kline after a forty-five-minute argument in his chambers about the admissibility of the eggs. Fearing that we must have had some scheme to use the eggs to our advantage, Levine objected that the coagulation of eggs was absolutely irrelevant. He added his own Section 352 objection – that the "probative value" of the eggs would be outweighed by the prejudice of Len's testimony. My argument was admittedly thin, the strongest point being this: The eggs related to time of death. As this was a murder trial, even slightly probative evidence should be permitted because there would be no prejudice to the jury in allowing it. Judge Kline, noting that he saw little purpose in allowing the testimony, nevertheless permitted it in a case so strong for the prosecution that he wanted zero risk that some appellate court would second-guess him.

After David's testimony, the prosecution rested its case. Judge Kline took a short recess before we began our defense. During the break, Len went across the hallway to use the bathroom, where he encountered David Delinquent just before David left the building. When Len returned, he told me excitedly that he was sure David was high, almost certainly on speed, or methamphetamine. Before and during law school, Len had worked for three years as a drug counsellor at one of Northern California's best and most well-known treatment centers, Walden House. After working with hundreds of clients, he knew about drug-users and the drugs they likely were taking. When Len said he was sure David was high, I knew it was true. In about thirty seconds, I decided to try to authenticate Len as an expert on drug use and have him testify about David.

Under the laws of the state of California, a witness may be called to give an expert opinion if the witness has "special knowledge, skill, experience, training, or education" on an issue that is not the subject of common, everyday knowledge, so long as it will help the jury understand the issue. Federal courts and most states have similar standards. Whether someone is on drugs is not necessarily something the average person would know without some specialized training and knowledge. That means that a qualified expert could be called to give an opinion about it. I thought Len clearly met the expert witness qualifications, because they don't require *super* special knowledge, skill, etc., just a reasonable amount of it, which he clearly had.

Before the jury returned to the courtroom, I alerted the judge and DA that I planned to call Len to the witness stand not just about the eggs but also to give his opinion about David being on drugs. For the first time, I saw Hugh Levine get angry. He objected vigorously to this testimony. He argued that I hadn't told him about Len being an expert, but of course I hadn't known about the evidence until ten minutes earlier. Next, he argued that this mere law student didn't meet the qualifications required of an expert. That was fine with me because under the law, he was entitled to *voir dire*, or question, a proposed expert to test his expertise. And so, with the jury still out of the courtroom, he called Len to the witness stand to ask about his "special knowledge, skill, experience, training, or education." After five minutes, it was clear that Len more than met the qualifications. Judge Kline ruled that Len had the requisite expertise, the jury entered the courtroom, and Len took the stand.

My examination was brief and to the point. Did Len have the opportunity to observe Mr. Delinquent right after he testified? What did he observe? Why did he conclude David was on drugs? Len cited several factors in support of his opinion: pinprick eyes, jerky, excitable demeanor, repetitive motions, and so on. I sat down to listen to Levine's cross-examination.

Levine was obviously still angry, perhaps because he didn't like surprises, not that any lawyer in the midst of an important trial would. But in truth, Len's testimony was fairly collateral to the issue of Simon's guilt; evidence that David was high might affect his credibility with the jury, but it wasn't as if we could prove David had lied. Still, Levine came on very strong with Len: rapid-fire questions, insistent tone, aggressive posture, the works. Len, who had a good sense of humor, looked like he was taking it all in stride, and I, feeling that this boxing match was not scoring points for the prosecution, leaned back in my chair and relaxed as if I were at a Sunday picnic. The last thing I wanted to do was object to Levine's argumentative questioning.

Levine ended with a last attempt at a knockout punch. Addressing Len's testimony that repetitive movements are one of the indicia of drug use, he asked whether Len had noticed Judge Kline's habit of periodically stroking his moustache during the trial testimony. Len said that he had. Then Levine, turning up the aggression, asked, "Do you think *Judge Kline* is on drugs???" It was, at its heart, an argumentative and even offensive question, but I was not about to object. Len turned to look at Judge Kline, for perhaps just a half second too long, then turned back to Levine and said, "No." But that extra half-second caused Levine to jump on my poor law student: "Do you think this is *funny*, Mr. Mastromonaco?"

Len looked in my direction. I was still in my Sunday picnic mode and I did nothing. And that was the end of Levine's cross-exam. I stood up and said, "No further questions," and Len, more than a little ticked off at my failure to protect him, got off the stand. But Judge Kline was puzzled, and called for a side bar, a *sotto voce* conversation at the side of the judge's bench away from the jury. "What about the eggs?" a puzzled Kline asked me. "I decided to not do it," I replied. Kline didn't seem to fully appreciate that I had simply made a strategic decision. While we had spent almost an hour that morning arguing over the admissibility of the eggs, as things stood Len's testimony was much better without my putting any eggs in that basket.

Simon takes the witness stand

My biggest decision in the case was whether I should let Simon testify. I say "let" despite that it was Simon's decision alone – his right – about whether to testify. Still, almost without exception, my clients took my advice on this issue, and while Simon wanted to testify, I expected he would go along with my recommendation. Arguing against his testifying was his admission that he stabbed Renato, his "Krazy" moniker, and an excellent DA ready to cross-examine and rip holes in his story. On the other hand, Simon claimed that the two had argued and that Renato was stabbed during a fight. Perhaps more importantly, Simon was the only person who could testify that he did not intend to take Renato's jacket until after the stabbing. That could negate the felony murder rule.

Simon took the stand right after Len. His testimony was straightforward enough. No, he did not tell anyone he was going to take his knife and steal Renato's jacket. By his account, he went to Renato's room to settle an argument from the previous night. The two of them started yelling and then scuffling, which escalated into a battle royal during which Renato was stabbed with Simon's pocketknife – the knife he always carried with him. After Renato was on the ground,

Simon decided to take that nice leather jacket. Simon held up reasonably well on cross-examination, consistently sticking to his story. Except when Levine asked Simon why he would take a jacket that didn't belong to him. Simon said, simply, that Renato was not going to need it anymore. Not good.

In deciding to put Simon on the witness stand, I gave relatively little thought to whether his testimony was truthful. Did I believe him? Had I thought about it at length, I would have answered that I probably did not. But by this time in my legal career, I was past spending much time on that issue. My ethical requirement as a criminal defense lawyer was clear. I was not there to be my client's judge but his advocate. The question was only whether I knew the testimony was *perjurious*. Absent clear knowledge – tantamount to proof – that my client would be testifying falsely, I was ethically forbidden to allow any personal doubts or negative assumptions about his testimony to affect my duty of vigorous advocacy. In the criminal defense community, allowing one's own opinions to affect one's representation is called "playing God."

That meant I had to use Simon's testimony to his best advantage: in this instance, that Simon's testimony raised a reasonable doubt whether he intended to steal that jacket before the altercation. When added to Dr. Satten's testimony, I hoped it might just be enough to avoid murder in the first degree.

Using a client's testimony that the lawyer doesn't truly believe – required by the ethical duties of confidentiality and vigorous advocacy – is one of the most difficult things for non-lawyers to understand. To many, this can seem like justice denied, not justice served. Like almost all my colleagues, I was aware of the irony that for those of us defending the accused, the truth of the defendant's guilt was secondary to the lawyer's duty of vigorously representing the client. But without lawyers playing that difficult role, our criminal defense system – the presumption of innocence, the protection of constitutional rights – would fall apart. Years ago, here's how I suggested a criminal defense lawyer might explain that role:

Look, most of the clients we represent have never had much of a chance in life: poor, poorly educated, no intact family. I'm the one person whose job puts me on their side. At the very least, I treat my clients with dignity and respect. And if I don't speak for them, who will? After all, on one side, you've got the power of the state, the legal authority of the D.A., the police department, the sheriff. On the other side? Just one poor, scared son of a gun. And me.

In order for the state to be put to its proof, people like me are necessary. But if I'm just going through the motions, am I really testing their case? Our justice system is like the carnival strongman who says, 'Hit me with your best punch.' If I don't use my best punches, it defeats the whole purpose.

Please understand: I'm not defending what people do when they commit serious crimes. I worry just like everyone else about dangerous people going free. But the system doesn't work if I don't do my level best....

I confess that while I practiced criminal defense for years in the beginning of my career, well over half my time in practice has been spent since I abandoned that work. But I still believe strongly in the principles that guided me as a young lawyer, and in moving from criminal law to civil work I've never abandoned those principles. Rather, my move had far more to do with the extraordinary stress involved. Of course, part of that stress is adhering to the difficult role the criminal defense lawyer must embody.

"Sleepy Joe" and "trying the victim."

It's not unusual in a criminal trial for a defense lawyer to try to turn the tables and put the victim on trial. In sexual assault cases, this strategy can be both patently offensive and fraught with danger. But in other cases, especially those with overwhelming evidence, it may be one of the few options defense counsel has. Here, of course, one difference was that the victim we were going to attack was dead.

To implement this attack, I needed Joe Satten's testimony. Satten had learned his craft from Dr. Karl Menninger, perhaps the most well-respected American psychiatrist of the twentieth century and the father of forensic psychiatry. By the time I first met Joe Satten in late 1973 to ask him to discuss the psychological pressures on people incarcerated in places like "the Hole" in San Quentin, he'd had twenty-five years of forensic psychiatric experience. My access to this extremely busy doctor was facilitated by his close relationship with my father – they'd "shared a cadaver" in med school, kind of similar to being at the same graduate-school workshop station – and had remained close, perhaps because of their similar backgrounds.

Joe and my dad were both sons of immigrant Jewish families from Brooklyn, and each went to one of the New York

City public colleges, Joe to Brooklyn College and my father to "CCNY," or City College of New York. Each graduated near the top of his class. But they both faced an anti-Semitic hurdle getting into medical school. The best New York med schools, including NYU, Columbia, and Cornell, took only one Jewish student a year from the city colleges, despite those public colleges' acclaimed reputations. But after Pearl Harbor, with the country in desperate need of doctors, the quotas gave way to the requirements of war.

In a perverse way, both my dad and Joe benefitted from the anti-Semitism. The Army signed them up as first lieutenants and picked up the tab for their education. And they were put in a special three-year, year-round expedited program instead of the usual four years, to get them out into the field as quickly as possible. True they first had to wait. Before the war, Joe had been sidelined for a year, while my father, a few years older, had to sit out four years and had begun another career as a behavioral biologist. But the final irony of the school's exclusionary policies was that they and their classmates graduated on almost the same day as VE Day, Germany's surrender in Europe, and they were in basic training at Fort Sam Houston, Texas, when Japan surrendered. They'd gotten their med school admission and a free education, done their duty, and missed the war entirely.

Once in the service, these newly certified Army doctors found less discrimination than they'd suffered before the war, and much less than what Black soldiers faced in the still largely segregated Army. When Lieutenant Jackie Robinson was arrested in 1944 for not sitting in the back of an *integrated*

Army bus, he was court-martialed not for that lawful activity but for insubordination, which amounted to talking back. Though he was eventually acquitted, I was always reminded of this story when my Black clients faced resisting arrest charges after it turned out there were no bases for their arrests in the first place.

After doing his post-war US Public Health Service work in the federal prison at Leavenworth, Kansas, Joe Satten became the chief forensic psychiatrist at the Menninger Clinic in Topeka, the largest and most important psychiatric center in the country. In addition to studying the pathology of murderers, he introduced Truman Capote to the two men who became the subject of *In Cold Blood* and worked closely with Capote on the book. By the time he moved to San Francisco in 1971, Satten knew more about the psychology of murderers than perhaps anyone in the United States with the possible exception of Karl Menninger himself. I couldn't have had a more credentialled expert, particularly given that his testimony in our case was quite a bit different than his usual assignment. But my direct examination of him went less well than I expected, because Joe Satten had one drawback as a witness.

Dr. Satten was a brilliant physician with a fundamental understanding of what made someone like Renato Franco a dangerous man with a propensity for violence. His testimony presented the clear opinion that Franco had that violent, dangerous propensity. But his classmates didn't call him "Sleepy Joe" for nothing. Satten had an exceptionally soft-spoken and deliberate manner of speech, almost a caricature of the consulting psychiatrist, listening to the patient on the analyst's couch, then stroking his beard in deep thought before slowly – agonizingly – giving his opinion. He said all the right things, but was the jury still listening? I was disappointed and worried. I doubted the jury had gotten much of the substance of his testimony.

But for the second time in the trial, Hugh Levine made a mistake. He'd again been surprised. He'd done his homework and knew that Joe Satten was a renowned expert on the pathology of murderers. But he'd assumed that I was calling Satten to testify to Simon's "diminished capacity" – that Simon was not able to form the requisite specific intent for murder. While I had explored that possibility early on, we had no evidence to support this theory. But Levine didn't know that.

Once again, Levine was forced to wing it in cross-examination, though he would have been much better off asking no questions after the weak presentation we had made on direct. Levine couldn't know for sure how the jury perceived Dr. Satten, so he went after Satten aggressively, as he had with my law student, Len. That did not work. The more he questioned the reasoning behind Joe's opinions, the more Joe strongly and ably defended that reasoning. He was able to repeat more than once how his conclusions about Franco had a clear underlying basis in the medical evidence. By the end of Joe Satten's testimony, I was feeling much better about what we had accomplished to create the possibility of avoiding first degree murder.

We quickly proceeded to argue the case, Hugh Levine emphasizing the clear legal standard for first degree felony murder, while I focused on Renato's character, the generally weird and unreliable scene at the SRO, and an argument based more on equity than on how concrete legal principles should be applied to the case. After two and a half days of deliberation, the jury came back with a verdict of murder in the second degree. This was not my first second-degree conviction, but it was the first time I felt that it was the best I could do.

This case served as a reminder to me that average, ordinary people (like jurors) perceive outliers – or people who are clearly not like them and seem inherently strange – differently than those who are at least superficially more familiar. I could see that Simon was off-putting to several of the jurors. My way to combat that was to show my own friendly relationship with him, with in-court gestures and chit-chat. (Simon's sexual preference, which back in those days could have been another outlier factor, was irrelevant to the case and never came up.) Fortunately, by trial's end, Renato Franco was likely more of an outlier than Simon. That may just have helped avoid murder in the first degree.

EPILOGUE

Simon was sentenced to sixteen years to life in state prison. I heard nothing from him for over twenty years, until he became eligible for parole. By then, he had become quite religious, a saving grace for many behind bars, and a ruse for others hoping to use religion as a vehicle to get paroled. In Simon's case, I strongly suspected it was the real deal. He had never fed me any bull, and to me, didn't seem to possess that gene.

Apparently, the parole board agreed; Simon was paroled in 2013 and four years later was discharged from parole. I spoke to him after his discharge, and our conversations further convinced me that he'd turned the corner. He abandoned both drugs and the punk rock world and was living quietly in a western state, remorseful about his past life and the Franco homicide, but relatively content and peaceful, protected by caring friends.

Hugh Levine continued his high-level prosecutions for several more years, always as one of the most thorough and effective DAs I'd seen. I felt lucky to have caught him on a case where two surprises, especially Dr. Satten, threw him off his feed.

I continued to see Joe Satten and his wife Norma from time to time over the years. The last time was at a celebratory dinner at my sister's home with my parents in town from New York. Joe told a long and involved story about how he, Norma, and Harper Lee were in a taxi with Truman Capote in Topeka in 1960. Capote was giving extensive instructions to the driver to find a specific location in a dark and semi-deserted part of town. Finally, Capote said, "Stop, we're here!" and the party all descended into a gay bar in the basement. It was an interesting story. Turned out Sleepy Joe could deliver a good tale upon occasion.

Len Mastromonaco passed the bar and hung out his shingle. Fifteen years later, we became law partners, and remained so for over a decade. To this day, we remain good friends. We've told the story of his testimony many times in many places. Although Len clearly understands that my duty back then was to do my best for my client and not to protect him, he always chides me about how I hung him out to dry on the witness stand.

We both run across Judge Tony Kline once in a while at one local event or another. We're lucky to have him as an appellate judge, something that has been a better fit for him than the trial bench. At times when I've seen him, he'll look at me with a twinkle in his eye and then stroke his moustache.

8

Escort Service or Call-Girl Ring?

People v. Robert M. "Max" Forrest

*A former client who ran a licensed escort service hired me to repre-
sent him on a charge of "pimping and pandering." The evidence
was hardly overwhelming, less than in many cases I'd defended
successfully. But we had a problem. My client was a Black guy,
an ex-con operating his business in a largely white town, arrested
with an attractive, young white woman co-defendant, and with a
wife/business partner who was also white. Besides, in all honesty,
Max was close to fitting some people's stereotype of the slick Black
pimp. In wealthy, lily-white Marin County, that could be fatal to
our defense.*

An old client returns, is arrested, and gets searched

When I began practicing law with David Mayer after the San
Quentin Six case, he had almost no ongoing business after
spending several thousand hours working only on that one
case. Our goal was to practice criminal defense, but first we
needed to make enough money to pay the rent. We tried to
stay true to our principles, including representing the little
guy and not big corporate interests or insurance companies.
That was easy enough: None of those big-bucks folks were

looking to hire us anyway. A successful family law firm run by three great women lawyers who liked David's skills and natural empathy referred many smaller domestic cases to him, and those cases helped pay the bills. Beyond that, David's reputation as a prison rights lawyer gave us another stream of cases: parole hearings for guys on the inside. It didn't pay much, usually a few hundred dollars apiece gathered up by relatives, but that was enough to get us back out to San Quentin to take our best shot. David handed off a good portion of those cases to me, and I soon developed the skills needed to make reasonably compelling presentations to parole boards, and even wrote a booklet about how to do it.

In the mid-70's, rehabilitation was still considered an important part of a prisoner's experience, and parole hearings happened more frequently, as often as once a year. Often, prisoners with good in-prison records and no "115s," or disciplinary writeups, were complimented by parole board members before being told to go back and complete this or that rehab program and apply again in a year. Prisoners who followed the board's rehab conditions each year were given a path to parole. If they successfully completed Program X, were then told to complete Program Y the next year, did that, and were then told to complete Program Z and did that too, we could argue at the next hearing that by the board's own standards, "This guy has done everything you told him to do, and done it successfully. You have no reason to keep him." Our rate of getting parole in those cases was pretty good, and even when we lost, we had some success filing *habeas corpus* petitions to ask courts to release these clients based on their successful completion of all the rehabilitation the parole board had demanded.

Robert M. Forrest was one of my first successes. After his release from prison, I didn't hear from him for a couple of years. When I did, it was because Max, as everyone called him, had been busted on felony charges of "pimping and pandering." "Pimping" is a term familiar to most everyone, while "pandering" is procuring someone for sex or facilitating an arrangement for sex without requiring a money element. Max told me that he had been running "Elite," an escort service in Marin County, and had signed up a group of women willing to accompany out-of-town businessmen to cocktail parties, business dinners, or occasional dates. He said he'd gotten a state license and had been doing legitimate business for a year and a half. He had recently interviewed a woman for a job as an escort when, in the middle of the interview, the police barged into his office and arrested both him and his office manager, Jenny Bahr, who was also present. After he made bail, his next call was to me.

It turned out that the woman he was interviewing was an undercover police operative wearing a "Fargo unit," a device that back then was the state-of-the-art police wire. A Fargo worked by taping a microphone to the body and transmitting the audio feed to a police tape recorder nearby. It didn't take a PhD in police science to figure out why the cops decided to send someone undercover into this particular business. Max was an ex-con and a good-looking young Black guy; he was "articulate" in the racist vernacular of the day. Instead of going back to Southern California, he had stayed in Marin County, where the Marin Sheriff's Office kept an eye on all the San Quentin guys who stuck around. Besides, Max was not keeping a low profile; given his nature, he couldn't have if he had wanted to. And to run an escort business, he had to do some promotion.

Deputy Public Defender Glenn Becker was assigned to represent Jenny, the office manager. I had known Glenn for years, ever since I had been a law student in the PD's office and he was a rookie deputy public defender there. By the time of Max and Jenny's case, we'd become good friends. One morning over coffee, as we pored over the police reports and listened to the audiotape from the Fargo unit, we quickly understood both why the pair was arrested and why the case had enough holes to give us a decent chance to win. The bad evidence was pretty bad: Max telling the undercover operative, "We're in the business of sex here. Sex is our product." But the bulky Fargo unit, with two wires, one for the mike and another serving as an antenna, was hard to conceal. The bust occurred on a chilly evening in late November, and the undercover was wearing a coat. In mid-interview, when Max asked the woman to "take off your coat so I can look at you" – not her clothes, just her coat – the cops in the undercover police car at the curb jumped the gun, racing into the escort service's office to bust Max and Jenny rather than risk the wire's being exposed when the coat was removed. This created a case of "undercover interruptus." Why the cops placed the wire so it could be so easily discovered was something I never understood. But despite the cops having interrupted their own investigation before it was completed, Max and Jenny still got charged with felonies.

Not only was this Fargo unit bulky, but much of the audio that it transmitted was garbled. When we heard the audiotape, we could hear Max say, "take off your coat" and "business of sex," but it was impossible to understand much of the rest. This concerned me and Glenn a great deal, because it would mean that Detective Sergeant Arkasian, listening in the patrol car, or the undercover operator herself, could claim that the conversation that we couldn't understand was far more explicit than what we could make out on the tape. And it might not be hearsay. Ordinarily, what a person says outside of the court-room is hearsay, but if the person makes a statement about committing a crime – an "admission" in legalese – that's not hearsay and anyone overhearing that statement could be allowed to testify about it.

Max had made bail and Jenny was released on her own recognizance, or promise to appear in court, so that the prelim-inary hearing was put off five weeks down the road. Timing for prelims for in-custody defendants always had priority because people who were sitting doing jail time while their cases were pending had the right to a speedy trial under the California and United States Constitutions, and that included these hearings. For others, the courts – and the lawyers – could take more time. And usually, for us defense lawyers, this provided more time to prepare and develop a case.

In the aftermath of the arrest, the sheriff's deputies combed through every nook and cranny of the Elite offices – desk drawers, closets, banker's boxes – and gathered up everything they thought might be evidence. We had the right to examine everything that was taken, and soon agreed with Mike Elliot, the DA assigned to the case, on a time for us to sit down and go through all that the cops had gathered. But even before we had a chance to do that, Glenn and I knew we would be filing a motion to suppress evidence. Motions to suppress, "MTS" or, in California number lingo, "1368 motions," named for the relevant Penal Code section, are common in criminal court. Here, we thought there was a clear violation of the constitutional requirement to be free of any "unreasonable searches and seizures," in the words of the Fourth Amendment. That was because the police had secured and had control of Elite's premises and thus had all the time in the world to get a search warrant from a judge to permit a complete search. While occasionally a search of a premises is justified by "exigent circumstances," usually a matter of urgency, no exigency existed here. The Fourth Amendment also says that "Warrants shall issue ... upon probable cause." Here, the cops almost certainly could have gotten a warrant and shown probable cause, but they didn't. And that made this a bad search.

We'd file a motion to suppress right after the preliminary hearing. But first, we sat down to review what the police had taken from Elite's premises, and in truth, we found very little that had any evidentiary value one way or the other – except for one item: a green spiralbound notebook. Inside, someone had written out a page for each woman who had signed up to be an escort listing her "likes and dislikes." To our delight, any concern about what "likes and dislikes" really meant was quickly put to rest by the content of the pages: "Likes music; doesn't like sports"; "Likes to dine, loves classical music, doesn't like jazz"; "Likes to go dancing, likes baseball, but hates football"; and so on.

We had just uncovered a great piece of evidence to show that Elite was exactly what Max said it was: a legitimate escort service.

Preliminary Hearing

As we got to the preliminary hearing, both Glenn and I were feeling pretty good about our case as a result of that green notebook. But we still had one huge concern. Given the opportunity, what would the cops say about the parts of the conversation between Max and the prospective escort that couldn't be heard on the tape? To prevent being surprised at trial, we subpoenaed Detective Sergeant Arkasian to the preliminary hearing.

First, though, the deputy DA called the undercover police employee, who turned out to be a dispatcher and not a police officer, to testify about her conversation with Max. Then Detective Low, who was involved in setting up the tape recording, was called to verify that there was a tape made. These witnesses alone supported the very low threshold of probable cause needed to bind over Max and Jenny for trial. But Low, though he agreed that part of the tape was unintelligible, wasn't in the patrol car when the conversation took place, and so didn't hear the conversation live. Arkasian was the officer who recorded the garbled tape and heard the entire conversation live from the patrol car. Although in his police report he admitted that some of the discussion was garbled, we didn't have any idea what he was going to say – or claim – he heard in the car. We had to have Arkasian's testimony to pin him down as to what he heard and, just as importantly, what he didn't hear.

When I called Arkasian to the stand, the DA said nothing, but Judge Robert Mansell, who could be crusty and sometimes obstinate, insisted, "I want an offer of proof." An "offer of proof" is a statement from a lawyer about what the witness is going to say. I couldn't give any kind of accurate offer here because Arkasian had refused to speak with me before the hearing, and I had no idea what he would say; that was the whole point of calling him to the stand. Back then, a very important principle of law concerning evidence at a preliminary hearing – one that made matters fair for the defendant – was that if a witness had evidence that might overcome the prosecution's case or establish a defense, the defense was permitted to call that witness. The idea was that if the prosecution had held a witness in its back pocket rather than present the testimony, fairness required that the defendant could still call the witness to find out what the witness knew.

Unfortunately, despite numerous California court cases that supported this right, in 1990, a state proposition called the "Crime Victims Justice Reform Act" did away with it and other rights of defendants, supposedly in the interest of protecting victims of crime. In fact, though, the proposition was written and supported by district attorneys interested in turning preliminary hearings into wide superhighways leading to a finding of probable cause. This "reform act" resulted in defendants losing other rights that should be guaranteed by the Constitution, including: to confront the witnesses against them under the Sixth Amendment, because eyewitnesses might not have to be called when police officers could testify to hearsay; and to be provided information about the basis for a defense, in violation of both the Fifth and Sixth Amendments. This proposition, passed during a groundswell of law and order concerns, has severely handicapped those accused of crimes ever since.

At the time, though, the law allowing me to call the detective sergeant was clear. Clear, I suppose, to everyone except the judge. When I explained that Arkasian was "in position to listen to the conversation in the patrol car," the judge responded, "Well, so what?" When I amplified that Arkasian had both made the tape and knew what was on it, the judge gave me a five-minute recess to find out what was said or else he'd exclude the witness. But Arkasian had no interest in talking to me voluntarily. Nevertheless, when Mansell got back on the bench, I made an offer of proof speech outlining in general what little I knew: Arkasian came to the scene "equipped with an electronic sound device," heard the conversation "in the nature of an employment interview," observed Max leave and come back in a few minutes with a young woman (presumably Jenny), and then heard further conversation.

The judge pronounced my offer "completely inadequate," and said that I had, "Apparently, no knowledge of what an offer of proof is." He wanted me to stipulate that Arkasian would testify to the generalities I'd outlined. Stipulating, of course, would defeat the entire purpose of my calling the detective in the first place – pinning down his testimony – so I refused.

The judge was irate. But the deputy DA, knowing that we were right on the law and not interested in a defective prelim that could overturn a conviction later, said she would waive any objection. And Mansell caved in, with one parting shot: "It certainly would help if we had attorneys in the courtroom."

As it turned out, Arkasian's testimony was essential to our defense, and we may well have lost had I not insisted on calling him. I played the garbled tape for Arkasian and asked what he could understand. He came up with the same bits of conversation – "we're in the business of sex," "sex is our product," and ultimately "take off your coat" – that were intelligible on the tape and that were also highlighted in his police report. I then asked him, after the usual preliminaries about how important his report was and how he would write down everything significant, the typical cross-examine-a-cop question – whether there was anything important that he was able to understand from the garbled conversation that he didn't write down in his report. He naturally said no. So, there it was: Arkasian would be unable to say later that a more explicit conversation took place. The evidence for the prosecution came down to "We're in the business of sex; sex is our product." Not ideal, but ambiguous. And we had the green spiral notebook.

Superior Court motions and trial

The first thing Glenn Becker and I set about doing after Max and Jenny were arraigned on felony charges in Superior Court was to file that motion to suppress. Usually, either the lawyers for each defendant make their own motion, or one lawyer writes it and the lawyers for the other defendants join in. For some reason, probably having to do with our close friendship, we wrote a *joint* motion to suppress. What this meant is that both of our names and law offices appeared on the single pleadings, the motion and the brief, and we both appeared in court to argue the motion. It didn't seem like a big deal at the time, especially because we were so confident on the law, but it became a major issue at the trial. Motions to suppress are generally hard to win, but we knew this one was a likely exception, since the cops' lack of a warrant that could so easily have been obtained made the issue clear.

The motion and the trial were assigned to the Honorable E. Warren McGuire. McGuire was a strait-laced conservative Republican who was one of the best trial judges I ever appeared before. He did something extremely important that so many judges don't do: He left his personal politics, biases, and opinions at the door to the courthouse and once on the bench, did his best to apply the law as it existed. He quickly suppressed all the evidence the police had gathered from the Elite office. DA Mike Elliot was not at all surprised under the circumstances and simply accepted the ruling. And although we had moved to suppress the state's ability to bring anything, including the green notebook, into evidence, that wouldn't prevent us from bringing it in ourselves to support our defense. After all, we were not the ones who had wrongly seized it.

As all jury trials do, this trial began with *voir dire* of the jury, the opportunity to ask the potential jurors questions in an attempt to determine whether they can be fair to our clients. Or as was usually the case for many of my clients, particularly people of color and especially in upscale, lily-white Marin County, whether they were less likely to be unfair. In a case like this, I had two goals in *voir dire*. One was to get at the biases of jurors and either bring them out sufficiently to be able to get the judge to excuse them for cause, or to excuse them myself through the "peremptory challenges" – those exercised without having to give a reason – each side is given. The other goal was educational. Given the way Max came across, it was important for me to show the jury that any inherent biases they might have about a young, good-looking, somewhat stereotypically "slick"-looking Black guy should not cause them to start out with any negative feelings whatsoever about him or the evidence in the case.

During this particular *voir dire*, a somewhat strange event occurred that I thought did wonders for my efforts to educate. When I asked one potential juror, Mr. Marvin, what he saw when he looked at my client, he said he frankly saw someone who looked a lot like his image of a pimp. We discussed his stereotyping Max, and he was quite candid about it. He cited the way Max was dressed, even his demeanor in the courtroom. I then furthered that stereotype by suggesting, in a lighthearted way, that "all Mr. Forrest would need is a big, wide floppy hat, right?" and Mr. Marvin agreed. This juror was so candid about this all being just a stereotype, and that he'd be careful not to hold that stereotype against Max, that I decided to leave him on the jury. Ordinarily, I wouldn't want to trust someone presenting such bias even after a candid acknowledgement, but Mr. Marvin had been so honest. Besides, he'd been important in educating all the other prospective jurors, almost all of whom, like him, were privileged and white. I was afraid of a possible juror backlash if I removed him.

The trial proceeded fairly normally, at least once I'd asked Glenn to tell his client to close one more button on her blouse to make it less revealing. Our constant mantra was that Max ran a legitimate escort service, and that his comment "We're in the business of sex" was merely a candid and truthful statement – that the male business clientele wanted an escort who would be eye candy. With nothing further in support of the prosecution, given the aborted undercover effort, we felt we had quite a strong defense despite this statement. And we had the great evidence from the green notebook. We could put the notebook's entries into evidence either by subpoenaing the police officer who seized it and having him examine and read from it, or by having Max testify about it. But I felt that the best course would be to have Max's wife, Angela, testify about it. She was the one who started the book, and most of the writing was hers. Besides she happened to be a working RN, and, though her being white could cut both ways given her Black husband, on balance she came across as a credible witness with far less baggage than Max.

The prosecution presented its case in just a day and a half: the undercover operative, Detective Low, and Detective Sergeant Arkasian, and they played the voice recording. The cops testified that they feared for the undercover's safety when she was asked to remove clothing. But the clothing remained only her coat. I called Max to the stand as our first witness, and he did a good job overall of explaining that in fact his business was selling sex in a way, but not the illegal kind. Yes, he was a little too smooth and glib from my perspective, and I remained worried about what the jury thought of him. But all the same, his explanation of "the business of sex" made sense.

After court that afternoon, while thinking about Angela and the green notebook, I idly thumbed through the notebook's 200 pages. Only the first fifteen or so were filled out with the (exculpatory) likes and dislikes of the escorts. But about two-thirds of the way through the pages, with about fifty blank pages both before and after it, I caught sight of several lines of writing that took up just a quarter of a page. It clearly appeared to be the script of a voicemail message, and it didn't sound so great.

> Hello. You've reached Elite Escort Service. We can't answer your call right now, but we can certainly fulfill your needs for an escort. She can come to you at your home, your hotel room, or wherever you'd like her to come. Just let us know what you'd like, and we'll provide it.

I freaked out. Sure, the statement was ambiguous. No one was saying "she'll come to have sex with you." And no one spelled come "cum." But I sure didn't like the message much. I went off to find Glenn, and together, in the otherwise empty courtroom, I showed him what I'd found. We must have read it three or four times. We'd been confident about our case, and the green notebook had been our Get Out of Jail Free card. But now, I was worried about the jurors thumbing through, as I had, finding that page in the book, and drawing the conclusion that these escorts were call girls. Glenn disagreed. He pointed out, reasonably, that since we had gotten the evidence, including this notebook, excluded from the case, he doubted that the DA had seen that page or examined the notebook closely at all. He also felt it was unlikely that the jurors would stumble on it, since we would be talking only about the first fifteen very exculpatory pages. Besides, Glenn argued, even if the jurors read this page, the voicemail message was at worst ambiguous, and it would never outweigh the good evidence in the front pages of the book.

It was a Friday afternoon, so Glenn and I had a couple of days to chew on things and debate it some more. We agreed we'd talk on Sunday to decide what to do. This evidence had been suppressed by Judge McGuire as a result of our joint motion, so we essentially had veto power about whether to introduce it or not. In the two intervening days, I became convinced of two things: First, we could and in my mind probably would win with or without using the "likes and dislikes" in the notebook. The prosecution's case had always been thin, saddled by undercover interruptus. Max's testimony had gone well, as had his explanation of "the business of sex." I felt there simply wasn't enough to convict anyone beyond a reasonable doubt. Second, I became convinced that putting the notebook in evidence with a voicemail message that sounded more damning every time I read it was creating an unnecessary risk. Keeping the notebook out was the safer move given the weak prosecution case, and I told this to Glenn in our Sunday phone call. But by then, Glenn, a good lawyer and an independent thinker who could be stubborn when he felt it necessary, had decided he wanted it in evidence. It was going to be a strange and unusual Monday morning with us on opposite sides.

Before Judge McGuire got on the bench Monday, we alerted him that we had an issue to discuss outside the jury's presence. For the next half hour, Glenn told the judge that he wanted to use the green notebook in evidence, and explained why he should be able to, while I objected, noting that I had successfully moved to suppress it. McGuire was understandably puzzled: "Who made the motion?" We told him that we both had. Glenn argued that although the evidence was illegally seized by the police, the prohibition of its use in evidence should only apply to the *state* introducing it, and not to one of the defendants. I argued that I had moved to suppress it for all purposes, so that it could not come into evidence whatsoever for any reason unless I agreed, and that's what the Fourth Amendment was all about. Throughout this, deputy DA Elliot looked like a fan at a tennis match, swinging his head back and forth, with little interest in the outcome and, actually, no information about why the argument was even taking place. McGuire asked for cases on point. We told him we could find none. The judge took a recess in his chambers, resumed the bench, and, falling back on the Constitution, ruled in our favor.

As a result, we were down to the simplest of cases: Could the state prove, beyond a reasonable doubt, that Max and Jenny were involved in "pimping and pandering" as opposed to running and working for a licensed escort service? The jury deliberated for two days, a surprising length of time for such a brief trial, and the foreman sent a note to Judge McGuire saying that they had a verdict on one person but were locked up on the other. The judge asked them to try a little longer, and they did. But the next morning, the foreman wrote another similar note. McGuire called the jurors into the courtroom to ask whether they were irrevocably deadlocked.

I must state at this point that when a jury is deadlocked, if you are defending a criminal case the assumption is *always* that they're deadlocked against your client and that a hung jury is, all of a sudden, a great result. That was my state of mind when the judge asked the jury foreman whether they were completely deadlocked. Mr. Marvin, now the foreman, stood up and said that they were as to Max. Immediately, the other jurors started speaking with raised voices – essentially that Mr. Marvin had promised to tell the judge that they were *not* deadlocked and would continue to work on coming to a verdict. But I, based on training and experience and fearing the worst, was ready for the mistrial that would result. Judge McGuire asked for quiet from the other jurors and asked the foreman again whether there was any way the case could result in a unanimous verdict. "No," said Mr. Marvin in a clear voice. McGuire declared a mistrial as to Max, and a moment later announced an acquittal for Jenny.

Then something unique in my experience happened. The jurors rushed the bench to explain to the judge that Marvin had promised them that he would not declare a mistrial but would continue to deliberate, and that he, the foreman, was the only holdout for a guilty verdict, plus there was no real evidence against Jenny or Max, and that Marvin's own biased view of Max was standing in the way of a fair verdict. You could have knocked me over with a feather. I had reacted as any criminal defense lawyer would have reacted and was totally wrong. And I was even more wrong for leaving a guy on the jury who had stated such racist views.

"Now what?" Max whispered to me.

"Now what?"

What I learned after the verdict reminded me of the racist attitudes of the Marin District Attorney's office at that time. Not everyone was that way, of course. Mike, the trial deputy, would have loved to see this case dismissed after the 11-1 vote to acquit Max. He was a good lawyer and knew the case was fatally weak. But the higher-ups in the DA's office wanted Max's hide and absolutely refused to dismiss the case despite the nature of the mistrial. In a bit of overkill, they sent the chief assistant DA to each court appearance to argue against every post-trial motion I made. But Judge McGuire wasn't a whole lot happier than I was about the DA's refusal to dismiss, and it showed. First, I asked for Max to be released on his own recognizance, avoiding further bail. Granted. Next, I asked to be appointed counsel at state expense, because Max had spent the last of his money on me in the first trial; since being charged, his business had gone down the tubes, and he was now indigent. Granted. Then I asked the judge for some money for investigators. Granted. A month in, I went back into court for an expert to testify about linguistics – basically, as to what the reasonable meanings of Max's words, "We're in the business of sex," could be. The judge didn't grant that one but did order the DA to file a brief on the issue. And the judge kept putting off setting a date for the retrial.

Meanwhile, the reporter who covered the courts for the Marin daily, the *Independent Journal*, had picked up on the case and had written a couple of small pieces that asked why the DA was so insistent about trying Max again. When I filed a request to have the court reporter transcribe her notes of what was said in court the day the jury came back with its non-verdict, the DA finally capitulated and dismissed the case. All the office had done in the eight weeks between the end of trial and dismissal was to make themselves look foolish in the eyes of both the judge and the community.

EPILOGUE

Max, an ex-con, something of a con artist, and often in and out of trouble, was far from an innocent soul. He was multi-talented, though, so this time he started a new business repairing electronic equipment out of a storefront in San Rafael, the county seat. About eighteen months after his 'pimping and pandering' dismissal, and with the eyes of the police always on him, he caught another felony – a fraud case. This time, shortly before trial we discovered evidence that almost certainly completely exonerated him. When cases go out to trial, there's almost always a little in-chambers discussion first about whether the matter could be resolved by a plea bargain. In our morning pre-trial conversation, I presented our evidence to the deputy DA and our judge, Richard Breiner, the same man who years earlier had represented Fleeta Drumgo of the San Quentin Six.

The deputy DA asked for time to go speak to his boss, the same chief assistant DA who had refused to dismiss the pimping case. The deputy came back with a much better deal. We said "no, not good enough." Instead of beginning to pick the jury, the deputy asked for still more time, went back to the chief, and came back with an even sweeter deal – a plea to a misdemeanor charge with no jail time and no probation, just one more (minor) offense on a pretty long rap sheet. But when I talked to Max, he was concerned that the misdemeanor could cause him to lose the license for his new business. I took that back to the DA and judge in chambers, and Judge Breiner went to the Government Code, found the applicable law, and said, "Look, I'll put on the record that this offense is not one that can result in the suspension of a license. Not only that, but I'll write a letter on your client's behalf saying exactly that."

Well, I thought that should do it, and told both the DA and the judge that it sounded great to me. For many people, a misdemeanor crime on their record would be a huge deal, but for Max, who had more than one felony conviction, it seemed trivial. No fine, no jail, no probation. Go back to his shop. You can't do better.

By this time, it was the lunch hour, and Max and I had plenty of time to discuss things. I told him all the many reasons why this was a great result, an almost perfect deal that he couldn't possibly turn down. He kept on saying, "Richard, I trust you. You're going to win this case. I have no doubt. I don't want to plead guilty to anything." I replied that there is *always* the danger of losing, which in a criminal case is inevitably true. But Max then told me this: "You know, there comes a time in every man's life when you gotta draw the line. And this is that time for me. I am not pleading guilty to anything."

We went back into open court after lunch, with the prospective jurors waiting in the hallway. Judge Breiner turned to me expectantly and said, "Does the defense have a motion?" meaning to set aside Max's not guilty plea and enter a plea of guilty. "No," I replied to everyone's surprise save Max. And the DA then stood up and dismissed the case.

Representing Max taught me an important lesson and reminded me of two others. The lesson was that no matter what, if you are a lawyer and you're right about something and it's important, you cannot back down in the face of authority, even when that authority is very angry. My completely non-violent mother tried to teach me this when I was a kid, with the phrase, "Stick to your guns." At the preliminary hearing, Judge Mansell was furious with me and was close to holding me in contempt. But I knew I was right on the law and, even more important, needed to call that police witness to protect my client's interests. The odd thing is that the judge had always liked me, even back when I appeared before him as a student practitioner. As it happened, the next day, doing part-time work as a special public defender, I was in his courtroom for another hearing. Judge Mansell called me up to the bench and told me he knew I was a good young lawyer, and I shouldn't think otherwise. A nice and rare thing for a judge to do.

The first reminder was this: My clients were entitled to their own autonomy. I had pushed Max very hard to take this deal. I saw no downside to it at all. But unlike with Gypsy, who I finally convinced *not* to plead guilty, I couldn't convince Max. And, as it turned out, he was right. But even if he had been wrong, his dignity as a human being required that he be able to maintain his autonomy. And although he attributed his refusal to take a deal to my skill as a lawyer, I think it was really about his right as a person to decide things for himself.

The final reminder, of course, was that racism runs deep. I had thought that through our long conversation in *voir dire*, Mr. Martin's acknowledgement of bias was a statement of fairness – that he could truly set aside his stereotyped assumptions about Max and treat him objectively. But while Martin may have educated other members of the jury, it turned out he had not educated himself. In the face of weak evidence and eleven others who saw how weak that evidence was, he couldn't get over his internalized animus towards Max, even to the extent of lying to his own fellow jurors. Yes, racism runs deep indeed.

9

Divorce Kings of Marin County

In re Marriage of Betz

In re Marriage of Duarte

One important lesson I learned as a young lawyer was that if you don't control your law practice, it will surely control you. That's how I found myself representing Chief Petty Officer Ernie Betz in his divorce case, one of many domestic cases I handled in my early years of practice. Ernie decided the marriage was over when his wife Margie came after him with a butcher knife. He fled his house, took refuge in a bunk on the aircraft carrier where he was stationed, and then called me. I tried to salvage something for him, his ex-wife, and his dogs, in roughly that order.

I handled the challenging Duarte case at around the same time. Unlike my experience with Ernie, I found myself with a client who was not only difficult to deal with but who simply refused to play by the rules, to devastating effect.

Developing a "book of business"

By 1980, David Mayer and considered ourselves the Divorce Kings of Marin County. We didn't plan it that way, but in order to keep the doors open and food on the table, those $500 family law retainers came in handy. Besides, at least we were working instead of staring at the walls, waiting for a criminal case to come in. The domestic cases started as a trickle, but within a couple of years, we'd developed an extensive family law practice. David already had an excellent source of cases – what lawyers call a "book of business" – from his friends at Marin's first and first-rate all-women family law firm. About a year later, I developed my own book of family law cases referred to me by the Judge Advocate General's office at the Presidio of San Francisco Army base.

My relationship with the Presidio JAG office didn't start entirely smoothly. I had been retained by Joseph Monk, an Army enlisted man, on a felony in Marin County. With the help of a good psychiatrist and a sympathetic judge, I'd been able to get him a misdemeanor plea and probation, subject to his entering a treatment program. The Army had set court-martial proceedings against Joseph, and he hired me to represent him on those too. Joseph was also entitled to an assigned Army counsel, and having never done a court-martial, I wanted all the help I could get. I asked around and found that everyone at the Presidio said the best lawyer on the base was a Captain Beau Billingslea, so I called him. Billingslea made it clear that he had absolutely no desire to get on Joseph's defense team. But I knew from listening to David's Air Force JAG stories that if a JAG officer is reasonably available, he cannot refuse the assignment. I put that to Billingslea, and he reluctantly agreed to help.

Once Beau got on board, he not only did his best, but he was also quite good. With his help, I was able to pull off a minor miracle and get Joseph a general, rather than dishonorable, discharge. During the course of the case, Beau and I became buddies. We were a good legal team and also enjoyed just hanging out. Beau was a charming and strikingly handsome Black guy in his mid-thirties who had acted in the soap opera *The Young and the Restless* in New York while going to law school in Connecticut. He hated the Army, and to prove it walked around "naked," as he put it, wearing no medals of any kind on his uniform, not even a good-conduct medal. When I met him, he was trying to lie low awaiting his discharge so he could head to Hollywood to make it as an actor. Once we had become friends, he made a strange request: He wanted to learn how to play tennis. He thought that a decent tennis game could help him in LA. I wasn't much of a tennis player, but I'd played as a kid, so he and I played quite often on the Presidio's hardcourts.

While Beau gained a tennis partner, I gained a referral source. I was hoping for criminal referrals, but that was not to be. Still, military marriages broke up all the time, many involving doctors working at the base's Letterman Army Hospital. Doctors, all commissioned officers, and their spouses frequently turned to the JAG officers for advice about finding a lawyer, and Beau and his buddy, Art Grant, a Harvard-educated JAG officer, started referring me lots of cases. For about three years, this became my greatest book of business — if only it had been the kind of business I was looking for. But I was making money, learning a lot, and getting a lot of trial experience.

David and I were both criminal defense attorneys and had even gotten formal State Bar certification as specialists. But we wanted to be successful, too. And to one extent or another, "success" is measured by a sustained, busy, income-producing practice. So instead of putting a cap on domestic cases, we kept taking them in. We even had a contest between us each quarter year about who was bringing in more income, with the prize being a nice dinner and bottle of wine. In the process, though, we made a mistake many young lawyers make – we let these cases – often contentious, and too often forced out to trial by angry clients who'd be better off settling – run our practice and, to a large extent, our lives.

In re Betz and Betz

As word spread around the Bay Area military community, my source of cases expanded. Ernie Betz was Navy, not Army, and looked every inch the part: small, wiry, with tattooed arms, and a bowlegged walk. He was a recovering alcoholic who worked as a drug-abuse counselor on an aircraft carrier. I'm not sure how he got hold of me, but when we met, I found I liked him better than most of the doctors and their wives who'd become my most frequent (and best paying) domestic clients. Ernie's wife Margie was a bartender and twice his size, and she was definitely not in recovery. After she came at him with a butcher knife, Ernie understandably decided to call it a day, and fled to his carrier, berthed in Oakland. By then, it was quite clear he was petrified of Margie.

Ernie and Margie didn't have much. Their home was a rental on Mare Island, then a Navy base in Vallejo, part of Solano County, an exurb of San Francisco. They had a couple of used cars, a little savings in the bank, an old Winnebago, and two purebred beagles, Buffy and Lady. That's about it.

By the time Ernie came along, I'd gotten pretty experienced in these cases, which in 1970 in California had become "no-fault dissolutions" instead of contested divorces. I knew that most everything would be divided fifty-fifty, and that Ernie and Margie had so little that it wasn't worth fighting over. The major issue was spousal support, as alimony had come to be called. Each county had its support guidelines based on the income of the parties, and Ernie was fine with going along with those guidelines. Anything not to piss off Margie again.

Margie's lawyer Ken Larrabee seemed like a nice guy and a reasonably decent if unexceptional lawyer: no world-beater, but competent enough. But he didn't speak with much authority or confidence. He and I talked a few times on the phone and had little difficulty coming to an agreement between us about what would be a fair deal. The only sticking point in the case was the dogs; both parties really loved those dogs, which they had bred more than once and then sold the pups. Ernie was really fond of the male, Buffy, and wanted to keep him. But when Larrabee took the proposal to split up the dogs back to his client, she was adamant that she would not settle without getting both dogs. Larrabee and I went back and forth with a couple of possible solutions, but Margie was unmoved: She wanted both dogs.

In the few years I'd been doing military divorces, I'd seen some very minor items become symbols of disagreement between husband and wife, and these sometimes drove their cases to trial for the silliest of reasons. A Japanese wood-cutting of a horse; a vase that a couple had purchased in a little shop in Germany. I knew that dogs could be far more important than seemingly trivial inanimate objects, but after a few back-and-forths with both the lawyer and Ernie, I suggested that given Margie's volatility, he might be better served by just giving her both dogs. He didn't like that and said he'd have to think on it.

Meanwhile, the case got set for trial up in Fairfield, the Solano County seat about an hour northeast of San Francisco. As in most counties, family court had one particular judge assigned on a rotating basis. The family court judge at the time was David Sherwood, whom I'd heard about because he had a well-known reputation for misogyny. I knew that if Ernie took the case to trial, it was very likely that Margie would get a very bad result. Fortunately for Margie, on the day before trial, Ernie called me and said he'd thought about the dog and decided reluctantly to give Margie Buffy just to avoid the pain of a trial. Since Ernie was being more than reasonable about the amount of support he'd pay, it looked like the easiest pre-trial settlement ever.

We didn't count on Margie.

One-day trials in Solano, as this was, weren't scheduled to begin until 10:00 a.m., to give the parties a last-minute chance to work things out. On the morning of trial, Larrabee and I met at 9:00 a.m., and I told him Ernie was willing to give up the dog. Larrabee was sure that would clinch the settlement and went off to get his client's approval. Five minutes went by, then ten, then twenty. I started to wonder what was going on and went out in search of my opposing counsel. When I found him, he was visibly upset: "Margie won't agree unless Ernie gives her another $250 a month in support." I told Larrabee that Ernie simply couldn't afford to do anything close to that and still have enough to live on, and that Margie made a decent living tending bar: "You're getting what the court's income guidelines say, and a bit more." "I know that," said Larrabee, "but she's adamant."

"Do you know about Judge Sherwood?" I asked.

"Not really," he replied. He was clearly not a lawyer who did all his homework.

"He has a history of being very tough on women," I told him. "If we can't work this out, this judge could really screw your client."

Larrabee went to talk to his client again but made no progress, so off we went to trial.

I should mention at this point that it was not my obligation as Ernie's lawyer to protect Margie's interests. In fact, if Ernie had wanted to squeeze as much as he could out of the case, my ethical obligation would have been to say nothing to Larrabee that might have helped Margie out. But Ernie, bottom line, was a nice guy who only wanted his share, and understood that much as he loved that dog Buffy, if giving up the dog was what it took to settle peacefully, it was worth it.

We went off to trial with predictable results. The butcher knife incident never came up; it simply wasn't relevant under California's "no fault" law. But Judge Sherwood, ruling from the bench as soon as testimony was over, awarded Margie $150 a month less than we had offered in settlement (and $400 less than she wanted), and gave Ernie the choice of their two cars, which he hadn't even asked for, and the camper as a bonus. Then, the judge, having saved the dogs for last, said, "I hereby order that Mr. Betz gets the male, Buffy, and that Mrs. Betz gets the bitch, Lady." It sounded to me that he gave a little extra emphasis to the "b"-word. Screaming, "Not my Buffy!!!" Margie charged the bench and attempted to strangle the judge. In all my trials, even the hairiest criminal trials, I'd never seen anything like this. The bailiff tried to pull Margie off the judge as three other bailiffs appeared from out of nowhere to drag her away. Somehow, they released Margie from custody, and I never learned whether she was criminally charged.

At the end of the day, Ernie and I went to pick up Buffy, escorted by a sheriff's squad car, and with Buffy in tow, we both got a sheriff's escort all the way to the far side of the Carquinez Bridge and out of Solano County.

The difficulties of a family law practice

By the time of the Betz trial, I knew that my practice was controlling my life, rather than the other way around. About this time, I looked at my list of cases and saw seventeen active family law matters. These cases kept us alive financially, but in some ways, they were much more difficult than criminal cases. Sure, life and liberty were at stake when our clients were charged with a crime. There were no higher stakes, and no higher level of anxiety for me personally. But there was nothing that brought out a client's raw emotions more than family law issues. Too often, I'd find myself on deadline for a criminal motion or doing trial prep the week before a criminal trial when I'd be interrupted by a phone call from a domestic client needing "desperately" to speak to me about something "extremely urgent." Those interruptions were, in truth, rarely urgent and were usually desperate only because of the client's own emotional state. But these were my clients, so I'd take the call, then find myself in a half-hour conversation about a visitation that started ten minutes late or one spouse calling the other a bad name, while my mind was on how to avoid years of prison time for my criminal client.

David and I both found that in family law cases, an essential ingredient of the lawyer-client relationship was often missing: "client control." By client control, I don't mean forcing our clients to do what we wanted. I mean that after active listening to understand a client's perspective followed by some reasoned and collaborative dialogue, persuading them to look at what we saw as their best interests and the best course of action to achieve those interests. It might seem illogical that criminal defendants were better listeners and collaborators than the average family law client, but David and I both found this to be true. Perhaps it had to do with criminal defendants' more realistic expectations. Perhaps there were ways in which we were able to build trust with our criminal law clients that we couldn't accomplish with our family law clients. Perhaps our criminal law clients, no matter how streetwise, sensed that they were out of their depth in the courthouse, while our family law clients – on average more educated, more monied, and more often white, thought they knew their way around the court system better – even though most of them didn't have much of a clue.

Whatever the reason, there's no question in my mind that on average, it was easier for me to get on the same page with my criminal defense clients than my domestic relations ones. And while it might sound counterintuitive, I liked most of my criminal defendants (except for the drunk drivers, who tended towards entitlement), but I had many domestic clients whom I didn't care for at all.

I knew by the time of the Betz case that difficult clients in domestic cases were hardly unusual; they came with the territory. And to a certain extent, they needed not just my advocacy but my protection. In my very first domestic trial a year into practice, I'd represented a Mrs. Sennett, a depressed sixty-something who felt abandoned by her husband, who'd moved into San Francisco and come out as gay. She was more unhappy and depressed than angry, but still angry enough to be a difficult client. But in her case, apparently her husband was every bit as hard to deal with. Every time I talked to Donald Beech, Ralph Sennett's attorney, Beech told me what a pain in the butt his client was. Ralph's behavior mirrored his wife's, but I never said a bad word about her. Not, I should emphasize, because to do so would be unethical – although I would soon learn as I began teaching legal ethics that it would be just that – but because it seemed to me that it gave us a strategic advantage to remain silent. In trial, that proved to be correct.

But representing Mrs. Sennett and others like her was still no picnic. As it happened, when the Betz case went to trial, I was also deeply enmeshed in the disastrous Duarte case involving the person who takes top prize as the least cooperative client I ever had, Giselle Duarte. If I had needed any more proof about my need to get out of domestic cases, Ms. Duarte provided that in ample supply.

Dr. and Mrs. Duarte

Hannibal Duarte was from the Philippines, where he joined the United States Army with the promise that he'd be brought stateside to do his four years of medical school, all expenses paid, in return for a post-grad term of service as an Army doctor. Giselle Dobson met Hannibal when he was in med school at the University of Virginia. How they met is unclear. According to Giselle, they met at the campus bookstore where she was working while a junior at UVA. According to what I was told years later by Hannibal's lawyer, they met in "a brothel." Hannibal was small, dark, and good-looking, a bit brooding and exotic, perhaps making him more exciting to a young woman from Virginia, whatever her background. In a year they were married, and they soon had two kids, a girl and a boy. By the time Hannibal was assigned to the Presidio's Letterman Hospital to finish a post-residency in neurosurgery, the children were five and six, and the marriage was dissolving.

Giselle was referred to me by my friend, Beau, at the JAG office. When she came to see me, she brought a $500 retainer and a healthy dose of deep-seated anger. Giselle described

Hannibal as a repeatedly unfaithful husband who did little to help in the home or even to bond with the kids. Giselle told me he spent all his time either at the hospital or out with his friends. This was nothing I hadn't heard before – in fact, nothing out of the ordinary for an Army case – so since I knew that there was enough money from a doctor's income to pay my fees as well as his own lawyer's, I was happy to sign up Giselle as a client. Then I went along for the ride down her own personal rabbit hole.

Unlike the depressed Mrs. Sennett, Giselle was not only angry but vengeful. She wanted to get back at Hannibal in any way she could. Had I known she'd be this adamant about revenge, I never would have taken her on. But by the time I understood this, it was too late to withdraw without damaging her case. All lawyers, particularly early in their careers, take cases they later wished they hadn't. But I felt that if I guessed wrong, that was on me, not the client. So, I stuck it out.

Giselle and Hannibal argued about all the usual trivial-but-symbolic tchotchkes that people gather during marriage. But their disagreements were far more vitriolic than most, particularly at Giselle's end. Giselle ranted and raged. She broke things, just for spite. She occasionally feigned reasons why one or another visit between the doctor and his kids couldn't happen that week. And she invaded the doctor's private papers.

Much of her angst focused on visitation with the children. Hannibal didn't want to share equal physical custody, since his post-residency required at least eighty hours a week on the job. But Giselle was insistent on giving Hannibal the least amount of visitation possible. Though she insisted that he was "a lousy father in every respect," she had no evidence to back it up, just her generalized unhappiness. No physical abuse, no spanking, no verbal abuse, not even yelling at the kids or calling them stupid. Giselle still wanted to permit Hannibal no more than every other weekend with the kids – a traditional but by-then outmoded father-visit schedule that had lost favor with the courts. That was unacceptable to Hannibal, who wanted to have the kids for an overnight visit at his place at least every week. That meant the case was headed for trial. And for a visitation battle we were very unlikely to win.

About six weeks before trial, Giselle came into my office to tell me that she believed Hannibal was going to abscond with the children. She said she'd learned this when she went to pick up the kids at Hannibal's apartment, where they'd been left in the care of a babysitter because Hannibal was on a graveyard shift at the hospital. Giselle said she took that opportunity to rummage through Hannibal's desk, and that she'd found one-way plane tickets to the Philippines for Hannibal and the kids in just a few weeks' time. This news, of course, was deeply troubling. First, if this claim were true and Hannibal had no intention of returning, then he would be kidnapping the children. But second, in order to get this information, Giselle had improperly and possibly criminally rifled through Hannibal's papers.

I was left with a serious dilemma. I certainly didn't want anyone absconding with children under any circumstances. On the other hand, how could I reveal Giselle's true behavior to my opposing counsel or the court without violating my strict duty of confidentiality? After much serious thought and a consultation with David, I decided that I should rely on the good relationship I had developed with Bruce Berger, Hannibal's lawyer. Unlike Mrs. Sennett's lawyer, neither Bruce nor I had ever said a bad word about our own clients, despite the obvious antagonism of the parties and the almost inevitable "difficult client" vibes that emanated from such cases. That helped me form my sense that he was an honorable and fair-minded counsel.

I risked a phone call to Bruce to tell him that Giselle was afraid that his client was going to take the children and flee the country, never to return. Bruce reacted by saying that the idea was ridiculous, and that Hannibal still had almost three years remaining on his tour of duty with the Army. But because we had built up a healthy measure of trust, Bruce didn't completely dismiss my concerns out of hand. And although he asked what Giselle's suspicion was based on, when I told him I wouldn't and couldn't reveal that, he didn't insist on an answer and remained willing to listen. This willingness was the key to reinforcing my positive impression of my colleague, and also reinforced in my mind the importance of developing good relationships with opposing counsel wherever possible. In my experience, good relationships with the other side's lawyers were the exceptions rather than the rule, but when those exceptions occurred, as here, they could be extremely valuable.

I told Bruce that I agreed that the chances of the good doctor taking the kids and fleeing the jurisdiction were relatively remote. But if Bruce was so sure that Hannibal had nothing of the kind in mind, then Hannibal shouldn't object to Bruce holding his passport for safe keeping in Bruce's office. Bruce said that he was willing to discuss the matter with his client and get back to me with some assurances of safety. The next day, he called me and told me we could rest assured that Hannibal would not take the children out of the country, without telling me exactly what those assurances were based on. Just as he had to trust me without revealing the source of my information, I now had to trust him when he said, "rest assured."

I did trust Bruce, but my client did not, and didn't trust me enough to overcome her continuing concern. Her anger never abated, and we went off to trial with two angry clients, though most of the anger was on my side of the table.

The two-day trial was predictable. The couple fought over a list of objects de marriage that the judge refused to rule on, choosing instead to require each party to list their three most important items and present them to an arbitrator if they couldn't agree. As for the children, it was no surprise that the judge ruled that while Giselle could maintain custody, Dr. Duarte was entitled to have the kids at least one-third of the time, including on overnights and some weekends. While I'd told Giselle innumerable times that this was and had long been the likely outcome, she was still furious.

After the trial and the granting of a dissolution of marriage decree, which can occur before all of the property in dispute is divided, Dr. and the former Mrs. Duarte were finally able to resolve their disagreements over the remaining items in dispute, though it took months. I then closed my file and only spoke to Giselle once thereafter.

EPILOGUE

Ernie Betz: Three months after his case was over, Ernie called me and told me that he was going to give Buffy the Beagle to his ex-wife Margie. He told me his ex-wife kept sending him messages through friends he used to hang out with before he became sober that Margie was distraught that the dogs were not together. "I love that dog," Ernie told me, "but it just ain't worth it to keep 'em apart. So I had a friend drive Buffy over to her place." There was regret in his voice, but he told me he felt more at peace than he had since before marrying Margie.

Beau Billingslea went off to Hollywood as he said he would, and I never saw or heard from him again until I reached out while writing this chapter. I don't know if his tennis game improved, but I do know that he left the Bay Area with all his considerable charm and good looks intact. Beau carved out a good career for himself in Hollywood. He never became the star that he wanted to be, but he hit the ground running, with dozens of parts in TV series and movies throughout the late 1970s and then the '80s and '90s. After 2000, he split his work between television parts, voiceovers and anime, including the voice of Jet Black in the critically acclaimed Japanese anime *Cowboy Bebop*. At age seventy-seven, he's still working constantly.

The Duartes: It was standard procedure for lawyers to withdraw from domestic cases once they settle or get a decision at trial, particularly with children involved. Otherwise, attorneys could remain "of record," potentially stuck in cases for years should they go back to court. About six months after

I'd withdrawn, I got a call from my opposing counsel, Bruce Berger, who told me that Giselle was moving with the kids back to her family in Virginia. Bruce told me that he was headed to court to get a modification of visitation to ensure that the children could come out to California each summer and spend alternate Christmas, Thanksgiving, and Spring Break weeks with Dr. Duarte, who had decided to remain in California permanently. I thought I should call Giselle just to remind her she still had to abide by whatever custody arrangement the court ordered. She assured me that she would, though I confess I was not completely convinced.

By then, Bruce and I had become friends and I even referred him a couple of domestic cases as I tried to wean myself from that part of my practice. After a couple of years, we lost touch for some time. That was the last I'd heard about the Duartes until decades later, when Bruce and I had reestablished our friendship. Before writing this chapter, I called Bruce to ask whether he knew what had happened to his client, Hannibal. Bruce told me that Hannibal had a successful private practice and that he and Hannibal had remained friends, lunching once a month for years. But he also told me that Giselle had ignored all communications from the court about visitations, had never complied with the visitation schedule, wouldn't let Hannibal talk to the children on the phone, and had apparently destroyed any piece of mail that Hannibal sent. Hannibal never saw his kids again.

I can't say that this news entirely surprised me, but it saddened me greatly and angered me too. I felt somehow complicit, even though Giselle's behavior was beyond my – or anybody else's – control. And I wondered whether this result would have happened had Giselle been Filipina and Hannibal white. One can never have a good feeling about a case or client that turned out like this.

Our law practice: After spending five years allowing the law practice to control us, David and I decided to stop allowing the tail to wag the dog. We put a cap on the number of family law cases we'd take, reduced that cap over time, moved our principal office into San Francisco (from where we could no longer be the Marin County Divorce Kings), and gathered as much criminal and non-domestic work as we could. By 1986, I had done my last domestic case. That meant I was back where I wanted to be, representing those for whom access to the courthouse was a challenge, not a given. My domestic cases were not all clients with means and status – Ernie Betz was a good example of someone who had neither – but on the whole, those clients had far more money, social status, and entitlement than the other people I represented, either criminally or civilly. Representing entitled people like Giselle had never been my cup of tea. I was, frankly, happy to leave that practice in the rear-view mirror.

10

A Doctor, a Patient, and the Molestation Question

People of the State of California v. Joseph Sing, MD

I handled only a few sexual abuse cases over the years, only one of which went to trial, and the timing was not good – it came at a moment when everyone assumed that a child's accusations were invariably true. Although the state had a weak case, my client was almost convicted. So, for retrial, we hired a jury consultant, who taught me not just how to ask questions of prospective jurors but also how to speak the truth – both to the jurors and to myself. I learned my lesson well, but only after experiencing the worst day of my professional life.

Sexual abuse and ignorance and in the 1980s

When it came to understanding sexual abuse in our society, America of the mid-1980s was still in the Neanderthal days of ignorance. Awareness of the pervasiveness of sexual assault was not on the agenda. Widespread exposés of molesting priests, gymnastics coaches, and others were years, even decades, in the future. On issues both modest and major, our attitudes then towards sexual offenses had more in common with the

1950s than the 2020s. American tourists in Italy were expected to be pinched on the behind, and not only accept but "like" it. More gravely, while the phrase "date rape" had entered the vocabulary, notably in a 1982 *Ms. Magazine* article, it wasn't until the late 1980s that anyone seriously examined how common an occurrence it was. As for #MeToo, that phrase wouldn't come into existence for another twenty years. The prevailing attitude remained that anyone who wore clothing that was deemed "too suggestive" or had sex when inhibitions were lowered was "asking for it." Accusations of rape by acquaintances and strangers alike routinely either went uninvestigated or were investigated by people, usually police officers, mostly male, who had little or no training on how to sensitively deal with victims.

But in 1984 when it came to children's complaints, ignorance had the opposite effect. The prevailing wisdom was that a child's accusations about molestation were invariably true, and everyone charged with child molesting, from child-care workers to parents and teachers, was presumed guilty.

Decades later, we've learned that children are highly suggestible, and instead of always being truthful, what they want most is the approval of the adults who question them. We've learned that those evaluating suggestible people must take exceptional care not to feed or imply an answer, or lead a child to a particular response, even if the leading is completely unintentional. An entire discipline of psychologists, clinical social workers, and sexual abuse specialists has grown up in the days since the 1980s, resulting in a much-needed professionalization of how we deal with child accusers – and the parents and others who carry the accusations for them.

But back in the mid-1980s, the country was in the grips of what commentators later described as "child sexual abuse hysteria." The first major manifestation of this hysteria came in 1983 in Bakersfield, California. Recently elected Kern County District Attorney Ed Jagels began racking up convictions of accused child molesters, at least twenty-six in all, getting sentences cumulatively totaling thousands of years in prison. The cases were all based entirely on the accusations of children interviewed by police and prosecutorial investigators. The accusations themselves were of the most sordid sort: parents having sex with their children, siblings forced to have sex with each other, adult-child orgies, and eventually, stories of Satan worship, and children who were beaten, hung on hooks, and forced to drink blood.

Significantly, these prosecutions and convictions occurred without any physical evidence. The children were simply believed.

That same year, an extensive investigation began into the McMartin Daycare Center in Manhattan Beach, California, just outside Los Angeles. The location of the McMartin case was crucial. Unlike the Bakersfield cases, the LA media market offered front-page newspaper exposés and torrid local television coverage that resulted in national headlines. The word "McMartin" swiftly became the most visible and distressing symbol for the false wisdom that children are always to be believed.

The McMartin case began when one parent claimed that her son had been sodomized by daycare teacher Raymond Buckey. In response, the local police sent out form questionnaires to over 200 families, stating: "Our investigation indicates that possible criminal acts include: oral sex, fondling of genitals, buttock or chest area, and sodomy…." The questionnaire set off a panic among parents. The police, with little expertise in interviewing children, turned that job over to an outside agency, which interviewed 400 children and concluded that 360 of them had been molested.

On February 2, 1984, KABC-TV reporter Wayne Satz broke the big story: More than sixty children "have now each told authorities that he or she had been keeping a grotesque secret of being sexually abused and made to appear in pornographic films while in the preschool's care…." That story kicked off a media frenzy; both print and television news jumped to report the latest – almost all assuming guilt. *People Magazine*'s headline screamed, "California's Nightmare Nursery"; The *LA Times* ran many stories, an early one with this headline: "McMartin School Brutality Disclosed." National TV was right there: The *Today* show's Jane Pauley asked, "Are you as sickened by this as we are?" *Nightline* was perhaps the most extreme: "something was terribly wrong" at McMartin where "no one knew about the terrible secret that the children here were afraid to tell." "This is a story," concluded *Nightline*, "about how even the very young children have to be listened to and believed…."

In March 1984, Los Angeles District Attorney Robert Philibosian obtained indictments against seven McMartin teachers, including daycare founder Virginia McMartin, her daughter Peggy McMartin Buckey, who ran the school, and her grandson Raymond Buckey. They were ultimately charged with 321 counts involving forty-eight children. If convicted, the defendants would face thousands of years in prison. The evidence was based solely on the statements of the children and a handful of medical experts whose opinions were that the children had been molested. Just as in Bakersfield, there was absolutely no physical evidence.

Yet, "the sanctified slogan of the moment," as a *New York Times* reporter wrote years later, was that the children must be believed.

Joseph Sing, MD

With exquisitely awful timing, into the midst of this hysteria and into my office came pediatrician Joseph Sing, MD. Dr. Sing had been charged with two counts of sexually molesting a patient named Daisy Wong while in his examining room. His office was in the middle of Chinatown, where he was the regular pediatrician for many Chinese American families in San Francisco. Dr. Sing came in to see me with his mother, a brother, and a sister. Fourth generation Chinese Americans, the siblings had followed their father, also a pediatrician, into successful careers. Joseph's mother was particularly striking: a woman in her mid-seventies, elegant in dress, speech, and manner, an impressive family matriarch. And Joseph's office was the same office in which his father had had his pediatric practice. His father's name remained in gold lettering on the door, above his own.

Like the Kern County and McMartin cases, there was absolutely no physical evidence supporting Daisy's accusation. In fact, after my investigator and I had thoroughly reviewed the case, there were many circumstances that pointed to the accusation being untrue. It's not that Daisy was lying, any more than the children in other "abuse hysteria" cases. Rather, she was victimized by pressure from adults and the prevailing circumstances in 1984: Children were always to be believed.

There was only one unsettling fact. Unlike the Kern County and McMartin children, Daisy Wong was not a preschooler or kindergartener. She was fifteen, having immigrated from Taiwan with her family five years before. But placed in a real-world context, it was clear to us that there was a strong parallel between the suggestibility of younger children and the pressures put on this naïve and timid immigrant teenager. Here's what happened:

One Friday afternoon, Daisy went alone to Dr. Sing's office for her annual pediatric check-up. During the check-up, the doctor showed her how to do a self-examination of her breasts to detect lumps – standard pediatric procedure at that time for any doctor whose patients had reached puberty. Apparently, this part of the examination upset Daisy quite a lot, though neither Dr. Sing nor his staff noticed anything about her behavior. But when Daisy got home a few blocks away, she ran into the bathroom crying. That's when things began to go off the rails.

Daisy's mother tried the bathroom door and, seeing that it was locked, screamed repeatedly to her daughter in Chinese: "What did Dr. Sing do to you?" Why Daisy chose to answer that he had touched her breasts *inappropriately* is something even Daisy herself might never have known, but perhaps it was due to her embarrassment about a routine examination and a desire not to contradict her mother. In any event, that's what she said. And from there, things escalated.

The next morning Daisy's father burst into Dr. Sing's office, found the doctor, and punched him in the mouth. He returned home, and he and Daisy's mother insisted on taking the reluctant Daisy to the local police precinct to tell her story. Along the way, both parents badgered her for more details, and by then, Daisy said that the doctor had touched her lower down than her breasts. Later that day, Daisy sat in the passenger seat of a squad car while a middle-aged, white, male police sergeant sat in the driver's seat and asked Daisy a lot of questions. Sitting in the back seat of the squad car was her father. By the end of the questioning, all in her father's presence, Daisy's story had evolved: While she was on the examination table, Dr. Sing had put his mouth on her private parts and licked her. And that was the statement that we had to confront at trial.

The first trial

Everyone involved in this case was acutely aware of the McMartin case and its supposed lesson about children telling the truth. The idea of suggestibility and the desire of children to parrot what adults said made sense to us, but it didn't exist in the eyes of the general public. Besides, Daisy was fifteen, not six. I knew I would need a lot of help, despite the absence of any evidence beyond Daisy's evolving statements. My first call for help was to Dr. Irving Schulman, another of my father's med school classmates, who became the first Chief of Staff of Stanford's famed Lucile Packard Children's Hospital. I filled him in and said I needed help from an expert, preferably from a woman pediatrician with a background in adolescent medicine. Dr. Schulman told me he had the perfect person: Dr. Iris Litt, who founded and directed Stanford's Division of Adolescent Medicine and later helped direct the Institute of Research on Women and Gender. As an expert in adolescent sexuality, she later told me that if I hadn't come to her through her much-admired chief, she wouldn't have even spoken to me. But after I'd briefed Dr. Litt, she was fully on board.

My first concern was whether it was normal and appropriate for a pediatrician to be treating fifteen-year-olds. Dr. Litt's answer was "absolutely": She emphasized that it was better to give children continuity of care by a trusted doctor until they were college aged. My second question for my expert was whether there was anything inappropriate about the setting of the examination, including no third-party presence. Her answer was a clear no: Dr. Sing had followed the regular standard of care, in which privacy was paramount. Years later, the rules about privacy evolved to both prevent inappropriate conduct and claims of such conduct.

Of course, Dr. Litt couldn't say whether Daisy's ultimate recitation of what happened was true or not. Neither could anyone else, except Dr. Sing. But my investigator and I went out looking for the next best thing. I had done some research on an issue criminal defense lawyers almost always want to stay away from: character evidence. Character witnesses are allowed testify about a criminal defendant's "conduct in conformity with … a trait of character." A typical character trait might be honesty, trustworthiness, or even lack of violent behavior. But to my surprise, I discovered that California law allowed character-trait evidence about almost anything that could be reduced to a word or a phrase. The exact wording of the character trait I decided on was whether Dr. Sing was "the kind of person who would hurt or molest a patient." Odd? A bit, and verbose and awkward. But clearly allowable under the law. The problem with use of character witnesses at trial was that even one other witness found by the DA who contradicted my witnesses would devastate our claim about character. But I felt these witnesses were a necessary risk, given the McMartin cloud of presumed guilt hanging over everything about the case.

It has been my experience that women often are better investigators then men – that by and large, they have more empathy, and that people, both women and men, are more willing to trust and open up to them. I was lucky to have an excellent investigator, Cathy Kornblith, whom I'd worked with in the San Quentin Six case and had used regularly since. Cathy was charged with visiting with some of the teenage patients Dr. Sing recommended to find three who would testify firmly that he had the character to always behave appropriately with his patients. Finding them was easy; all five girls that Cathy interviewed not only readily agreed with the statement but said they'd be willing to testify. "Great!" I thought.

We developed several other witnesses, including nurses and assistants who worked in Dr. Sing's office. Dr. Sing shared his office with another pediatrician. Like most locations in Chinatown, the doctor's offices were very small – small waiting room, small private offices, and three tiny examination rooms – significantly smaller than most doctors' offices in other parts of the City. The staff told me that many supplies were kept in the storage drawers in each examining room, or drawers underneath the examination tables themselves. When I asked what they did when they needed supplies, they uniformly told me that they would knock on the examining room door and then just go in without waiting for a reply. The crowded nature of the scene was another point in our favor, and I lined up a nurse and two assistants to come to court and testify.

Then, crucially, there was Joe Sing himself. Joe was a shy man, an introvert, almost timid, and getting up in front of a jury was not something he relished doing. But in this case, his testimony was vital. He had to describe what actually happened during the examination and do it as confidently as possible. We spent a great deal of time going over his testimony. First, an abbreviated life story: how he was a fourth generation Chinese American; how his father had been his hero, working at Joe's grandfather's dry cleaning business to put himself through college and then medical school; how in his father's honor, Joe kept his father's stenciled name on the street-level glass door to the second floor offices; how Joe had studied hard in high school to get to a college where he could take pre-med to follow in his revered father's footsteps; how he was able to practice with his father for just two years before the older Dr. Sing passed away. Then, the routine details of a physical examination of a female patient and, more specifically, an adolescent patient. How he took pains to reassure his teenagers about the examination, to always say what was going to happen next, to check in to make sure they were comfortable, and so on.

The trial went well. The key witness for the prosecution, of course, was Daisy Wong. She testified to what she "remembered," which by now was firmly embedded in her conscious memory. But she also acknowledged that she hadn't told her mother the same story when she was in her family's bathroom after coming home from the examination. And she acknowledged both that her mother yelled, "What did Dr. Sing do to you?" several times, and that she heard her father rage at Dr. Sing when he came back home after punching the doctor, which her father described as a necessary matter of honor. She admitted that she was uncomfortable sitting in the patrol car with the middle-aged male officer, especially with her father sitting there watching. She said she held her father in high regard as the respected head of the family, and that she would never want to disappoint either her father or mother.

Deputy District Attorney Peter Hart also called the police sergeant to the stand, to testify about how experienced he was and how careful he had been in questioning Daisy. Hart smartly got out on direct examination what I wanted to go after on cross – that Daisy's father was in the squad car. The officer told the jury that Daisy had been very nervous and wanted her father there. I wasn't sure I believed this, because Daisy had said nothing about it during her examination. But it left me without much to focus my exam on except the cop's lack of training in dealing with sex crime allegations and asking why a woman officer was not found.

Hart's final witness was Daisy's mother. When her mother asked, "What did Dr. Sing do to you?" Daisy blurted out that he had touched her inappropriately. A spontaneous statement like that is an exception to the usual hearsay rule that would exclude the statement from evidence. Hart may have felt it showed that Daisy mentioned inappropriate conduct from the very beginning. But since the conversation was not specific, was in Chinese, and did not imply what Daisy ultimately told the police, I wondered why Hart felt the mother's testimony was necessary. Maybe he wanted to show the mother's honestly felt anger. But I felt the mother helped our case because she was *so* angry that she couldn't really be objective. And she too admitted asking what Dr. Sing had done several times. This seemed to me to make Daisy's reply more of a response to a parent rather than an objective statement about what had occurred.

So, I was feeling reasonably confident when it was our turn. First the nurse and assistants described how the bustling, crowded office worked, with everyone on top of everyone else and little time or space for the privacy that might have been easier in a larger, less hectic office. This work environment was then and still is typical in Chinatown – what John King, the *San Francisco Chronicle*'s longtime urban architecture critic, calls "magnetic density." After the nurse and assistants our next witness was Dr. Iris Litt, who testified that fifteen-year-old children were better off in the care of a pediatrician's practice, and that Dr. Sing checked all the right boxes in terms of who his patients were, how he treated them, and how the examinations worked. She was unimpeachable; deputy DA Hart asked her no questions.

Then it was time for Dr. Sing. I could tell he was nervous, but we moved slowly through his testimony, and it was thoughtful and sincere. I believed that his family's history had made a major impression on the jury. Finally, saving them for last, there were the three pretty, pleasant, smiling teenage girls. I had to fight to get their testimony in, with Hart strongly objecting that my character trait for "not the kind of person who would molest a patient" was not, like honesty or trust-worthiness, a legitimate subject for testimony. But the law was clearly on my side, and the judge, Mary O'Connor, who by then had made it clear that she didn't like my client or my case one bit, nevertheless had to let it in.

Part of what a witness is allowed to say about a character trait is why the witness believes what she does. So, at the end of each girl's testimony, I asked each of them, "Why do you believe that Dr. Sing has the character of behaving properly and not molesting his patients?" Each answered, in turn, "Because he never molested me."

The case really couldn't have come in better.

While the jury retired to deliberate, I sat with Joe and his mother, the widow of the family's first physician, in Zuka's, one of the crummy restaurants across the street from the Hall of Justice. We were all cautiously optimistic, although for me, any optimism was tempered by my usual approach of expecting the worst. We sat there all afternoon without a peep from the jury. Judge O'Connor dismissed the jurors for the night at

4:30 p.m. and told them to report back at 9:00 a.m. the next day. They did and so did we, spending the day cooling our heels in the Hall of Justice corridor, outside of a couple of brief walks around the block to get some fresh air. By 4:30 p.m. on Day Two, the jury had still said nothing. No requests to read back testimony or to see evidence, no questions for the judge, nothing. The judge again sent them home for the night.

Finally, just before 3:00 p.m. on the third day of deliberations, the bailiff came out in the hallway to tell us that the jury foreperson had written a note to the judge. Along with the DA, we scrambled into the courtroom to hear the judge read the note: "We the jury are irrevocably deadlocked. We cannot reach a unanimous verdict." This did not make anyone particularly happy, especially Judge O'Connor. But hung juries are always supposedly better for the defense, and even though I thought we'd put in a great case, I knew that the times we then lived in didn't give defendants much if any wiggle room. We could do worse than a hung jury.

There's something of a ritual when hung juries come into the courtroom to explain themselves, and Judge O'Connor followed that ritual. First, she asked the foreperson whether he felt the jury was absolutely unable to resolve the case. He said yes. Then the judge asked, "Without saying which way you all have voted, please tell me what the split in votes is." The foreperson said, "9 to 3." The judge then suggested that 9-3 was pretty close to a resolution, so she asked each juror individually whether they might be able to "really try a little harder." Defense lawyers don't like that kind of talk at all, because they generally assume it's a majority for conviction and would like to leave well enough alone, get a mistrial, and start fresh. But I thought we might be winning, given the weak evidence. Either way, each juror, when polled, said that the jury was irrevocably stuck, so Judge O'Connor, left with little choice, declared a mistrial. Which meant starting all over again.

Between the trials

We were allowed to chat with the jurors after they were excused, and a few were willing to speak with us. Which way, I wanted to know, was the 9-3 vote. In favor of conviction, I was told. Despite my training, inherent skepticism, and understanding the "children must be believed" times we lived in, I was shocked. There was simply no supporting evidence to bolster Daisy's narrative, and there was clear evidence of three things: first, that her story was in response to her mother's accusatory question; second, that that the narrative grew over time; and third, that her father, whom she deeply respected, not only punched the doctor but was present while Daisy was interviewed in that most uncomfortable of venues – a police squad car. Wasn't that enough to at least raise a reasonable doubt?

Besides, we had so much of our own helpful evidence, in addition to Joe's testimony. The busy, bustling office, with people entering examination rooms with just a quick warning knock. The testimony of the esteemed Dr. Litt. And the three teenaged character witnesses.

We had almost three months before the second trial. But I was despondent. I couldn't figure out what went wrong and concluded it must have been me; with so little evidence, that near conviction must have been my fault. Although by this time I had a rather high opinion of my trial skills, I was ready to withdraw and get Joe to a better attorney. I called my friend M. Gerald Schwartzbach and asked to sit down with him to discuss the case. Gerry was – and still is, today – one of the very best trial lawyers I've seen, and he specialized then – as he does now – in criminal cases.

When Gerry and I sat down to lunch, his first point of emphasis was telling me to let go of what he considered the "ridiculous" proposition that I had screwed up the trial or that he would do a better job. "It's the times," he said. Over lunch, we schmoozed about what else I might do that I hadn't done. One major topic of conversation was Judge O'Connor, a hard drinking, opinionated, and stubborn former newspaper executive who had made it clear during the trial that she did not like my client or our case. The local court rule in San Francisco was if there was a retrial, the judge who sat on the first trial would also sit on the second. This scared me, as I feared O'Connor might be tempted to place her thumb just a bit on the scales of justice – and not in our favor. Then Gerry came up with a great idea. Since the doctor's office was so small, why not suggest to the judge a site visit for the jury? "And call it a "field trip," Gerry offered. "Mary loves field trips." And by this point in our lunch, I was feeling much better, ready to go fight another battle.

We moved on to discuss whether it might be a good idea to hire a jury consultant. Jury consultancy was then relatively new but increasingly common, after having begun in occasional cases during the 1970s. Despite my sense that I was pretty good at picking a jury – I avoided questions that pointed to the "right" answer, I knew all the names of the jurors when addressing them, and I formed seemingly comfortable relationships with most – I readily acknowledged that only two potential jurors had admitted that they or someone they knew had ever been molested or assaulted. That seemed to be too low a number. Were there things they simply were uncomfortable sharing? A jury consultant could be my way to open up this key issue on *voir dire*.

I took that idea back to Joe and his family, and they were skeptical. They were, by nature and background, frugal people, and their first reaction was to say, "It's so expensive." I knew that three months would fly by, and that it would take a good deal of ramp-up time to get the best use of a jury consultant. So, I pressed the point pretty hard. After all, if Joe lost this trial, life as he knew it would be over. His life as a physician would be gone in a flash. The choice was between spending more money on one hand, and his life on the other. He and the family ultimately agreed, and they loosened the purse strings.

Many of the early jury consultants started out advising lawyers in left-leaning political trials. That was how Oakland's National Jury Project got its start. The NJP soon became one of the very few respected consultants in this new field. I knew most of the women involved in running NJP through Bay Area progressive political circles. I reached out to my friends there about working on our case, and got a cordial but very firm, absolute "no." They wouldn't even consider working on a case in which the accused was charged with any kind of sexual offense. I wasn't sure whether they, like seemingly everyone else in those days, assumed guilt, but they weren't taking any chances. So, my next call – something of a Hail Mary – was to the only other credible consultant I knew of: Cathy Bennett.

Cat

Cathy Bennett, known to all as "Cat," had a most appropriate nickname. She purred like a cat in her sweet, slow Georgia drawl, while simultaneously acting like a cat on the prowl, with claws out, searching to unlock the secrets among the twelve to eighteen strangers sitting across from her in the courtroom in the jury box – something she did with remarkable success.

Cat was not a lawyer, which served her well. Rather, she had a master's degree in psychology and a strong instinct for ferreting out the true feelings of complete strangers in an environment hardly conducive to candor: a courtroom. Along with the NJP, she was *the* pioneer in jury selection techniques. The key technique sounded simple: "Ask open-ended questions," something counter-intuitive to any trial lawyer. But how to *use* that key to unlock the door to honest and effective jury selection took more than a three-word catch phrase.

Cat started young; at twenty-three she was working on jury selection in the trial of Oglala Lakota tribal leaders who, under the banner of the American Indian Movement, had seized and occupied the South Dakota town of Wounded Knee. The standoff ended in a shootout with federal law enforcement officers, and its leaders were soon indicted. With that jump start, Cat went on to work on many high-profile cases, including civil lawsuits against the Ku Klux Klan and the skinheads of the White Aryan Resistance Group, the fight over Howard Hughes' will, and the successful defense of former chief GM car designer and DeLorean car creator John DeLorean, who was charged with cocaine trafficking. By the time of the DeLorean case, Cat Bennett had become a celebrity.

It took a couple of weeks after our hung jury to convince Joe Sing to pay the substantial sum Cathy Bennett required. But my timing in calling Cat was fortuitous. She had just finished the DeLorean acquittal, and at the moment had nothing on her immediate agenda. She quoted a large retainer and I immediately agreed. But a week later, she called back to beg off the job. My impression for her cold feet – and perhaps her huge fee – was that while still in her early thirties, Cat had gotten used to working almost exclusively with famous lawyers, celebrity defendants, and infamous cases. I didn't qualify as a famous lawyer and didn't have a personal "in" with her at all. And Joe Sing was certainly no celebrity and, happily, not infamous – there had been no lurid local press and, thank goodness, no press at all. Desperate to keep her on board, I told her a war story or two that she laughed at and then volunteered that my then wife and I would fly down to Houston at our expense to meet with her and her new husband, Robert Hirschhorn. "We'll buy the wine at dinner," I offered. She agreed: a three-day crash course on jury selection, helped along by three nights of eating and drinking. Perfect!

When we got to Houston, I found I had a lot to learn. First, Cat wanted to broaden my understanding of why it was so important to ask jurors open-ended questions. I knew enough to know that I needed to be careful and circumspect when "*voir dire*-ing" a jury, because most people will simply tell me what they think I want to hear. If I were to ask, "Now you don't have any biases against Chinese Americans, do you?" I would almost never get anything but agreement: "No, of course not." Yet this is how most lawyers were told to do jury selection. When it came to reasonable doubt, criminal defense lawyers were told to ask something like, "Would you agree that as he sits here today, without any evidence against him, Mr. Jones is not guilty?" "Yes, ok, sure." "And if the DA doesn't present evidence of guilt beyond a reasonable doubt, what will your verdict be?" "Hmmm…, not guilty." I knew that these kinds of questions gave me no real information about the true views of the person answering them.

What Cat reinforced is that my own views, from proof of guilt to far more subtle issues, had to become irrelevant, and that my goals in the questions I asked needed to focus on the only thing that counted: the juror's feelings. This was especially true when it came to individual biases. Cat emphasized that since we all have biases, the idea was to put jurors in the position of acknowledging theirs without feeling threatened or criticized for having them.

Next, I had to learn to internalize the *real* meaning of "open-ended questions." In principle it's very simple. Let's say someone says, "Sometime after dinner, I went to the store." If that person is a witness, then the lawyer cross-examining her will want to pin her down: "It was about a quarter to nine went you went to the store, wasn't it?" Asking something more open-ended ("When did you go to the store?") would give the witness too much wiggle room. But Cat taught me that when questioning a prospective juror, "When did you go to the store?" was not an open-ended question at all, because it assumes that "when" was important to the speaker. Even "What happened when you went?" was not open-ended enough for Cat. Lawyers want to get exact answers from witnesses: who, what, where, and when, and get them precisely, often with the answers *we* want to hear. But during *voir dire*, lawyers want to accomplish the exact opposite – to learn as much as possible in a short space of time, and to hear the unspun and unvarnished *truth*, not what we want to hear, but what's real.

It's surprisingly difficult at first to turn off this cross-examination mindset. The key is to internalize the goal – to learn something important about complete strangers, things that are important to *them*, not us. Put in that context, "What happened at the store" assumes way too much. Why did something have to happen? And why did it have to be at the store? Maybe something happened in the car *en route*. Maybe nothing happened but suddenly the speaker had a feeling – of dread, happiness, absolutely anything. When I internalized my understanding of why "What happened?" is not truly an open-ended question, I was on the way to jury-communication enlightenment. And not only jury enlightenment, but given the active *listening* that's required, on the way to greater personal enlightenment as well. Thus:

"Sometime after dinner, I went to the store."

"I see. And...," or

"Tell me about that....," or

A silent expectant pause.

If this sounds like a therapist listening to a patient, it's because there's a great deal of similarity. After all, Cat's field was psychology.

We spent the afternoon of our first day in Houston going over the basics, followed by a wonderful dinner with great food, wine, and laughter that cemented a friendship. That mood carried through the next two days of hard work and serious jury planning. We started with Cat asking how *voir dire* was conducted in California, both under state law and common local practice. California law has long allowed liberal *voir dire*, particularly in criminal cases, but California judges, concerned as are most state judges about efficiency and their lengthy calendar of cases, have long tried to minimize the *voir dire* they had to put up with. Judge O'Connor, like most of her colleagues, liked to seat twelve jurors and a "six-pack," prospective jurors numbered 13 through 18. This saved a bit of time calling out new names, and it set up a rotation so everyone knew who was coming into the jury box next: When one of the first twelve was excused or challenged by one of the parties, Juror No. 13 would take that person's place and so on, until the six-pack was exhausted and then re-filled.

Cat and I decided on using a hybrid of her usual jury-selection questioning method modified to account for the six-pack. Since speed and efficiency – or at least their *appearance* – were essential, we decided that I should ask the judge to let me pose a series of general questions to all eighteen prospective jurors at once. On the surface, that seemed a surefire way to save time by avoiding repeating the same questions to each person. But in reality, these carefully chosen eight questions, each of which ended with my asking the jurors to raise their hands if the question applied, would be the seeds from which an entire *voir dire* would grow for each juror. Also, we felt that on a sensitive subject like this, it would be way easier to raise a hand in a group than in the spotlight of a question asked individually. This method made a lot of sense to us both, and I was sure it would work. Ultimately, it became the method I used from that case forward in every jury trial.

Cat and I spent the rest of our two days with me writing down absolutely everything I could think of that I wanted to know about the jurors, and Cat focusing globally on the main issues. After we had fully brainstormed, our last four hours were spent implementing "The Plan." There would be three parts:

First, an introduction, done within a couple of minutes. Judges always gave a bit of leeway for lawyers to introduce themselves and do a little throat-clearing. Given the subject matter, that throat-clearing was important. For one thing, judges all seemed trained, at trial-judge school I guess, to tell people that when they were called as jurors, they must leave their biases and prejudices "at the courtroom door." Cat had reinforced something I already knew: Jurors can't do that successfully, any more than any of us. So, the first thing I wanted to tell the jurors was something like:

> Everyone here is looking for impartial jurors in this case. We all have biases, different ways of looking at things. That's true of all of us, certainly including me. The most important thing to all of

> us here is that each of you be open and honest. So, if you're not 100% certain you can be completely fair and impartial in this kind of case, that's ok. Some people may feel that their duty as a juror will fit better on another kind of case rather than on this one. And that's fine.

Then there was the main issue: This was a sexual molestation case. So, we planned for me to say:

> I'm going to be asking you some very personal questions. Some of them will be about yourselves and people that you know. I know this will be hard for you, and I hope you will forgive my intrusion. I also hope you can be as candid as you can. If you are uncomfortable in answering any of the questions in the courtroom, we can do it in private. And if you feel that prying questions like these are unfair to you, please tell us, either now or when you're asked individual questions.

Second, the "seed questions," tailored for this case. Of the eight, several were softballs, designed to make it easy to answer and have people relax a little, while a few were the real keys to the jury selection. I would ask all these questions to all eighteen prospective jurors at once, while Cat and my law clerk jotted down who raised hands. Then, I would go back and *voir dire* each juror individually about their responses. My open body language in asking these questions would be important, as was my usual, more "accessible," warm brown sports coat and slacks rather than the standard lawyer "trial uniform." I would be asking these questions while nodding expectantly and raising my hand as I asked them to raise theirs. My delivery would be slower, with elongated sentences to try to make things more conversational and accessible, asking multi-part questions slowly enough for people to think each part through, and hopefully encouraging people to raise their hands along with mine. And above all, I'd do it all with kindness. Here are those questions:

1. Are any of you familiar with the Chinese American community in Chinatown?

2. Do any of you have any training in medicine? Or work with doctors? Or work with children, perhaps?

3. We're going to be describing pretty serious sexual matters, charges about particular sexual conduct, references to private parts, or sexual acts. Do any of you feel that this may upset or disturb you to an extent that it concerns you?

4. While I know it's difficult, I have to ask if you or anyone close to you has ever been the victim of a sexual molestation or sexual offense?

5. Do any of you belong to an organization that involves medicine, or maybe holistic medicine? Do any of you have strong opinions about doctors? Or pediatricians?

6. Are any of you members of an organization that seeks to reform or change people's attitudes about sexually related crimes? Or hold any beliefs about reforms or change?

7. Have any of you ever been accused of something, not necessarily a crime, but in a situation where someone accused you of something you did not do?

8. Have you heard anything about this particular case?

And a closing question: "If there's anything else that you'd like to tell us, either now or later when we speak individually, would you please raise your hand?"

Again, the only goal with these general questions was to encourage people to raise their hands to form the outline of their individual *voir dires*. Of these questions, none were entirely without importance, but the most important question was clearly number 4. Would people be willing to raise their hands in this more user-friendly framework? The idea was to build to Question 4 through two easy questions and an important but more introductory third question, and then to back off some, though Questions 5 and 6 had importance too. Number 7 was a particularly important question, because anyone who'd been falsely accused might be favorable to us and might have valuable things to say about their experience. We intentionally wanted to separate this question from numbers 3 and 4 to give people a break in between the most important questions.

Part three of The Plan was the individual *voir dire* based on who raised their hands to which questions. With all my practicing on asking open-ended questions ("Uh huh," "tell me about it," etc.) I felt that this part would be the easiest in a way – just chatting one on one with another person, listening and following the conversation. I was much more worried about whether anyone would raise their hands than I was about discussing it with them it later. I was mistaken.

There was one more important piece of the individual *voir dires*. With a few of the jurors we liked best, I would ask a series of questions about reasonable doubt and the presumption of innocence. These would not be open-ended but strongly directed and conclusionary, asking for promises from those jurors to abide by the presumptions in favor of a defendant:

- Can you accept without hesitation that it is the DA's obligation to present evidence and bear the burden of proving his case beyond a reasonable doubt?
- Can you promise me that as Dr. Sing starts out today, he is not guilty and will remain so unless and until the DA *proves* each and every element of the charges?

With the trial two weeks off and Cat set up with a week at a nice hotel in San Francisco, we were ready for trial, and my confidence had been restored.

Retrial and finding truth

Cat joined me, Joe, and my law student at counsel table to begin the re-trial. We had already scored in chambers that morning when my suggestion of a "field trip" to Joe's office that sounded like a delightful idea to Judge O'Connor, with DA Hart putting up only token resistance. But before the bailiff brought in the jury panel, I introduced Cat to the judge, and by the time Cat had finished saying "Good mornin', Your Honor," I could see that the hard-living Irishwoman on the bench had already formed a dislike for the sweet Southern belle at counsel table, and that the judge would toss her out of her courtroom if she could. But she couldn't and didn't, so we began.

I was super-prepared for this jury selection, and it started out just as we had planned. The twelve prospective jurors and the six-pack were selected, and I got to do my introductory pitch to them all. Everyone seemed attentive and concerned. Two people raised their hands and said they didn't think they could be fair on this kind of a case and were excused by the judge. One was named Ms. Broadmore, and I jotted down her name for future reference. I moved on to the general questions, and again, everything went smoothly. In fact, it went better than I could have hoped, with lots of hands in the air from the start. When we got to questions 3 and 4, many people's hands went up and I made sure, calling them by name, that we noted each one. By the end of the general questions, we had the beginning scripts for each individual *voir dire*. And at the end, when I asked if there was anything else anyone would like to tell us and mentioned the honesty and courage of Ms. Broadmore telling us right in the beginning that she could not be fair on this particular case, two more jurors raised their hands and asked to be excused. Boy, I thought, this is such a far cry from any jury selection I'd ever done.

Then, after the mid-morning recess, it all went off the rails, and I experienced by far the worst day in my life as a lawyer. By 10:30 or so when I began my individual questioning, to the moment the judge recessed at 4:30, I was destroyed, humiliated by the judge, embarrassed by the panel of sixty prospective jurors sitting behind me in the courtroom, and at a total loss about how this brilliant plan had gone so wrong.

I had such great material for each juror and plenty of questions to ask each of them. It very soon became apparent, though, that this method of selection was not going to make *voir dire* more efficient or quick. I was doing okay asking open-ended questions, particularly about sensitive topics, just as Cat had taught me, but it all took an agonizingly long amount of time. I spent over a half hour talking with Juror #1, and I had barely started with Juror #3 when we got to the lunch break. By then, Judge O'Connor was looking at me with disgust and the panelists in the back of the room were beginning to mumble discontentedly. By early afternoon, the darts fired at me from the judge's eyes got sharper and the rumblings of discontent behind me turned into loud and constant heckling that the judge was clearly not going to stop. By day's end, I'd finished interviewing only six of the eighteen prospects, my focus waning during the course of the afternoon's toxic atmosphere until the importance of my questions began to get lost.

My wife, our law student, my longtime lawyer trial assistant John, and Cat got me back home as quickly as possible where I downed three glasses of red wine in about ten minutes. After I had settled down, I asked, "What now?" Everyone took a turn at answering, each one encouraging me, reinforcing that I knew what I was doing and that it just took time. Until we got to the last person, Cat.

"Richard," she said in her sweetest possible drawl, "you always look like you're in such control in the courtroom." I guessed that despite my churning internal emotional turmoil, I had managed to keep my outward poise and look as confident as ever, something I'd always strived. And I told Cat just that.

"Well, bless your heart!" Cat smiled at me. "You did keep such good control. But let me ask you: How did you really feel about what was going on in the courtroom?"

"Terrible," I replied. "It was horrible. All that heckling and the judge just letting them get away with it. I feel like shit."

And then Cat said this: "You're asking people to tell you the truth about the most private and personal questions anyone can be asked. You want people to answer you honestly and candidly. But you're hurting inside, and you showed them nothing; none of the honest hurt." Then with one question, Cat taught me more about being a good lawyer than anyone ever had, before or since. "Richard, how can you expect people to tell you the truth about their real feelings and emotions when you're not showing them your true feelings and emotions? Isn't that the least that you could do?"

I can't say that the heavens opened up and I got struck by a bolt of lightning, but it was pretty damn close. Cat's message was about so much more than lawyering; it was about hubris, honesty, and humility, and the danger of acting like you know it all. It's a message that I've carried with me every day since.

Cat and I got down to work on how I could best change the courtroom atmosphere with, Cat insisted, the very first words out of my mouth. The next morning, after we were called to order, I stood to address Juror #7, Mr. Bentley. As I came forward into the well of the courtroom, I asked him in my most sober voice whether he had heard all the heckling from the back of the courtroom the previous day. Looking a mite surprised, he said that he certainly had.

"And Mr. Bentley, can you imagine how terrible that made me feel?"

"Yes, I suppose I could."

When I asked him whether he could also appreciate that I understood "how much it was bothering everyone to sit through all that talk," he again answered affirmatively. And then I asked him this:

"Can I ask you to appreciate that even though I know everyone's unhappy about this and even though I feel really bad about it, I'm just trying to do my job, to do my best for my client, Joe here, the best way I know how?"

Again, Mr. Bentley looked a bit surprised, but he responded by saying, "Yeah, sure."

And in that moment, with my "thank you," the entire atmosphere of the courtroom changed. I hadn't done much, really; no disclosure of intimate life events, horrible past experiences, fears, hurts, or concerns. I'd just spoken the honest truth. And that was enough.

The second time around

We spent three more days picking the jury, but the atmosphere had flipped. We were now a group of concerned citizens discussing each other's welfare. Many people spoke honestly, and in open court, about events in the lives of their loved ones, and in their own lives, with a simplicity and candor I found extraordinary. Many admitted that based on their own experiences or what they'd heard on the news, they didn't think they could be fair. A few people spoke of how they'd been falsely accused of doing something wrong. I was particularly taken with the story told by a tall, thin, young gay Black man, his name now lost to posterity, whose friends in his college dorm accused him of taking a stereo. He was a keeper for sure.

By the time we said we were satisfied with the jury, the DA had run out of challenges, the only time in all my criminal trials that happened. Cat headed back to Houston, and we launched into the evidence – the same evidence as the last trial, except that this time, we took a field trip to Dr. Sing's office.

My opponent, Peter Hart, was an excellent lawyer, not prone to the mistakes I saw most lawyers make in trial. But he made one when it came to the field trip. He said he'd drive over to Chinatown in his own car. Meanwhile, the rest of us rode the same sheriff's bus – judge, jurors, alternates, bailiffs, my client and his family, and me and my law student. And we had a great time, pointing out the sights and laughing at the strange looks from passers-by who thought we were in-custody prisoners being transported somewhere. In short, a bonding experience. As for Dr. Sing's office, it was far more crowded in person than it sounded from the witness stand, and of course with twenty-odd people rummaging through it, it seemed even smaller.

Only one issue still bothered me: With several references to other testimony and a prior transcript, it was obvious there'd been some other trial. I wanted Judge O'Connor to tell the jury that there had been a mistrial. Otherwise, I feared the jury might think that Joe had been convicted and gotten a reversal on appeal. But the judge hadn't warmed to our case at all, was still angry about four days of *voir dire*, and if anything seemed more convinced than ever that Joe was guilty. She refused, warning me not to bring it up. But when the opportune time arose in the middle of a witness examination, I did it anyway, slipping in the "mistrial" word as subtly as I could. The judge seemed to take no notice, but Peter Hart did, and when the trial was over, he upbraided me for it. I liked Peter and we eventually became friends, but on that one occasion, I admitted to myself – but not to Peter – that I strayed across the ethical line because I felt the need to protect my client. Peter asked me years later if I would do it again. Probably, I told him.

After the lawyers' arguments and the judge's instructions to the jury, the jury started deliberating at about 10:30 a.m. They stayed through the lunch hour, ate their sandwiches and salad, and, led by the young man who'd been falsely accused, came back by 2:00 p.m. with a not-guilty verdict, and hugs for my client and his mother and family. The two trials featured the same evidence but could not have been more different.

EPILOGUE

Joseph Sing went back to his pediatric practice, making sure from that day forth that there was always a nurse or assistant in the examining room when he had a female patient. His mother lived into her mid-nineties. I ran across her some years later – still elegant in every respect.

Cat Bennett returned to Texas, moving to Galveston with her husband Robert, and together they developed their nationally renowned jury practice. Tragedy was not far away for Cat, though. By her late thirties, she'd been diagnosed with breast cancer. It soon metastasized, but she insisted during her last months on continuing to work on the case she had at the time – perhaps her most widely publicized case – the defense of William Kennedy Smith, nephew of President John F. Kennedy and Senators Robert and Ted Kennedy. The case was one of the first to be televised gavel to gavel on Court TV. Smith was accused of rape. He was acquitted. Cat died a few months later at age forty-one.

The Kern County cases: District Attorney Ed Jagels' team convicted at least twenty-six people. The first four were found guilty in 1983, and convictions followed in seven other cases over the next three years. In one, seven defendants charged with 155 counts involving thirteen children were convicted after a six-month trial on each and every count, and sentenced to between 285 and 405 years in prison. By the time of the last trial, in 1986, a man convicted of sodomizing his own daughter, some people had begun asking questions about why there were so many abuse prosecutions.

The cases began to unravel with a 1986 investigation by the California Attorney General's office and a series of articles by *Fresno Bee* reporter Jim Boren. The Attorney General's report, wrote Boren:

> concluded that local authorities had used "suggestive" questioning that led children to give answers that they wanted.... [S]ome alleged victims were simply parroting what they were told in questioning or what they heard other

children say. In many cases, young children were
interviewed numerous times by authorities until
they finally admitted to being molested. In one
case an alleged victim had been interviewed 35
times before giving the "right" answer....

In 1990, the seven defendants convicted of 155 counts had
their convictions thrown out based on the actions of Deputy
DA Andrew G. Gindes. After a 115-page description of "a
mere fraction of [Gindes'] misconduct," the appellate court
described him as "an overzealous prosecutor who, in his blind
quest to convict, forgot or ignored his constitutional and ethical duties...." By 1994, all of the child witnesses had recanted,
saying their testimony was coerced.

The other cases ended in similar fashion, many only
after long periods of imprisonment. The first four convicted
were not freed until 1996, when a judge cited "interviewing
techniques ... fraught with undesirable consequences." The
daughter who testified that her father had sodomized her
recanted her testimony almost immediately. But he remained
in prison until 1999, when a judge concluded that those interviewing methods were "likely to generate false and unreliable
accusations." The last innocent victim was not released from
prison until 2004. In all, twenty-five of the twenty-six accused
had their convictions reversed, all except a serial sex offender,
convicted of sex crimes both before and after the trumped-up
mid-80s cases, who remains in custody.

The victims in these cases were both the accused and the
child accusers, often their own children, most from poorer
working-class communities. The perpetrators were the Kern
County DA's Office, and DA Ed Jagels. In the aftermath of the

Kern County prosecutions, there were numerous exposés of Jagels' office's misconduct, including a book, *Mean Justice*, by Pulitzer Prize-winning journalist Edward Humes, a documentary, *Witch Hunt*, produced by Sean Penn, and even a *Lifetime* movie. But Jagels, while widely excoriated, remained proud of his record, including his claim that Kern County had the highest per capita prison commitment rate of any county in California. He remained Kern County DA until 2010.

The McMartin aftermath: Unlike in Kern County, the McMartin cases fell apart before and during the trial. First, after an eighteen-month-long preliminary hearing, new DA Ira Reiner dismissed the cases against five of the seven defendants, calling those cases "incredibly weak." That left only Ray Buckey, the first person accused, and Peggy McMartin Buckey, Ray's mother and the director of the daycare center her mother had founded.

These two went to trial on sixty-five child abuse counts in what became the longest criminal trial in California history – longer than the San Quentin Six case. The result? Peggy was acquitted on sixty-four of sixty-five counts, Ray was acquitted on fifty-two, and the jury hung on thirteen counts, twelve against Ray and one conspiracy charge against them both. After retrial, neither mother nor son stood convicted of anything. In fact, *no one* was ever convicted of a crime in the McMartin case. But its chilling effect was apparent across the country. Meanwhile, Peggy had spent two years in custody before raising bail, and Ray spent five years in pre-trial custody.

What went wrong in McMartin has been the subject of much after-the-fact analysis by psychologists, sociologists, and journalists. First, the DA and police took a single accusation from a person with a long history of mental instability and alcoholism at face value and with little scrutiny. Had even a modest amount of attention been paid to the accuser's claims – one example: "At the armory it was a ritual-type atmosphere [where] Ray flew in the air [and] the goatman was there...." – the case may never have begun. Second, the police primed the pump by sending a highly suggestive questionnaire to over 200 families that implied the most grotesque, inappropriate behavior.

Even then, however, had the interviews of the children been carried out in a way that carefully avoided suggesting the "right answers", the McMartin case may have ended there. The atmosphere in which 360 of 400 students reported abuse was, said one team of psychologists who examined the case, "the result of children ... interviewed in a highly suggestive manner by social service workers." A 1998 study cited the "infected" interviewing techniques: "At first most of the children denied being molested. But in extensive taped interviews in which anatomical dolls were used, the children were told that other children had divulged "yucky secrets" about the school and were urged to do likewise." Today, it's well recognized, as a third set of experts noted, that "an abundance of research reveals that children are particularly susceptible to suggestive questioning, and hence the formation of false memories."

A final factor was the attitude of both the print and television press. David Shaw, an *LA Times* reporter during the McMartin case, wrote a series of articles in 1990 on how the press, including his own newspaper, had played a "pivotal and sometimes distorting role" by abandoning their usual skepticism at an early stage, and then sensationalizing the case and presuming the accused to be guilty. And that story spread like wildfire into nationwide headlines.

More than any other case, the McMartin Daycare case led to huge reforms about the way in which children are interviewed about possible molestation and abuse, and the fallacy of the inevitability of children telling the truth.

As for me, as I look back at this case today, I see similarities in the way Dr. Sing and many of my other clients were perceived in court. Joseph Sing's case came at what was absolutely the worst time during my years as a trial lawyer for an innocent person to be accused of molestation. The default perception of almost every prospective juror was that the accused must be guilty. I'd seen this presumption of guilt in many other courtrooms. It came with Simon Stanley's "Kenny Krazy" moniker, with Max Forrest's appearance and demeanor, and of course with the San Quentin Six appearing in prison jumpsuits, chained around the waist, wrists, and legs: "They must be guilty."

More recently, I've realized that the same "presumption perception" also exists outside the courtroom – in the police squeezing the life out of a large Staten Island man as he lay on the ground fighting for breath, in a man shooting and killing an unarmed Black teenager wearing a hoodie, in a Black man being shot seven times in the back by a police officer, or in Chinese Americans being spat at on the street for being the "sources" of the Covid virus. The perceptions made by those at the scene about Eric Garner, Trayvon Martin, Jacob Blake, and countless others are also based on stereotyped presumptions that have only been seriously examined after another Black man, George Floyd, died, suffocated under the knee of a white policeman. And now, over a year after that event, some of us may be in danger of allowing these presumption perceptions to sneak back into our consciousness, unless we take serious steps to prevent it.

Finally, on a more personal note, the lessons Cat Bennett taught me were ones that I brought to many jury selection trainings I did at law schools and for public defender and legal services groups over the years. Perhaps more importantly for my own health, these lessons helped me to speak out publicly at continuing education seminars for other lawyers about the pressures of law practice that had led me to two periods of major depression. Talking candidly and truthfully about this in public was one of the most liberating and healthful things I've done and, I hope, may have helped some other people get in touch with their own truths. None of this would have been possible without Cat.

11

Death on a Houseboat

People of the State of California v. Curt Kalliner

*What happens when someone brings a gun into a dwelling but
is so loaded on heroin that he has little idea of where he is and
what he's doing there? In this case, my client and his sometimes
girlfriend went onto a drug dealer's houseboat, supposedly to get
heroin. He had a gun the girlfriend had given him, and in a
struggle for the gun the dealer was killed. It soon seemed clear to
me that a conviction of anything more than manslaughter would
not only be unlikely but unfair. But things did not work out as
expected. This case was a harsh and depressing reminder that not
every case goes as expected, and not every client gets a fair result.*

A houseboat homicide

One night at about 10:30 p.m., Carl Kalliner, whom everyone
called "CK," found himself walking onto a houseboat with his
sometimes girlfriend in front of him and a gun in his hand.
I say that he "found himself" doing this because he was so
loaded on heroin that a toxicologist later testified that he was
amazed Carl could walk along the narrow planks from the pier
to the boat without falling in the water. He followed behind
Lindy James, who was in search of both heroin and retribution

for a heroin buy gone bad. When their visit was over, drug dealer Bobby Caracci was dead, and the gun was still in Carl's hand.

The police soon took Carl and Lindy into custody, where Carl gave a heavily slurred statement to the police in which he admitted that the gun went off during a struggle with Bobby. Two days later, Judge Dave Baty, my longtime favorite judge, appointed me to defend Carl because the Public Defender had declared a conflict of interest since the office had represented Caracci on several occasions.

From my first interaction with Carl, I found him one of the least likely murder suspects I'd encountered. Mild-mannered and soft-spoken, with an almost gentlemanly manner, "CK" could have been a real estate broker or an auto mechanic – any one of a number of things – had it not been for the dreaded consequences of his heroin addiction. Although he was on some kind of maintenance program administered by the Marin County jail, his discomfort was palpable.

The story CK told me sounded more believable than most all the stories I'd heard from a client in custody. He said he and Lindy, whom he described as a "sorta girlfriend," often got high together. Lindy had searched him out on the afternoon of the homicide to tell him that Caracci had ripped her off in a dope deal, selling her heroin so heavily cut with flour or baking powder that it produced almost no high at all. CK didn't see this as his problem, but Lindy promised she'd get him high if he'd go with her that night out to Caracci's houseboat in Sausalito. CK liked the part about getting high, so he agreed.

As he told it, Lindy got him high that evening, handed him a gun, and told him to put it in his pocket and follow her. She drove her car up to the houseboat area known as Gate 6 on the Sausalito waterfront, just across the Golden Gate Bridge from San Francisco, gave CK another heroin hit, and instructed him to follow her down through the maze of piers and walkways out to Caracci's houseboat. He did as he was told, though he was loaded and nodding off. He remembered afterward that while on the boat, Lindy was really angry at Bobby and kept demanding her money back for her last heroin purchase. He didn't remember whether the gun was in his pocket or his hand, but he did remember that he and Bobby were both grappling for the gun, and that Bobby got ahold of it and was pointing the gun at CK's privates when he just "lifted up" as the gun went off, and Bobby fell to the ground, dead.

A day or two later I received a copy of the audiotape of the statement CK gave sheriff's officers an hour after his arrest. The narrative he gave me was entirely consistent with the tape. The taped statement was clear even if CK's voice was not. Speaking very slowly and heavily slurring his words, CK described the same events: Lindy had gotten him loaded, given him the gun, driven up to Marin County, told him to hold on to the gun no matter what, given him another hit of heroin, and then had him follow her to Bobby's houseboat. They both went inside. He remembered Lindy and Bobby yelling at each other and Lindy demanding money. And he remembered struggling with Bobby to gain control of the gun. "He was going for my balls," CK repeated several times in a slow, barely intelligible voice. "And I just lifted up…. and it went off."

CK's prior record – his rap sheet – was remarkably mild for a long-time, forty-year-old addict. The only arrest and conviction on his record was a drunk driving several years before. CK had told me he'd held down jobs in the past several years and did fine at them. His wife, from whom he was separated but on good terms, verified that employment history. It seemed to me that CK was for the most part a functioning addict. By that time, I'd seen a fair number of them. From my subjective view, his statement to the cops and his minimal record enhanced the credibility of his story. It felt to me as if Lindy was using CK, like the gun, as another tool to get back at Caracci.

I suppose I might have had a drop or two of naivete left in me, but from everything I could see, it seemed to me that the "bad guy" here was Lindy, not CK, even though CK had the gun when it went off. Supporting my view was a very disturbing statement the sheriff's investigators had taken from a witness, Barbara Barnett. According to Barbara, Lindy had told her on the day before the shooting that she would score some drugs for them both. When Lindy returned from the houseboat and the heroin was too weak for a decent high, Lindy got furious and told Barbara, "I'm gonna get a gun and my boyfriend and blow that motherfucker Bobby away." Sure enough, the next day she had a gun, which she gave to her "boyfriend" CK, and the result was that Bobby was blown away.

To a large extent, this one sentence was the key to the entire case against both Lindy and CK. It was direct evidence of an admission by Lindy of both her intent to kill and premeditation. And the statement was also devastating as applied to CK, because it supported the prosecution's theory of the case – that the "boyfriend" CK willingly complied with Lindy by taking the gun on board the houseboat that night. But properly understood and with good reason, the statement should never have been admissible as evidence against CK, only against Lindy.

If believed, Lindy's statement to Barbara about getting her boyfriend and gun and blowing Bobby away would be serious and strong evidence against her in the murder trial. But CK was not around when it was said, not responsible for what Lindy said, and was therefore unable to refute it. The statement was *her* admission of guilt, not his. As to CK, Lindy's statement was pure hearsay, a statement made outside of court by someone introduced as evidence to prove CK's involvement. Any judge would know that her statement was admissible only against Lindy but not CK. And any judge would instruct the jury to ignore Lindy's statement as it related to CK's guilt. But instructing the jury to consider the statement as to one defendant and disregard it as to another asks jurors to do the impossible. And in circumstances like these, it's particularly unfair not only because the statement was hearsay as to CK but because CK's lawyer had no opportunity to cross-examine Lindy about the statement's veracity. This inability to cross-examine violates the "confrontation clause" of the Sixth Amendment to the Constitution, which gives all criminal defendants the right to confront and cross-examine all the witnesses against them.

On the other hand, if Lindy's statement was not placed in evidence, the case against her would be much weaker. Evidence of the malice and premeditation required for first-degree murder would be almost entirely absent. The evidence of first-degree "felony murder" – a killing without malice or premeditation but occurring during the course of a felony – would also be much weaker. And while the state might still prove that CK brought the gun on the houseboat, the case against him would be primarily focused – as it should have been – on the struggle over the gun rather than the explanation of why CK was there in the first place.

It was for reasons like these that in 1965, in a case called *People v. Aranda,* the California Supreme Court decided that it was not enough for the judge to instruct the jury to disregard an admission made by one defendant as evidence against another defendant. Rather, the prosecution would have a choice: not use the statement at all or give each defendant a separate trial. In separate trials, Lindy's statement would come into evidence only in her case, and never come up in CK's. A few years later, in a case called *Bruton v. United States*, the United States Supreme Court agreed. This so-called Aranda/ Bruton rule was based in part on the hearsay nature of the statement but mostly on the confrontation clause. Here's what the US Supreme Court said:

> The risk that the jury will not, or cannot, follow instructions is so great, and the consequences of failure so vital to the defendant ... where the powerfully incriminating extrajudicial statements of a codefendant, who stands accused side-by-side

with the defendant, are deliberately spread before the jury in a joint trial.... [This] is intolerably compounded when the alleged accomplice, as here, does not testify and cannot be tested by cross-examination.

So as soon as I could, I made an Aranda/Bruton motion to either exclude Lindy's "boyfriend/gun" statement from our trial or to grant CK a completely separate trial. Working in our favor was the law of the highest courts of both California and the United States. Working against us was the unwillingness of the District Attorney's office to recognize and accept the clear law on point, and the reluctance of any judge to grant a separate trial, thus doubling the considerable resources that would be expended in any murder case. My motion was denied. So clearly was this ruling erroneous that I took a writ. That effort, always up to appellate court discretion because of the availability of appeal after the trial, was also denied. This exponentially increased the degree of difficulty we would have in being able to show that CK was guilty of manslaughter at most.

Getting CK's story before the jury

As was true in most serious cases, I realized that putting the relatively unsophisticated and uneducated CK on the witness stand would be a serious risk. Besides, I already had the best possible testimony I could have: his statement to the cops right after his arrest. The statement was the most compelling confession I'd ever heard. Because the sheriffs had taken him to a substation just five minutes' drive from the houseboat, instead of driving him all the way to the jail and booking him,

CK was still so loaded and out of it that it was obvious to anyone listening. So was his distress and despondency. The tape sounded like it had been recorded at an extra slow speed, so that everything he said was elongated, especially the key moment: "He was gooooing for my baaaaaaaaaaaaalls...," which he repeated many times over.

This confession showcased three important things. First, CK was definitely loaded on heroin, necessary if we were going to claim that Lindy got him loaded to use him as a tool, just like the gun. Second, it showed that in that state, CK could not form the specific intent to kill anyone; he was just too messed up. And third, it showed that the shot happened in the midst of a struggle over the weapon between CK and the drug dealer. While it was true that the DA would argue the felony murder rule, as they had in Kenny Krazy's case, the felony being Lindy's effort to rip off the drug dealer, the statement was so compelling for our side – a struggle for the gun between Bobby and the obviously loaded Carl – that the DA decided not to introduce it in evidence.

At first, I thought I could use the statement myself, but after a bit of research, I realized that a criminal defendant could not introduce his own statement into evidence, even if he admits guilt, because it would be self-serving. But the statement was by far the best evidence I had to show that CK was merely another tool in Lindy's hands. After giving this some serious thought, I concluded that if I could make the statement the basis of a psychiatrist's testimony that Carl was so wasted that he couldn't form the specific intent required to commit murder, I might have a way of getting that audiotape in front of the jury. I asked myself if I could in good conscience get the jury to hear the statement through this psychiatric side door, when the real purpose was for them to understand the obvious distress in CK's voice and how loaded he was.

My answer was clearly "yes." My job here was to get my client the best possible verdict – manslaughter – which is what I believed was the most punishment he should receive. The difference between a sentence for manslaughter and murder was huge: six or seven years vs. either seventeen or twenty-seven years *to life* for murder, depending on whether it was first or second degree. So, I asked the court for funds to hire a psychiatrist, and once given a modest budget, I found Albert Keneally, a psychiatrist who was willing to examine CK in the jail, listen to the statement, and give me an opinion on exactly how impaired he was. If that opinion was helpful, I would call him as an expert witness. After Dr. Keneally had read the police reports, spent a couple of hours with my client, and listened to the taped confession, he reported that he thought CK was incapable of forming the specific intent to kill. And part of the basis of that opinion was the taped statement. "Great!" I thought. That should get the statement in front of the jury.

The Trial

As I readied the case for trial, I faced an ethical conundrum. I needed to persuade the jury that CK's state of mind made him far less culpable than Lindy. Under the law, CK was the alleged perpetrator and Lindy the "aider and abettor," the person assisting the perpetrator. But under these unusual circumstances, she seemed more culpable than CK. Had Lindy's counsel been someone I could discuss strategy with, we likely would have found a way of dealing with this issue in a way that helped CK's case but didn't hurt Lindy. Unfortunately, that was not the case. Lindy was represented by an old "lefty" lawyer, John Schell, then well over eighty and far past his prime. Schell hadn't read many of the police reports, relying instead on a smart but inexperienced paralegal to spoonfeed him information as he felt he needed it. As a result, his understanding of both the factual details and the applicable legal principles seemed fuzzy at best. And a lawyer simply can't competently try a murder case without a thorough understanding of both the facts and the law. In addition, he seemed to regard me as the enemy, rebuffing out of hand my efforts to come up with a workable strategy for us both.

With Schell's unwillingness to work with me and the failure of the motions judge to strike Lindy's damaging statement or give us a separate trial, I was left in the difficult position of having to paint Lindy as the heavy, to show that the whole incident was *her* idea, that getting CK stoned and handing him the gun was just part of her plan, and that under these unusual circumstances, if anyone was guilty of murder, it was she, not CK.

To take this position went against a strong criminal-defense code that lawyers defending the accused did not "snitch off" others, especially co-defendants. But without being able to work on a common strategy with Schell, I felt I had no choice. I'd have to go it alone and live with the consequences.

And so would Lindy. Fortunately, I thought, since Lindy was the aider and abettor, it would be unlikely for her to fare worse than CK, so manslaughter might be in the cards for both.

The trial went well, or so I thought. The prosecution's case was simple and straightforward: the coroner, the toxicology report on the decedent, the ballistics report on the gun, and the statement made by Lindy to Barbara about getting "a gun and my boyfriend and blow that motherfucker away." The trial judge was E. Warren McGuire, one of my favorites, the conservative Republican who was always careful and tried to be fair-minded. McGuire gave a clear limiting instruction to the jury about why Lindy's statement could only be considered as to her and not CK. But McGuire would not go as far as to grant my renewed objection and request for a mistrial so CK could get a separate trial. I think he simply didn't get it.

When it was our turn, I presented Dr. Keneally, and he presented the opinion that CK' s mental state and his condition at the time of his statement meant that he was unable to form malice or any specific intent to do anything. (Keneally diagnosed CK as suffering from a moderate form of "undifferentiated schizophrenia.") Because the statement played a part in his analysis, it was admissible evidence to support his opinion, and I was able to play it in its entirety. I could see its effect on the jury; many were significantly moved, and a few seemed to be tearing up. Then, by going over the specifics of the doctor's opinion about the statement, I was able to play almost all of it a second time.

Verdict and aftermath

Before closing arguments, Judge McGuire gave the jury a full day off so he could consider what jury instructions he should give. Instructions are determined by the judge, but each side has the opportunity to submit proposed instructions and a summary of the law on which those instructions are based. I had a whole series of requests for special instructions, and McGuire, ever conservative and cautious, considered each one seriously. He agreed to read most of them to the jury, noting over the DA's objection that he didn't necessarily agree with them personally, but that he felt required to read them under the law of the state as he understood it. He even made an offhand (and off the record) comment that, after listening to the testimony and arguing about instructions, he realized that he may have made a mistake by not granting CK a separate trial. "What a good judge," I thought, while recognizing that he'd made a bad mistake.

Ever since my first murder trial, Elvin Drummond's acquittal, I tried to have my efforts in each case live up to the lawyering I'd done in the Drummond case. No lawyer ever tries a "perfect" case, but I felt that Elvin's defense was as close as I'd ever come. I set a high bar for myself trying to achieve that level in each trial, probably being a bit tough on myself in pursuit a worthwhile goal. More often than not, I fell just a little bit short. But in CK's case, I felt I had met the Elvin standard. Argument to the jury went well, or so I thought. The District Attorney argued long and hard about the culpability of both defendants, lumping them together as equals in the same plot, and citing his best evidence for premeditation – Lindy's statement about getting her boyfriend and a gun. But each time that was mentioned, I got on my feet to make a "speaking objection" about why that evidence could not be considered against my client. In my own argument, the only significant problem was my discomfort in pointing the finger at Lindy as the main culprit, but I did it anyway, and in pretty harsh terms, convinced that this was the best path to CK's manslaughter verdict. After the jury retired to consider its verdict, and to my pleasant surprise, the jury asked to hear the tape of CK's confession, replaying it again in the jury room. Things were looking good.

Sometimes, though, a trial lawyer's sense of the case, no matter how strong, is just not in tune with what the jury is thinking. After three days of tense waiting during deliberations, the bailiff told us the jury had reached verdicts. CK's name appeared first on the complaint, so his was the first verdict read: Second degree murder. I was crushed, as, of course, was CK. Then the verdict against Lindy: Murder in the *first* degree. Incredibly, they had convicted Lindy, the aider and abettor, of a more serious charge. My defense had failed badly as to CK and also as to Lindy.

With the jury still present, Schell immediately demanded that Judge McGuire instruct the jury that it could not find his client guilty of murder one when the perpetrator was "only" guilty of murder two. McGuire seemed about to agree and thought about sending the jury back for further deliberations with that instruction. As often happens in trials, in the heat of the moment, I had only a few seconds to decide what to do. I felt that the best chance I had to get the judge to overturn CK's verdict on a motion for a new trial or to prevail on my separate-trials argument would be enhanced by the jury finding Lindy more culpable. So, I argued that the jury's first-degree verdict on Lindy should stand pending post-trial motions. McGuire ultimately agreed, saying that if the verdict was wrong it could be fixed later, before sentence was pronounced. Lindy and Schell were livid with me.

My taking this position made me feel extremely uncomfortable. Had I not spoken up, it seemed likely that the judge would have set aside Lindy's first-degree conviction that afternoon. I felt I was to blame for her receiving a verdict that could very likely result in her spending the rest of her life in prison, rather than the chance of eventual parole with second degree. I didn't like Lindy and blamed her for CK's involvement in the case. Still, I knew the deprivations of the prison system too well to feel good about anyone sentenced to a life behind bars. Despite my discomfort and the wrath of Lindy and her lawyer, I believed that I had done the right and necessary thing, both at that moment and later, after I had time to reflect about the whole situation. My abiding job, I knew, was to help my client to the best of my ability, and that meant doing anything within the law that would increase his chances of a better outcome. I'd always felt that one of the hallmarks of a good lawyer was loyalty to the client. My loyalty to CK required blinkers; my goal was to help him, and that meant setting aside the consequences to others.

Several weeks later, we came together for our motions for a new trial. Schell argued on Lindy's behalf that she could not be convicted of a more serious crime than CK, who was holding the gun when it went off. Unfortunately for her, it turned out that the law was clear: An aider and abettor *could* be liable for a more serious crime than the perpetrator. Her sentence remained first-degree murder.

My argument centered on the most damaging thing in CK's case – Lindy's statement about getting a gun and her boyfriend and "blowing away" Bobby, the drug dealer. I reiterated all the arguments I had made pre-trial, in the petition for a writ to the appellate court, and at the trial itself. I was hoping, based on his comment during our debate about instructions, that Judge McGuire had seen the light and would grant our motion. I knew that ultimately, even granting the motion might well make no difference. If we were right and CK should have had a separate trial, the remedy would not have been to reduce the verdict to manslaughter, but to throw out the conviction entirely and give him a new trial. I also knew Judge McGuire had the power to sit as the "thirteenth juror" and, based on the evidence as he saw it, reduce the conviction to manslaughter. I was hoping for that solution. But such reductions were exceptionally rare.

Even though we would have been happy to have CK plead guilty to manslaughter, granting a completely new trial was beyond where even this usually fair judge was willing to go. And reducing the verdict to manslaughter on his own motion simply wasn't in his playbook. Sadly, the motion was denied.

EPILOGUE

The day of CK's murder verdict was the darkest day of my legal career. I felt strongly that the wrong verdict had been reached, and that the Gods of Justice had conspired against this pleasant, reasonably well-functioning heroin addict to land him in prison for what could very well be the rest of his life. In those first few years after the trial, not many days went by when I did not think about this case, feeling alternately angry, depressed, and helpless.

CK stayed in touch with me from time to time, and when he became eligible for parole, I wrote letters on his behalf every year for many years, while the DA submitted letters saying, unfairly and inaccurately, what a heinous crime it was. Eventually, CK managed to find a fellow prisoner who was a good jailhouse lawyer, and with his help filed a *habeas corpus* petition in federal court. *Habeas corpus*, which literally means to bring the person's body before the court, is available not only to free someone or fix the conditions of confinement as in the San Quentin Six case. As the "Great Writ," the only such remedy mentioned in the United States Constitution, it's also available to challenge a conviction in federal court based on an error of law. Here, the error was in not following *Bruton v. United States*, the Supreme Court case that mandated a separate trial for someone in CK's circumstances.

One day I got a letter from CK saying that his petition had reached the federal Ninth Circuit Court of Appeal in San Francisco. This court was well-known for its good record on the rights of criminal defendants. The briefs had been filed, but CK had no lawyer to represent him at the oral argument, so I volunteered to do it *pro bono*. After all, by this time, I sure knew the issues. About a month later, I appeared in the beautiful, ornate Ninth Circuit courthouse on Seventh Street to argue on CK's behalf. I thought the argument went really well. The judges seemed to be clear on the law and understood how the law applied to the facts of CK's case. I eagerly awaited their decision, which came down about a month later. But it was "petition denied." Why? I have no idea. It served as a chance for me to feel angry, depressed, and helpless all over again.

Meanwhile, Lindy was meeting with more success in her efforts at parole. Like my client Stanley Simon, she too had cleaned up and become religious. After thirty years in prison – early on for someone sentenced to twenty-five to life – she was released on parole at the age of fifty-five, and in a few years successfully completed parole.

CK remained in prison, and he and I eventually lost touch. I was almost sure he would die in prison, but thankfully that was not to be. After thirty-four years in prison and now in his seventies, he was released. Prison records show that he too successfully completed parole, and as far as I'm aware, he is still alive. I hope he's found some measure of peace.

As for me, this case served as strong reinforcement of my growing disappointment with the justice system. The system failed in this case in so many ways. An overzealous prosecutor who not only pushed for a murder conviction but spent years writing letters opposing CK's parole, citing a non-existent danger to society. A generally good and fair-minded judge who didn't see the harm in leaving my client and his co-defendant in the same case, and then, when he realized his mistake, failed to make the right but expensive decision – a new trial for my client. A good man with a serious illness – addiction – who was seen by both the justice system and the prison system as a common criminal – a junkie and a murderer.

A few things have changed a bit since. Many people, if not most, now understand that addiction is an illness. While it can still foster criminal activity, treatment opportunities are more widespread and sophisticated than they were back when CK was an addict with few alternatives. Some district attorneys' offices have also become more understanding about addiction and treatment alternatives to incarceration, though they are still a relatively small minority. But not much in the attitude of the judicial system has gotten better, particularly as led by a Supreme Court that's the toughest on criminal defendants in my lifetime. Drug offenses continue to be prosecuted at alarming rates, and severe sentences remain common. The United States continues to incarcerate far more people per capita than any other developed nation, with an ongoing over-representation of black and brown people. Small baby steps have begun, but there is still so far to go.

12

Dora Takes on Chrysler

Dean v. Chrysler Motor Corporation

Dora Dean, a Latina housewife in her mid-thirties who was married to an itinerant roofer, got into her van to drive home after a Fourth of July neighborhood holiday party. When she tried to steer around a gentle curve on Mission Street, the main drag in a working-class neighborhood of San Francisco, the steering wheel turned but the van didn't, and she plowed into a building on the other side of the road. My friend Mark brought me into the case as the "experienced" civil trial lawyer — with one civil jury trial under my belt. But this products liability case was no ordinary civil trial. Had I known what prepping this case would be like, I might have simply passed. As it was, we were two rookies against the might of a gigantic corporation represented by the East Bay's largest law firm. Holding our own against them would not be easy, at least at first.

Mark and Dora

One day soon after the huge loss in CK's murder trial and not that long after Dr. Sing's second trial, I got a call from my friend Mark Rosenbush. Mark was one of the small number of lawyers for whom I had the greatest respect. As my co-counsel in Gypsy's case, he'd won the case by getting the alleged victim and his wife to cross each other up on what money was supposedly stolen from them. There weren't many lawyers I'd want to "go to war" with, but Mark was one.

Mark told me that he had a great case – he was a terrific salesman – in which his client found she couldn't steer her van even though the van had been recalled for a steering defect, and even though she had brought the vehicle in to get the factory repair just a couple of months before. Fortunately, Dora Dean was not seriously injured when she crossed three lanes of traffic and crashed into a building – she had a broken leg – but what attracted Mark – and what he used to attract me – was that the fix Chrysler had implemented was absolutely useless to correct the defect. At the time, my caseload was lighter than usual, and I needed a change of scenery from the criminal courts, so I figured what the hell, why not take the plunge? Mark and I agreed to split everything – the work, the trial, the costs, and the fees – fifty-fifty, and working with someone as talented as Mark made this a much easier lift. After all, in a products liability case, if there was a known defective product, that meant "strict liability," a predetermination that there was something wrong with the product. That gave us a big head start.

In truth, though, neither Mark nor I had any idea of the depth of the rabbit hole we'd jumped into. Mark previously had referred the case to a civil lawyer, but that lawyer had done nothing: no written discovery – the information-gathering process – about what Chrysler admitted or claimed, no depositions of Chrysler personnel, no demands for Chrysler documents that might show what the company knew and when it knew it. At least we got a written agreement from that lawyer that he would not ask for any fees if we prevailed.

I had no doubts that Mark and I could do a great job trying this case. But while I had tried one civil jury trial and taken depositions in a few others, I had virtually no idea about how to conduct discovery against a corporation, and absolutely no idea what to do if the other side refused to produce documents or information. And there was one other problem that Mark failed to mention until after I'd agreed to come on board: the "five-year rule." Like many states, California not only has a statute of limitations on how long someone has before filing a case, but another statute that limits how long we had from the time the case was filed until the jury was sworn in at trial. And this case had languished for so long that we had barely a year until the five-year statute expired and the case would be automatically dismissed. One year may seem like a long time, but when you know nothing about the case except that the steering was defective, and still – according to Dora – didn't work, you really don't know anything. We were ready to go to war, but this was unlike any war I'd seen.

We did the only thing we could do: We got to work. One of the great things about Mark was his favorite expression: "You gotta do what you gotta do," which sounded a lot like my mentor David Mayer. One of the first, and smartest, things we did was bring in my former law student, Len Mastromonaco, to take the lead on discovery. Len by then was five years out of law school and had done a lot of civil discovery. While products liability was new to him too, he at least knew about procedure, deadlines, and all manner of discovery options, and he was willing to take on the work for a modest percentage of our contingency fee – if we ever received one. At the same time, we launched into our own independent investigation. One of the strengths of a criminal law background is that you don't sit around assuming that eventually you'll get what you need from the other side. We went out and found out for ourselves.

Meanwhile, I got to know Dora. She was sweet and kind, an attentive mom to her two girls, six and seven, managing to keep her family grounded, and making do without much. When I first heard her narrative about not being able to steer the van, it was completely believable. She told us that she had spent most of the day at Our Place, a bar on Mission Street in the Excelsior District, a working-class area of the City, and a gathering place for many mostly Spanish-speaking friends.

San Francisco's main streets were then – and still are today – filled with neighborhood bars, many of which, like Our Place, are ground-floor storefronts in houses, with residential flats on the floors above and back-yard patios in the rear. Many of those bars served a bit of food and were gathering places on special occasions. On July 5, a Saturday, Our Place hosted a spaghetti feed to celebrate the Fourth of July weekend. Dora was there with her husband William and her two girls, who played with their friends in the bar's backyard. When the girls got tired, Dora's husband took them home. She followed later in her Dodge Sportsman van. After driving a block north on Mission, she steered slightly to the right to negotiate a gentle curve, but the van kept going straight ahead. She steered more, but the van still kept going straight. A block later she had crossed the southbound lanes and crashed into a building just two blocks north of the bar. She couldn't remember whether, in her panic, she ever put her foot on the brake.

Unfortunately, by the time Mark and I got actively involved in Dora's case, her deposition had already been taken and, between English being her second language and her being poorly prepared by her former lawyer, some of her deposition narrative was not helpful. Two issues in particular stood out. First, she testified that she had gotten to Our Place about noon and left at about 5:30 p.m. But the police officers who responded to the scene and pulled her from the van noted the time in their report as after eight o'clock that night. She was two-and-a-half hours off. Although Dora testified that all she had to drink at Our Place was one white wine spritzer, the depo transcript made it clear that the Chrysler lawyer didn't believe her. He asked her repeatedly whether she was sure that was all she'd had to drink. She said each time that she was sure. But we worried how she could be so far off about what time she left. The second issue was that when she was asked to draw the path her van took across Mission Street, she drew something like this showing her van going almost straight across the

roadway rather than moving in a straight line and gradually crossing traffic lanes as the road curved over two blocks.

Learning our case

As I was learning about our case's biggest weaknesses, we were doing our best to develop some strengths. In hindsight, we knew remarkably little at first. We knew that Chrysler had recalled over one million Dodge Sportsman and Tradesman vans like Dora's due to defective steering. We knew that Dora had taken her van in when she got the recall notice and had the fix done at a local Dodge dealership. We knew that she still couldn't steer the van through that Mission Street curve a couple of months later. We knew that Chrysler claimed the defect wasn't dangerous, but eventually agreed to do a formal recall, meaning that the principle of strict liability applied: Chrysler could not claim at trial that the part was not defective. But there was so much more that we didn't know. And we'd still have to prove that the defect is what caused Dora's collision.

Because Dora couldn't steer, we were quite sure that the recall had done absolutely nothing to fix the problem. The problem, in a nutshell, was this: Vehicle frames are boxes of steel, strengthened by being enclosed on all four sides. In these vans, though, Chrysler changed that design by separating, or unboxing, the frame forward of the left front wheel into two rails. In the "Y" created by the two separate rails – the longitudinal, or outboard rail and the interior, or inboard rail – Chrysler welded a bracket, then bolted the power steering housing onto that bracket. At the front of the van, the two frame rails were welded not to heavy-duty frame metal but to the lighter-weight radiator grille support. We believed that in splitting the rail in two, Chrysler had unnecessarily weakened the system. Imagine extending your index and middle fingers and placing a matchbox between them. If you keep your fingers rigid, the matchbox remains in place. But if you twist the fingers, eventually the matchbox will twist and finally drop out. But what did we know? We weren't engineers.

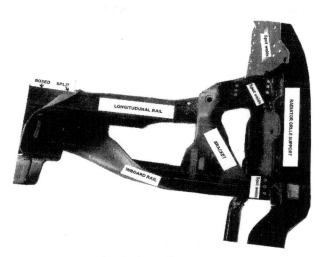

Underside of Plaintiff's Trial Exhibit 2,
steering system forward of left front wheel.

Soon after getting involved in the case, I asked my mechanic and life-long friend, Carlos Martin, if he knew who the best wheel-and-frame man in San Francisco was. He immediately replied, "Denny Quade." With Carlos's name as a reference, I headed over to Denny's shop on Bush Street. Denny told me that he'd started working on cars as a thirteen-year-old at his father's wheel-and-frame shop in Wausau, Wisconsin, dropping out of school after eighth grade. At eighteen, he joined the Navy, and when discharged, he found himself in San Francisco, where he opened up his own shop, which he'd run for over twenty years.

I explained the steering design to Denny, who seemed surprised. After asking me a few questions, he said he couldn't imagine why anyone would want to get "cute" by unboxing the frame, the essential foundation of all cars and vans. I told him about the recall fix that Chrysler had authorized: lift the van on a hoist, inspect it for cracks, weld any visible cracks, and if there were cracks then weld a round piece of cold-rolled steel to the underside of the "inboard" rail. Denny said that made no sense to him: "Spot welds" between the rails and the lightweight radiator support in front would pop right off, and the cold-rolled rod of steel, not welded to any other part, would do nothing. "What you have to do," Denny told me, "is fishplate it." "Without fishplating," Denny continued, "what happens is that the steering system is twisting and twisting, and over time, the steering starts turning the frame, not the wheels."

"Fishplating" was a term I'd never heard, so I asked Denny to explain. It meant re-creating a boxed-in frame by welding rectangular pieces of steel to both rails both above and below the bracket. Closing up the frame was necessary to withstand the torque of power steering, allowing the entire steering and frame system to operate as it should. Simple enough.

Meanwhile, we were working on finding out in discovery what Chrysler knew about the steering problem, and when they knew it, and if they knew how useless their fix was. We were told that Chrysler had sold NHTSA, the National Highway Traffic Safety Administration, on doing this fix after years of denial. By finally agreeing to do the fix voluntarily, Chrysler may have avoided having the understaffed NHTSA do its own testing to see for themselves if the fix actually worked. We knew that the Dodge dealer doing Dora's van's fix was paid sixty-four dollars by Chrysler, not much, and not nearly what doing it right would have cost.

Mark and I were confident that given time, we could learn the details of how to conduct civil discovery, and all the necessary procedures and deadlines we'd have to follow, deadly boring though those procedures might be. We had barely heard of things like "requests for admission," "contention interrogatories," or "motions to compel document production," but we didn't have the time and we were busy trying to pull the case together. We were grateful to have Len Mastromonaco take the lead. He'd worked for a lawyer who had a large plaintiffs' civil litigation practice, and he had learned the ins and outs of the arcane world of civil law discovery, which we would put to good use.

With Len doing the initial drafting, we used all these discovery avenues, while the associate assigned to defend the case at Oakland's Crosby, Heafey, Roach & May did her best to stonewall even the simplest requests. From the very beginning, Crosby's lawyers denied and delayed. Early on, when we asked for the recall notice, they said that our request was "ambiguous" because there were three recall notices: a preliminary notice, an in-house notice to Dodge dealerships, and a notice sent to the public. We had to make a motion to get a court order to give these documents to us. Our motion said, in essence, "C'mon! We want all three!"

It was the rule rather than the exception back then that big firms representing big corporations approached discovery as a war of attrition. Making us fight for each scrap of paper was a successful if underhanded strategy, born out of the assumption that most people on our side – clients and lawyers alike – would not be able to stay the course. The first

battle was a mere skirmish. In Dora's case, these battles continued through all four rounds of discovery. We needed the first
round of information to know what to ask for next. And
given the advance notice and time to reply that each round of
discovery required, Crosby was making us eat up a lot of time
we didn't have.

Among the recall notices, the one sent to the dealerships
was the most interesting. First, Chrysler gave each dealer
only ten reinforcement rods, hardly enough to weld them to
more than a small fraction of vans. Second, the recall notice
instructed mechanics to inspect only part of the steering
system. Denny Quade had made it clear to me that cracks
could occur *anywhere*. Most startling, though, was that Chrysler apparently expected most vans to need only a cursory
0.2 hours of visual inspection to look for cracks, and stated,
underlined, that "If no cracks are present, no further service
is required."

Meanwhile, we had found out that the Dodge vans were
often converted into mini-school buses. Those buses could
ferry twelve or fourteen kids in a much more efficient and
economical way than big forty-passenger school buses. In
those pre-Internet days, I looked up school bus companies
in the telephone Yellow Pages and found that the largest Bay
Area bus yard was out in Martinez, about forty-five minutes
northeast of San Francisco. I called the yard and asked if they
had any Dodge van conversions in their fleet of buses. They
said they had a couple hundred. Would they be willing to talk
to me about how they drove? Sure, if I could make it on out
there.

I drove out two days later, and was greeted by Jorge, an outgoing, fiftyish man who told me he was the yard's maintenance manager. He was happy to talk at length about how carefully his company dealt with safety issues, and clearly proud of the fact that he never even considered using Chrysler's official fix to repair the Dodge vans. I asked him what they did with those conversions, and he said, "We fishplate 'em. Box 'em in. It's the only safe way to go." I asked how his crew did the fix, and he described using two men – the shop had only men back then – one to slide under the chassis on a dolly, and the other to turn the wheel. When I asked why they did it that way, he explained that unless the wheel was weight-bearing, cracks in the rails and bracket might not be disclosed. He explained that his guys also spray-painted the area so cracks would be more easily seen when the steering wheel was turned. "We're carrying children around here," Jorge added. "You can't [mess] around with that."

Before I left, Jorge took me to a wall of the shop, where he pointed to a memo, by then almost ten years old, dog-eared with a partial greasy thumbprint in one corner, and said, "Look at this." As I read it, it was difficult to contain my excitement. "Do you need this?" I asked. "No, not really," he replied. "We fixed all these vans ten years ago. Go ahead and take it." I thanked him and left. I had found our case's first smoking gun.

The memo was sent from Captain E.E. Kynaston, commander of the Commercial Vehicle Section of the California Highway Patrol, to senior Chrysler personnel in Detroit on September 19, 1975, informing them of the steering defects in school bus conversions. First, the letter meant that Chrysler knew of the steering defect way back in 1975, almost five years before the recall. Second, despite that notice, they continued to manufacture those vans with the same defect for three more years. Third and most important, the memo said the inspection required two people, and had to take place "with weight of vehicle on its wheels," exactly the way Jorge's crew had done their inspections.

It was now clear to us that Chrysler had ignored the CHP's inspection advice from Day One right through the recall. It seemed Chrysler was more interested in minimizing the cost of the recall than in fixing the vans. Chrysler's recall inspection was done on a hoist, so the van was not weight-bearing. Jorge's inspections, following CHP guidelines, were weight-bearing, which meant that turning the steering wheel would disclose cracking to the person on the dolly below the van that simply would not be seen by the Chrysler inspection. And while Chrysler's recall looked only at a specific part of the steering system, Jorge had told me that his mechanics had found cracks "all over the place," just as Denny had predicted. Of course, if no cracks were seen, "no further service [was] required." It was no wonder Chrysler had sent each dealership only ten rods.

The long prep for trial

With the CHP letter, we felt the case had turned the corner. We now had enough proof to give us a good chance in front of a jury. But that was a long way from victory. We still had much information to learn in discovery. And now that we knew the truth, we wanted to know whether Chrysler would admit to having received warnings both about the steering defect and how to inspect for it.

Meanwhile, I set out to find CHP Captain Kynaston. At trial, in order to get the memo into evidence, it wouldn't be enough to have a copy. We'd either need to have someone from the CHP authenticate the memo from their own personal knowledge, or have a Chrysler executive acknowledge that he had received the memo – something we felt was highly unlikely.

I called the CHP central offices in Sacramento and learned that Captain Kynaston had retired several years before. But I caught a big break. In talking to people in the Commercial Vehicle Section, I learned that the memo was actually drafted by a member of Kynaston's team named Clifford Campoy. Campoy had also retired, but one of his old friends knew that he was living in Manteca, in the northern part of California's vast Central Valley, driving a truck on and off to add to his state retirement income. It was easy enough to track him down, and when I asked whether I could drive out to Manteca to visit with him, he said sure, if I wanted to drive all that way.

Cliff Campoy was a pleasant fellow of about sixty who met me at his door with his wife, invited me into his kitchen, and offered me a cup of tea. Campoy remembered the memo clearly, not only because the cracks in the steering system had been so obvious, but because Chrysler had written back right away blowing off the CHP's warning. I asked him about the memo: two people needed to check for cracks, the van weight-bearing on the ground. He told me that any experienced mechanic should know that, but Highway Patrol policy would be to clearly state what should be done and not assume the recipient would know the right approach.

Campoy explained that vans were considered commercial vehicles, or trucks. He described how various kinds of trucks should be inspected, and it was quite clear that he knew his stuff. At the end of our conversation, I asked him if he'd be willing to be an expert in our case. A modest man, he expressed surprise and said, "I'm no expert in anything." I replied that he certainly was – an expert in inspecting trucks and vans. He was initially hesitant, but his wife encouraged him, knowing that it could give him a chance to shine and display his special knowledge – something he would take pride in. I offered him seventy-five dollars an hour for his time. He found that generous and agreed to come on board. Things were falling into place.

On my drive back to San Francisco, I decided that we should see if Denny Quade would also be willing to be our expert. With his encyclopedic knowledge of frames, I thought he'd be terrific. As lawyers who'd made our living cross-examining cops, Mark and I both understood how effective ordinary working folks could be as witnesses, and we would never underestimate them. But we also recognized that we needed a "suit," an expert witness with a fancy engineering degree and credentials, if only to counteract the expert that Chrysler would undoubtedly call. Intuitively, we both sensed that this was as much a matter of perception as proof. But we couldn't afford to take any chances. Mark was put in charge of finding the credentialled expert, while I stayed on top of the guys who actually got their hands dirty. I asked Denny if he too would come on board as an expert for the same $75/hour fee. He told me he'd never been inside a courtroom in his life. But there was always a first time. Denny agreed.

Meanwhile, our discovery battles continued through a second and then a third round of document demands. Chrysler's lawyers, partner Patrick Becherer and associate Lori Schweitzer, did everything they could to slow down the stream of documents to a trickle, knowing that the more we knew when we took depositions of Chrysler executives, the more we would be able to pin them down to helpful testimony. So, they kept objecting, and we kept asking the court for rulings. The result was a slow but reasonably steady stream of previously undisclosed documents. And many of them were explosive.

First, we learned that before NHTSA ever contacted Chrysler with its concerns, Chrysler already had twenty incident reports about steering problems. Examples from Chrysler's own reports: "steering mounting bracket completely broken away"; "All of a sudden steering had an extreme amount of free play"; "steering gear box mounting plate had broken away from frame at welds"; and so on.

Next, we learned that Lynn Bradford, NHTSA's Director of Defects Investigation Enforcement, had contacted Chrysler in April 1979 demanding that Chrysler provide an extensive explanation about "failure of the bracket(s) holding steering gear box to vehicle frame," and that William R. Kittle, Chrysler's Director of Vehicle Safety and Emissions, replied as if Chrysler's twenty previous reports did not exist:

[T]he level of reporting to date indicates a low
frequency potential for existence of the subject
condition. There is no evidence to suggest that a
general problem exists.... The subject condition
does not present an unreasonable risk to motor
vehicle safety.

Kittle admitted only that problems with the frame and bracket
could cause "a 'spongy' steering feeling," but it would "result
only in increased free play, [not] loss of steering control." At
the same time, he managed to blame any problems on issues
beyond Chrysler's control: structural damage caused when
the vans were tied down for shipping; "high steering ...
loads"; and "vehicle operation involving a high frequency of
heavy steering system loading maneuvers...." These last two
amounted to a claim of driver error for what seemed to us like
regular use of a van. We wondered if twelve students would be
a "high steering load."

Through 1979, Bradford and Kittle exchanged further
correspondence with neither changing his position. Kittle did
tell Bradford that Chrysler had added some extra spot welding
between the frame and the "cross member" – perhaps a euphe-
mism to avoid admitting it was just a radiator support – and
that a December 1975 in-house "Technical Service Bulletin"
documented this. But what he didn't tell NHTSA was that the
bulletin was in direct response to the September 1975 CHP
warning letter from Capt. Kynaston.

We also found out that Chrysler held several compa-
ny-wide Vehicle Regulations Committee meetings about the
Dodge van steering system from late December 1979 to early
March 1980. While the first meeting resulted in total denial,
at the second, the minutes noted that "free play can develop

... in the range of 45° to 125°"– a lot more than the "spongy" steering Kittle described. In February 1980, the committee asked the company's Service Division to do a survey to study the extent of the cracking problem. And then, seemingly out of nowhere, at the March meeting, the minutes acknowledged for the first time a wider problem: "The frame cracking condition has been found to be more prevalent than first thought as many as 10% of the 1971 through 1978 population" of vans. Kittle wrote Bradford and said Chrysler would do a "voluntary" recall.

These documents had all of us excited. It now seemed clear that Chrysler had engaged in a pattern of denying a defect they'd known about for years, and only when they realized that they'd soon be exposed, accepted that they had no choice but to recall the vehicles – except they did so with a recall that neither inspected correctly nor fixed the problem. We began to think more seriously about punitive damages. We had their willful ignoring and stonewalling of the steering dangers, and their use of a recall they should have known wouldn't work. As we prepared to go back to Detroit to depose William Kittle and others, Mark and I were developing examinations designed not only to pin the executives down to untenable positions, but perhaps to also catch them in falsehoods.

And then, just before the discovery period ended and a week before our depositions in Detroit, we finally got the last batch of documents. Len got them first and immediately called me and Mark to shout, "You won't believe what we just got!" – dozens of internal Chrysler documents showing cracks throughout the entire steering system – the result of the Service Division's February 1980 survey.

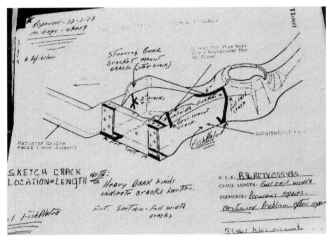

Chrysler diagram with inspector's drawing of steering system cracks, 1980

We had finally gotten what Chrysler most wanted to hide – smoking *guns* by the dozens: diagrams of cracks and surveys of governmental and private fleets with high rates of steering failure. The diagram above was typical. Chrysler's inspectors found failure rates of between 15% and 50%, even with their non-weight-bearing inspection. With proof of Chrysler's malicious disregard for safety and a clear path to punitive damages, we now felt we had all we needed to know. We were ready for Detroit.

As we took stock and looked back at the discovery process, Mark and I knew that opposing counsel's efforts to stonewall our discovery had completely failed. We assumed that Becherer and his team had simply grossly underestimated us, two criminal defense lawyers who must therefore not know what they were doing. We were also incredulous that they had directed *no* discovery whatever at us. They could have tried to develop witnesses who might have seen Dora "tipsy," or who would have been critical of her reputation, or who witnessed the crash. But they did nothing. We didn't know why, whether it was sloppiness, case fatigue, or simply that they felt in their abundant arrogance that they needn't worry about our factual presentation. My guess is that it was the last of these. The Crosby lawyers were neither stupid nor lazy, and Becherer's patronizing arrogance was becoming a theme in the litigation. But we will never know for sure.

Depositions

In California, Chrysler is a "foreign" corporation – one whose residence is in another state. As such, Chrysler had "diversity of jurisdiction" with Dora, meaning it could have removed her case to federal court had there not been another California defendant as a "resident," the local Dodge dealer. We much preferred San Francisco Superior Court to federal court, where we'd have jurors from the more conservative suburbs and where neither Mark nor I had ever tried a case. But when it came to taking depositions, we had no way of subpoenaing Chrysler executives to come to California. We still needed to either stipulate to deposition dates in Detroit or go through the arcane procedure of getting "commissions" from the court to allow us to depose people in Michigan. At first, Becherer gave us a hard time about a stipulation – my guess was he wanted to see if we could figure out how to get the necessary court order – but when it became clear that we would do what was necessary, he relented and agreed on depo dates for several execs. Otherwise, the execs would have had to show up on dates we picked, rather than those agreeable to both sides. So, Mark and I went off to Michigan, splitting up who would take on which executive.

Primary among the deponents were William Kittle, whom I got to examine, and Jim Tracy, the Service Division coordinator who ordered the 1980 survey, whom Mark questioned. We knew that unless Chrysler's lawyers decided to call these executives as witnesses, their deposition testimony would be all that we would get from them. We had no way to subpoena them to a trial outside Michigan. That meant that our deposition examinations would likely serve as our cross-examinations at trial. By this time, that was fine by us.

The depositions were something of an anti-climax. Mostly, we used them to "authenticate" documents – to establish the foundational proof we needed to get the documents into evidence at trial. Tracy couldn't very well deny what the survey documents and diagrams he ordered said. He also acknowledged that he had discussed the ultimate recall specifications at length with his boss, Charles Joiner, General Manager of Chrysler's Service and Parts Division. Joiner signed the recall notices limiting the fix to the cold-rolled steel rod on one rail despite the results of Tracy's survey.

Kittle couldn't deny his ongoing assertions to NHTSA's Bradford that the steering system was not defective, nor that Chrysler had ultimately admitted that 10% of Dodge vans had steering system cracks – a gross underestimate considering how the inspections were conducted. We did get a bit more from Kittle. We asked him whether he was aware of any governmental agencies other than NHTSA that had contacted

Chrysler with steering system concerns. He falsely said he was not. But Kittle knew about the CHP's September 1975 memo, and he also knew of Chrysler's written response and the additional welding ordered as a direct result of the CHP memo.

We also knew that the New York State Department of Transportation had contacted Chrysler about the steering system. In my last pre-trial investigative foray, I'd found a school bus yard in Suffolk County, New York, with over 900 Dodge vans, all of them fishplated to protect their drivability. I met Rich Henke, the manager of the school bus fleet, who insisted that almost every one of his vans showed cracks when inspected on the ground. Henke also gave me an important lead: the New York DOT had opened a file on the steering. So, on the way back to California, I made a stop in midtown Manhattan to talk to a group of DOT folks, and I was given copies of their own test results showing the dangers of both the defect and Chrysler's own fix. They too had contacted Chrysler, and that information would have been routed to Kittle as well.

When we returned from Detroit, it was time for expert witness depositions, usually the last major event before trial. Mark took their engineering expert's deposition and defended the deposition of our expert, ready to make objections as necessary. There was nothing surprising in their complete disagreement. We figured they would likely cancel each other out at trial. As for our other witnesses, Becherer had been disparaging them constantly before the depos, calling them "grease monkeys" who would provide no help to our case. It was my job to defend those depositions, and I confess that a tiny part of me was concerned he might be right. Mark and I thought that Cliff Campoy and Denny Quade would be great witnesses, but we were rookies. My civil litigation friends had emphasized the need for credentials. They also reminded us of Becherer's sterling reputation as a great trial lawyer – one of the two litigation stars at his large firm. By this time, I was relying on the principle I'd always used with David Mayer: If everyone says we're wrong but the two of us agree, then we're right. I was comfortable applying that rule to Mark. And neither of us was impressed with Becherer.

The Quade and Campoy depositions seemed to go great from our perspective. Becherer put them both through their paces, showing them lots of documents and asking a lot of questions designed to throw these "grease-monkeys" off course. But they knew what they knew and stuck to it. Only Marvin Jacobs, the sole practitioner who represented the local Dodge dealer, scored any points at all. Becherer was particularly patronizing to Denny, unable to help himself when he learned Denny had left school after eighth grade. He patronized me as well. At one point, I objected to a question as argumentative, a common objection, and we had a brief quarrel, which he ended by saying, "Right, I'm supposed to let *you* tell *me* how to practice law." I was furious, but instead of lashing out, I decided that I'd file that one away for another time and place when I could return the favor.

The Trial, Part One

During the two weeks before trial, my then-wife, Naomi, had taken Dora clothes shopping, because she didn't have outfits suitable for going to court. We got her a week-long wardrobe of nice, simple attire. In doing so, we may have been violating an ethical rule that stated that while lawyers could advance the costs of litigating a case, they were not permitted to pay for a client's personal expenses. Whether those expenses included outfits to wear to court was debatable. Either way, we simply didn't worry about it. The rule itself dated from the early days of the twentieth century, when lawyers from elite northeastern white-shoe firms wrote the original thirty-nine canons of legal ethics. In several respects, those rules were designed to protect those firms and their monied clients at the expense of ordinary people, who some rules-drafters called "riff-raff." If Dora was supposedly among the "riff-raff," I felt we this was a rule we could ignore.

Meanwhile, in the days immediately before trial, Mark and I met with a few civil trial lawyers we respected. We were concerned about two issues. First, we had lengthy multi-day depositions of the Chrysler executives, some of the depositions involving dynamite testimony, particularly those of Kittle and Tracy. But when a witness is not available for trial, we are not allowed to pick and choose what parts of the deposition to read. We'd have to read the whole thing, which could be endlessly boring. Second, the trial was scheduled for six weeks, and on the day of trial we were assigned out to the Hon. Daniel "Mike" Hanlon, who told us he had a long-planned, three-week, family vacation set after our fourth week, and he was not about to change it. Because we were coming up on the five-year statute of limitations, we couldn't put the case off, nor did we want to: We were more than ready.

Our friends were pessimistic on both counts. They couldn't envision how we could keep the jury awake reading page after page of deposition transcripts. And they thought that the jury would likely forget our "case in chief" – we'd be going first – after the break. They even thought it unlikely that after a three-week hiatus, the jurors would return to the courtroom rather than begging off with one excuse or another.

But Mark and I came up with an idea for reading the depos that we thought might work. First, we'd intersperse the readings among the other witnesses: the reporting officers, our engineer, their engineer (whom we'd decided to call in our own case because we didn't think he hurt us and we wanted to control the narrative), Cliff Campoy and Denny Quade, people from the neighborhood who frequented Our Place, and of course, Dora. Then, we decided that I'd read all the questions we asked – the defense had asked nothing, which was routine, as they could always bring their witnesses back for trial – and Mark would answer. Mark would have to answer in neutral tones. Anything else would be inappropriate, undoubtedly anger Judge Hanlon, and possibly tick off the jury. But I, on the other hand, could do a little acting. I could sit at counsel table for the boring parts, and then, for the juicy parts we wanted the jury to focus on, stand up, move forward, raise my voice a little, and use my hands, emphasizing those parts of the testimony.

As far as leaving the jurors out to sea for three weeks, we'd just have to do our best to get them interested in our case, try to time things to end around the break, and leave them with a big finish. And hope.

In those days, the court held last-minute settlement conferences in the days before the Monday trial call. On the Thursday before trial, we had a conference with Judge Victor Campilongo, one tough cookie, who made it clear he thought very little of our case. We had demanded $800,000 and Chrysler had offered far less than the costs Mark and I had spent on the case. Campilongo managed to knock us down to $445,000 and get Chrysler to $60,000, still less than our costs. Mark and I were worried. What were the weaknesses the judge and our opposing counsel saw that we simply didn't get? Was our principle of "If we agree, we must be right" just a bunch of hooey? Still, we rejected the settlement out of hand.

Campilongo did make one valuable suggestion: settle with Marvin Jacobs's client, the Dodge dealership, for a nominal sum. It was clear from our depositions that after Becherer spent a long time examining our witnesses and, from where we sat, getting nowhere, Jacobs would come in and in five minutes score more points than Becherer had all day. We liked Marvin, a smart guy who mostly defended elevator companies in accidents, and we'd formed a friendly relationship with him. It was apparent to us that he didn't have much more use for big-firm lawyers than we did. And frankly, we did not want him cross-examining our witnesses at trial. But we were extremely worried that if we dismissed his client after a settlement, the Chrysler lawyers would immediately remove the case to federal court, as was their right. Ultimately, we needed Marvin out, and took a chance by settling with his client on Friday. On Monday, we were still in state court, sent out to trial in Judge Hanlon's courtroom. Chrysler had not removed the case.

Department 19 in City Hall was a beautiful courtroom, and today it is one of the few old courtrooms in City Hall still preserved as a hearing room. I had mixed feelings about the place. I had tried Elvin Drummond's murder case in this courtroom with great success. But I'd tried another murder case there too – a hard one with terrible facts – and received a verdict that I hated: second-degree murder, fifteen-to-life. My client wasn't a horrible guy, and he didn't intend to kill anyone, but he and his buddy had tied up a man and placed duct tape over his mouth while they robbed him in his apartment, and the man suffocated and died. About six weeks after my client was convicted, he hung himself in prison, leaving a note that said, "fuck all this time." Both cases were the kind that stay with you for a lifetime.

The first day with Judge Hanlon was devoted to both sides giving him a case synopsis and discussing "motions *in limine*," motions addressing what evidence would or would not come in at trial. To the extent possible, Hanlon wanted to rule on the admissibility of evidence before we got started, so that it wouldn't interrupt the case's flow in front of the jury. This process took several hours. We began jury selection on the morning of the second day, and by 4:30 p.m. that afternoon had a jury that both Mark and I really liked. Having been schooled in the Cat Bennet art of jury selection, I did our *voir dire*, using the same method of asking general questions to panelists, getting them to raise their hands, and then engaging in specific conversations with each juror about their responses.

Sprinkled in among my seven general questions, including those about a defective product and a surprising experience while driving, was this one, which we felt was particularly important: "San Francisco is kind of famous for being a neighborhood city, with neighborhood bars and restaurants. Do any of you ever go to a neighborhood bar as a gathering place, or for a social occasion, where friends get together?"

With one significant but correctable glitch, *voir dire* went extremely well, and I felt a good connection with most of the jurors. As for the glitch, I mistakenly called a juror named Mr. Mah "Mr. Tam" by mistake. By now, I knew that it was imperative to honestly and immediately own my mistake. When I began his individual questioning, I started out by apologizing to Mr. Mah. He accepted graciously, and we went on to have a friendly conversation.

In my view, though, the best part of *voir dire* was the tone-deaf way Becherer conducted his jury questioning. Unable to break from his patronizing mode, he asked every juror whether they would follow the law and treat a corporation just as they would treat an individual. Given the question's phrasing, every juror, of course, said yes. To several women jurors, he then said, "Very good." I was so impressed by this lack of sensitivity that I noted it on the pages I kept for each juror. For Juror number 12, a Black woman who worked for the City as a social services eligibility worker who sat in the upper right corner of the jury box, I wrote "does not like PB." She actually turned and looked at the wall at one point. For Juror number 7, a grants writer for UC Medical Center, I wrote "He's lecturing her!" For Juror number 6, a Black high school teacher, I wrote a strong "yes" when she seemed to stare him down. Without empathy, Becherer didn't have a genuine conversation with a single juror. I couldn't believe he left some of the women he'd patronized on the jury. When we had both approved the twelve jurors and two alternates at the end of the day, we were overjoyed. We had a diverse, largely professional jury that lived mostly in the progressive parts of the City. I couldn't know then, but given the jury we'd picked, the case was all but over. My good feelings were reinforced when the next day, Juror number 12 came in with her hair in braids, which I saw as a small act of defiance.

The newly sworn jury had the next day off as we spent the day marking exhibits for identification and stipulating to the admissibility of a lot of evidence, including our Exhibit 2, a full-sized left front frame rail and extension, complete with power steering housing, that our engineering expert had gotten at a salvage yard and cleaned up and spray painted, marking all the welds with red dots. We began presenting our case on Day Four, and it went well. Mark gave our opening statement. We had prepared white poster paper listing sixty-five things that we would prove. Mark went through each of the sixty-five and explained to the jury how they all fit into our case. The jurors seemed attentive and interested. When we began with testimony from our engineer, we were feeling pretty good about things.

The next three weeks was taken up by our witnesses and what turned out to be over five days' worth of deposition transcript reading. But boring though that sounds, it all went according to plan. By getting up and approaching the "witness," Mark, who read from the Chrysler executive's transcript from the witness box, I was able to emphasize the important stuff and bring the jurors back to attentiveness. Meanwhile, on the stand, Cliff Campoy was straightforward and unimpeachable. Dora, who we put on last, was confident and clear, and Becherer's examination did not faze or fluster her.

Perhaps the best moment, though, came during Becherer's cross-examination of Denny Quade. Denny's direct examination had been great, as he explained in terms that any juror could understand why the Chrysler fix wouldn't work, what fishplating was, and how he would fix the van's steering so it wouldn't break again. Becherer had Denny leave the witness box and join him standing over Exhibit 2, the car part exemplar. As Becherer continued to ask Denny questions, he got to one that sounded confusing and had me concerned, though I can't remember now what the question was. I needn't have worried. Denny simply did not take the bait: "Excuse me, but you're trying to trick me!" he said. "Look here!" he continued, pointing his thumb – his greasy thumb, I must add – down into the interior of the car part. "*Here's* where the whole thing goes wrong!" Becherer, realizing he'd lost the battle, sat down, and the judge told Denny he was excused. Once Denny understood that he was free to go, he headed for the courtroom door, and as he got there, turned around and said to the assemblage, "Good luck to everyone!" and left. I'd never seen a courtroom exit like that before, nor have I seen one like it since.

We were wrapping up our case just as our four weeks before the judge's vacation expired. When we broke for the three-week hiatus, we could only hope that the jury had internalized our case and that, in the best-case scenario, they had already decided it in our favor, though the judge told them they must wait until all the evidence was in. The danger, of course, was the other possibility raised by our friends: that the jurors would forget everything we'd presented, and the defense would have free rein after our break. If they even came back at all.

The Trial, Part Two

Mark and I took some needed R&R time during our hiatus. But Mark became convinced that Chrysler would come up with some kind of trickery during our three-week break. I was dubious, but he had gotten the whiff of something in the air.

On the first day we returned to court, we looked in the jury box to see that all fourteen jurors and alternates were in their seats, not a soul missing. We were pleased, feeling that our presentation had kept them all interested. We rested our case. But Mark was right: Chrysler had a trick up its sleeve. Their first witness was their engineer, who launched into testimony about the proving grounds test he had conducted during the break in trial. He described how he had asked the maintenance team to cut through the longitudinal rail, completely separating it from the bracket, in order to replicate what our engineer said had happened to Dora's car. Using a fancy pointer that telescoped out from pencil size to a full three feet – I couldn't help but contrast it with Denny Quade's thumb – he introduced a three-camera video of his drive around the Chrysler proving grounds: one camera mounted on the steering wheel, one bolted on the frame to show the bracket where the cut was made, and one at distance to show the van driving around the track. The vehicle responded perfectly.

This demonstration had me worried, but Mark seemed cavalier about it, saying "No one is going to believe that this really means anything." Still, the video was well produced, if slick – although not as slick as that pointer – and, to my mind, quite effective.

Mark undertook a vigorous cross-examination that made me feel a lot better. How much damage was there in the steering system before it was cut? The witness didn't know. Were there any prior cracks? No. How many miles Dora's van been driven when it crashed? He didn't remember. If he assumed that it was 66,614 miles, could he estimate how many thousands of turns Dora's steering system went through? No. Could he estimate how much each turn of the steering wheel would fatigue the system, particularly when Dora's van was full? No, he really couldn't.

The rest of Chrysler's case was relatively brief and didn't add much. Mark and I believed that if the jurors had remembered what we presented, things were looking good. In closing argument, Mark went first, going through each of the sixty-five items on the sheets he'd used in opening statement. He explained how we'd proven each and every one: the existence of the defect, Chrysler's denials, the warnings from the CHP, the eventual admission of a system failure, the wholly inadequate fix and inspection method, and ultimately, that Chrysler knew that its own repair didn't fix anything, yet repeatedly denied it. After each item, he put a check mark next to the number until all sixty-five were checked. And he presented it in a way that was not at all preachy, more like a folksy high school teacher. Throughout, he exhibited his warm, accessible, slightly bemused manner – in short, someone very easy to like. It was one of the most impressive displays I'd ever seen in the courtroom.

We knew that Becherer would emphasize the proving grounds test that his expert had conducted, and we decided not to mention it until I argued in rebuttal. By this time, Mark had convinced me that it was no big deal, given the hundreds of thousands of times Dora's steering wheel had actually steered around corners, made U-turns, and otherwise fatigued the steering system over six years. I began my rebuttal by emphasizing the endless repetitive flexing of those frame rails over and over, *and over* again, during the course of 66,000 miles.

We were almost positive that the Chrysler team would focus on Dora's time in Our Place bar in their closing. We didn't know what else they had. We knew that we'd proven that the fix on her van would do nothing to help the steering, and supported Dora's testimony that the car wouldn't steer. But Becherer knew that proving a defect was not enough. We also had to prove that the defect, not Dora's behavior, caused the collision. That meant Becherer had to argue that Dora's not knowing what time she left the bar, drawing the path her van took as a line almost straight across Mission Street, and her eight hours at the bar, showed that she must have been impaired by drink, and that's what caused the crash.

But we were ready, and indeed we were counting on this attack. We knew from experience that once in a while, a case's greatest weakness can be flipped into its greatest strength. We thought that this was one of those times. If Chrysler accused Dora of being inebriated without any proof, our biggest weakness could become our biggest strength. We knew when to use our client's background to advantage – or, in this situation, to use the other side's privileged elitism against it. This was my job in rebuttal argument. It went something like this:

When the police removed Dora from the vehicle, no one gave her an alcohol test. You all saw the police officer on the witness stand. If he thought she was under the influence, he surely would have ordered her blood to be tested at the hospital, as often happens after a collision. But that didn't happen. So why is Chrysler saying she must have been drunk? There's no evidence of that, just talk, just demeaning innuendo. How dare they accuse Dora! Members of the jury, if you don't believe Dora, if you think she lied on the witness stand, then find for the defendant. But remember first that Dora was in her neighborhood gathering place for a spaghetti feed on the Fourth of July weekend. Maybe Chrysler executives like to hang out at the Grosse Point Country Club to celebrate Independence Day. Maybe they got drunk there, maybe they didn't. But for Dora and her friends, their celebration was at the Our Place bar in the Excelsior District. And that doesn't make Dora either drunk or a liar.

It did, though, make the jurors furious with Chrysler. It was not the first time I'd played the "race card," nor the last, but it was perhaps the most effective. After the jury had begun deliberations, feeling reasonably confident, and wanting to provide my own bit of patronizing, I went over to Becherer, shook his hand, and said, "You did a nice job on some of your examinations," damning him with faint praise. He could only thank me, though he was clearly ticked off by the comment. Two days later, Dora and I were sitting on a bench outside Department 19 wondering what the jury would do. I asked her how her two little girls were. She said they were doing well. I said, "Then it really doesn't matter much what happens here, right?" She agreed. Five minutes later, we were told that the jury had reached a verdict: $3,300,000, with fault distributed 100% to Chrysler, and zero to Dora. I was convinced then and believe to this day that the verdict would have been half that sum if Chrysler had not accused Dora of being drunk.

Lessons from the case

After verdicts, some jurors run for the courtroom door as fast as they can. More commonly, two or three, now free to discuss their impressions, stick around to talk to the lawyers. After Dora's verdict, almost every juror hung around. Chrysler had an in-house lawyer who sat through the whole trial. He approached the jurors and asked, "But what about the fact that she was in the bar all day?"

Mr. Mah, the juror whose name I had gotten wrong at first, was the jury foreman. He shook his index finger at the lawyer and said, "Shame on you! Shame on you for accusing her of being drunk!" Later, Juror number 12 told me that she thought the Chrysler expert had faked the three-camera proving grounds test and mentioned seeing his "little white thumb" on the steering wheel.

Despite laboring in the criminal courts for a dozen years, this trial was my first extended experience with elitism. It pervaded everything Chrysler and its big-firm lawyers had done, mostly in ways that helped our case. Fighting over discovery just steeled us to do better. Patronizing us did the same. Demeaning our witnesses diminished their value only in their eyes, and selling them short gave those witnesses star power at trial. I think to this day that Denny Quade may have been the most effective witness I ever put on a witness stand. Mark and I realized how insular both Chrysler and its lawyers were when it came to evaluating the case. How could they not see what we saw? How could they not want to settle rather than chance the bad publicity that going to trial could – and did – bring? How could the lawyers not understand the power of lay witnesses without initials after their names? We didn't know; our world was so different from theirs.

The defense's single biggest mistake was to demean and underestimate Dora. Chrysler's leadership team and principal attorney were all white men, and all acted towards Dora as if she were some kind of lesser human being whose straightforward testimony would not be believed by twelve other ordinary people. After all, despite all our preparation and proof that Chrysler ignored safety, if the jury didn't believe what Dora Dean said, we would still lose. But all twelve of them believed her without reservation.

While this pervasive caste-ism helped our case, it was also disgusting to witness. It brought me a deeper personal understanding of what today we call white privilege – not enough for an enlightened understanding that takes years, even a lifetime, to work through, but a more elevated understanding about the pervasiveness of the dominant white male elite culture of our society.

I also understood for the first time the depths of the prevailing attitude of a large American corporation. After this case, I had to conclude that a corporation like Chrysler would likely care far more about money than safety, more about reputation than consumerism, and more about stonewalling and dissembling than the truth. I had known that big American corporations were not our friends, but I had no idea to what extent. It took me a few years to realize that even with bad post-trial publicity, Chrysler saw this case as just part of the cost of doing business. It was better for them economically to either fight a case to the end or settle secretly. With enough roadblocks set up by their lawyers, they knew that just a few cases like ours would make it through to a jury trial rather than succumbing to the war of attrition. And even when we won, a few million in our case was far less of a financial blow than fixing 1.5 million vans properly. Events over the years have unfortunately reinforced this dark vision of the American corporation.

EPILOGUE

Dora Dean: Chrysler made a motion for a new trial, and Judge Hanlon decided to grant remittitur, which meant, as it had for Mrs. Friel, that the judge reduced the verdict sitting as "the thirteenth juror." When he lowered the amount for punitive damages significantly, Mark and I were both angry, and we felt we had a good chance of winning if we appealed the reduction. We had proven, in defense of the new trial motion, that given Chrysler's enormous yearly profits, the $3,000,000 punitive award (in addition to the $300,000 damages for her leg) was modest. But a couple of days later, we came to an important realization. *We* might benefit by appealing the case, but Dora might have to wait two or three years before seeing a dime. And our duty remained to Dora. We still had a result well into seven figures, and given her financial situation, Dora needed money now. There was plenty there to set her and her daughters up for a long time. We accepted the remittitur, and Chrysler cut a check.

We were representing the person, not the case, and so we suggested to Dora that she could buy a beautiful house for cash and still have plenty of money left over for a nest egg for her and her girls. She wanted a warmer climate, closer to San Jose, and picked the sleepy little town of Saratoga, a San Jose suburb. We found a beautiful four-bedroom house for about $350,000 in a neighborhood where houses now sell for $3,000,000 and more. We set her up with my financial advisor to take care of the rest of her award. We lost touch with her after a couple of years, and my recent efforts to find her were unsuccessful. I'm optimistic, though, that those two beautiful young girls turned into happy and successful grown women.

Mark Rosenbush: I would have thought it impossible for two skilled practitioners to work together every day for a year in true fifty-fifty partnership without a moment of conflict. Yet, that's what happened in the Dean case. Perhaps that inspired Mark to take on one more civil case with me – a wrongful firing of the manager of a Reynolds Metals can-making plant. That case also took us to out-of-state depositions, this time in Richmond, Virginia. There, walking along Monument Avenue, the boulevard filled at that time with the statues of Confederate generals, Mark turned to me and said, "I don't think either of our families will be moving here soon." He was referring to Richmond's Old South atmosphere and the fact we both had bi-racial children. Things in the San Francisco Bay Area were not as great as its reputation might have had it, but it was way better than Richmond in the 1990s.

Despite that second foray into civil trial work, Mark went back to exclusively practicing criminal defense, soon earning a coveted place on the federal court appointments panel, and eventually trying many federal cases in addition to his state practice. His wife died too young, and after his two sons married and almost 100 criminal trials, he retired. He told me recently that he doesn't miss it. He's too busy studying classical piano and playing with his toddler grandchild. He remains one of very few great trial lawyers with whom I've had the privilege of sharing a courtroom.

Patrick Becherer left the Crosby Heafey firm several years after the Dean trial and formed his own boutique firm with his former associate, Lori Schweitzer. I ran into Becherer a time or two after the case and we had brief but reasonably cordial exchanges. His new firm continued to focus on products liability defense and the defense of other complex cases. The firm seemed to be successful and maintained a good reputation among lawyers. But I have no idea if either he or Schweitzer learned anything from the Dean case – or whether, given the realities of defending big corporations, they even cared.

As for me, Dora Dean's trial amplified my view of the legal world in several significant ways. First, it further convinced me that what Cat Bennett had taught me about communicating with jurors – and, frankly, all people – was invaluable and abidingly so. Her lesson, to speak the truth and be unafraid to show your true self, continues to resonate with me. Second, I saw how extreme the other side of the litigation coin could be: judgmental, privileged, insular, and tone-deaf, a world that spoke and expected to be heard, but didn't know how to listen. I thought back on the DAs I had tried cases against, many of whom I had little respect for, and I realized in hindsight that most of them were at least well-intentioned, trying to do what they thought was best for society. I might have disagreed with their social philosophy, and I considered few of them to be great lawyers, but I felt nonetheless that the majority were sincere.

On a more practical level, the Dean case helped both my confidence and my career. After Dora, when I went out to trial, I did so more certain about my rather intuitive evaluation of cases, and I also knew I needn't fear either my opponent or the judge. Not long after Dora's case, I represented a guy named

Ken Barnhill, whose case tested both my evaluation skills and my new confidence. "Barney" was visiting from Shreveport, Louisiana when his car was hit from the rear by a taxicab on Nob Hill. He had less than $10,000 in medical bills and what injury lawyers call "soft tissue injuries," as opposed to a broken neck or hip. Lawyers almost always think such cases are worth little. But after Dean, I was done listening to what my expert trial lawyer friends thought. So, notwithstanding the obvious drawbacks, I took the case. More important to me than the size of the medical bills was that Barney was permanently disabled by a serious muscular condition afflicting his back and legs. He told us he had immense pain. If he was telling the truth and his doctors supported him, his case could be worth a lot.

When we went to trial, the jury awarded over $700,000, a huge sum under the circumstances. That reinforced my intuitive sense of looking at the people and the circumstances of a case – here, Barney and his relentless pain – not the data, like the dollar amount of medical bills. That's what gets to the core of a case.

Because Barney's doctors were back in Shreveport, I decided to use their videotaped depositions as testimony at trial rather than bring them out to California and subject them to cross-examination. When I played the videos in court, I set up a big monitor for the jury and a smaller one for the judge, Richard Figone. But Figone rejected the monitor. He spent his time during their videos taking notes on a big-money business dispute that he was presiding over without a jury – and that obviously interested him more than our case did. After the jury award, Figone, shocked by the size of the verdict, wanted to grant remittitur to reduce the amount, just as Judge Hanlon had done. This was grossly inappropriate, since he hadn't taken the trouble to watch the video testimony that explained how seriously Barney had been hurt.

I knew that this judge, unlike Hanlon, was ineligible to sit as a "thirteenth juror" precisely because ignoring the videos meant he couldn't judge the "nature and quality" of the testimony of the doctors, as the law requires. So, I filed a motion stating just that. The judge was furious. But he deserved it, and unless he held me in contempt without justification, I had nothing to fear. The defendants' lawyers, knowing I was right, worked with me to reach a favorable resolution with no appeals instead of suffering through an appeal of our award that they would lose.

During this time, in addition to teaching ethics, I was also teaching Trial Practice at the law school. I always told my Trial Practice students to be unfailingly respectful to judges, but never to fear them – a difficult road for students to navigate. But by the time of Barney's trial, I had fully internalized this lesson. The judge was just a person, his own power limited by the law he had sworn to uphold.

The final effect of Dora's case was that it inspired me to try to bring my two lawyering worlds – trial law and legal ethics – much closer together. I had not forgotten that I, the professor who taught my students to put the needs of the clients ahead of my own, had for a day or two thought about appealing Judge Hanlon's order reducing Dora's damages. I was angry at myself for this lapse, which served only me and Mark and not Dora. It was a mistake in priorities I vowed never to make again.

Merging my two worlds also moved me in the direction of specializing in legal malpractice cases and other cases involving attorney behavior. By then, I'd been around and established long enough in both arenas that I found myself going to trial less while still being able to settle cases for a reasonable approximation of their true value. Representing individuals against big law firms had lots of similarities to representing individuals against big corporations – the same insular, tone-deaf elitism was common in the legal profession. This work was a comfortable fit.

My ethics background also motivated me to take on an issue that, decades later, is still unfinished business. I started thinking about it after Dora's verdict came in and we were contacted by a consumer affairs reporter from a local TV network. Dora was shy about being on camera, but she encouraged our doing the show to explain what was wrong with her van. Soon after, Len Mastromonaco and I wrote an article about the defect in a widely read legal magazine. The information that Chrysler had tried so hard to keep secret was all revealed for the public to see.

But I soon realized that in cases that didn't go to trial, dangers like the Dodge van's steering would remain secret. Settlements usually required plaintiffs' attorneys to return all documentation to the defendants and remain quiet about what they had learned. This protected corporations, but many plaintiffs' lawyers went along for the sake of expediency to get what they needed in their own case even though it remained secret from everyone else. In the last decade, it's become more common for the lawyers to allow judges to issue "protective orders" to keep the discovery secret from anyone not directly involved in the case, which judges often agree to because they think it saves time. To me, it's fundamentally unethical for lawyers to conspire to keep secret information that, if known, would inform us all about direct threats to the public health and safety – and thereby save lives.

So, for the past twenty-five years my passion has been to advocate for what is called "sunshine in litigation," opening up all information contained in the discovery process and advocating for the public's right to know. I've found the time to write two book chapters, several op-ed pieces, and three formal law review articles (each one with too many footnotes) on this subject. I've testified before the United States Senate and various California legislative committees. And I've written legislation for both the U.S. House and Senate and for the California legislature.

Sadly, to date, my success rate in this endeavor has been far worse than my trial success rate. Making this information public seems like common sense to almost everyone, but the forces aligned against disclosure are powerful: big corporations, chambers of commerce, and other monied interests. Most recently, our planned 2020 bill was aborted when the California legislature closed due to Covid. But a new bill was filed in early 2022. Perhaps this is the year this necessary legislation finally passes.

I'm not in court nearly as much as I used to be. But this has given me more time to work for the poorest in our community, whose rights and remedies are routinely abused by the institutions they encounter during the course of their everyday lives. If I thought Dora had a hard time with those representing the institution she fought, I underestimated how hard it was to face similar institutions for people with even less power than Dora – who live on the margins, ill-housed if housed at all, often mentally ill. I have found it gratifying to be involved in their defense, and I hope to continue this work.

Epilogue – Same Old Same Old

Otis Benton v. Stani's Best Auto Repair

In the past twenty-five years, most of my work with the poorest Bay Area residents has come not through my private practice but through the pro bono work I've done in collaboration with San Francisco's famed Glide Memorial Church, where I ran a walk-in legal clinic for nine years, and with our local bar association's Homeless Advocacy Project, or HAP, which works primarily with people who are homeless or in danger of becoming homeless. After decades, I'm still surprised at the extraordinary amount of time many cases take, even when the injustices are crystal clear from the outset. The great gratification I've received by doing this work is balanced by the frustration that not much has changed in the way our society – and our justice system – deals with poor people, including the racism that continues to thrive even in San Francisco, the supposed mecca of progressive enlightenment.

Here's an example of what I mean: When I call a lawyer, or a layperson in authority like a bank manager, bill collector, or insurance agent, about a regular client in a regular dispute and tell that person I'm representing X, I am never, ever questioned about that representation. No one asks for proof. No one asks me to provide a document from my client saying that I really am the client's lawyer. No one demands that they talk to my client on the phone to get direct authorization. But when I'm representing a poor person, my bona fides are seldom accepted, and I'm asked to prove that I actually represent that person. Sometimes it's a minor pain in the neck; at other times, where time is of the essence, it's a serious intrusion. But at all times, it says volumes about the basic inequities of our system, and the indignities poor people put up with.

Then there's the added factor of ongoing racism, particularly towards Black people. Here's a brief story about Otis Benton that illustrates this point – a story that occurred not back during my criminal defense days but just a few years ago.

On the ground

One sunny Tuesday afternoon in July 2017, Otis Benton, a sixty-four-year-old disabled Black man, found himself in the middle of the street, face down on the pavement with his hands behind his back, surrounded by police with their guns drawn. His first thought: "What the fuck?" His second? "Same old, same old."

Otis had been driving his 2008 Pontiac Grand Prix down Stanyan Street by Kezar Stadium, once home to the 49ers, since converted into a jewel of a high school athletic field, when sirens blared behind him. Within seconds, he was on the ground, the police telling him the car – *his* car – was stolen. Pleading, he asked if he could go into his back pocket for his wallet, which contained the registration papers proving that the car was his. Fortunately, the cops let him do that, and upon seeing a valid current registration in Otis's name, let him up from the ground and let him go. What they wouldn't do, though, was give him back his car or any of his possessions.

The very next day, Otis walked into HAP's office seeking help. When HAP's director, Teresa Friend, learned the rudiments of the case – car mechanics claimed Otis hadn't paid for auto repairs and filed a mechanic's lien on the car, which under California law meant that after thirty days they could sell it – she called me. For many years, I'd been the go-to person for the odd, one-off cases that came through HAP's door. So, it wasn't surprising that when I told Teresa I had no idea how an auto mechanic's lien worked, she said, "Neither do we. That's why we're calling you."

The Story

To say that this story has a happy ending would be to ignore the eighteen months and hundreds of hours that the case took, not to mention leaving Otis without his car. I put in hundreds of hours myself and had help from a village full of law students, lawyers, and legal support personnel who gave generous and abundant time. It took well over a year for me to even understand the basics of what had happened, and after that, months more dealing with the nation's largest bank and one of our largest insurance companies before things got set right. And during that period, Otis, an indigent senior citizen, was left without his car and with a whole mound of grief.

Rather than give a full chronology of the chutes and ladders of the case, I'll just cut to the chase: what we eventually learned.

When his Pontiac stopped running, Otis brought it to Stani's Best Auto Repair. Otis needed the car; it served as his transportation and also as an occasional home after he'd fallen on hard times. He usually stayed with his daughter, but felt he owed her a little privacy break from time to time, so he'd take a week and live in his car. At the shop, after a diagnosis and estimate, Stani's placed the repair costs at just under $1,100. Otis only had $800 to pay for the car, but his brother loaned him another $300 in cash. The brothers went to pick up the car on June 16. Otis handed $1,100 to the head mechanic, Tariq, and Tariq handed Otis the car keys. Tariq told Otis that Stani had added another $135 to the estimate, but that Otis could pay it later. Otis drove off with the car, but without a receipt for payment or a clear understanding of whether it was payment in full. He had never signed off on an additional charge, or even agreed to it verbally.

Then, as we learned months later, Tariq took advantage of the situation, with some help from his older brother, Hamza, who owned the shop. I never learned whether Tariq told Hamza he'd been paid in cash and put it in the till or simply pocketed the money for himself. But he did lie and tell his brother that Otis had taken the car without his permission. The next day, June 17, Stani's Best filed a mechanics' lien on the car. Repair shops do that if a bill on a car is not paid. Filing the lien is supposed to trigger notification to both the owner and the title holder, in this case Chase Auto Loan. It also allows the shop to add storage charges to the invoice. But the notifications never reached Otis or Chase and likely were never sent. The lien-processing company Stani used requires that before sending out a lien notice, the repair shop must provide an estimate or invoice signed by the customer. Stani didn't have one, because Otis never signed one.

When a mechanics' lien is filed, it starts a thirty-day clock running. If the owner or the title holder doesn't claim the car from storage by then, the repair shop can hold a "lien sale" and offer the car to the highest bidder or, if no bidder, keep the car for itself. Of course, in order to charge storage and make the car available for bidders at the lien sale, the mechanics must have physical possession of the car. These guys didn't, and because they didn't, filing the mechanics' lien was a fraud, whether the repairs had been paid for or not.

Nevertheless, on July 18, the thirty-first day after the lien was filed, Tariq, claiming to have bought the car for $500 at the lien sale, registered the car in his name. Since he didn't actually have the car, Tariq filed a police report in San Francisco, claiming the car had been stolen during the night before the supposed sale.

Otis knew none of this, of course. He had paid the $1100, driven off, and heard nothing, not even a request for additional payment. He continued to pay Chase Auto on his car loan, and Chase continued to accept payment. On July 11, he renewed the car's registration and six months' auto insurance. Then, on July 22, he found himself face down in the middle of Stanyan Street. Although the police let him go when they saw his valid registration and deemed the situation to be a civil matter, he was out one Grand Prix. To make matters worse, a day later, on July 23, he got a call from Progressive Insurance telling him that on that same day one of its insureds had been in an accident … while driving his 2008 Pontiac. About a week later, after calls to Progressive, I was able to learn who was driving Otis's car: his name was Muzhir, and he had the same last name as the two Stani Best brothers.

Months went by as I tried to negotiate with Stani for the return of the car, with absolutely no success. I was flying blind, not knowing what I knew later, and having virtually no idea how vehicle mechanics' liens worked. Usually, my one-off cases, filled with a mix of unfairness and misunderstandings, got to a compromise within a few months. But this case was filled with lies and frauds, and my entreaties got nowhere. It took me three months to get Stani to agree to even give Otis back his personal belongings, including two plastic bags of paperwork. So, with HAP staff attorney Michael Spalding doing the heavy-lifting drafting, we filed a lawsuit against Stani in December. Six causes of action, eleven prayers for relief, eighty-six paragraphs of legal verbiage – it all came down to "Give Otis his car back, and all that it cost him in the meanwhile."

By having Otis verify the complaint, or swear to its veracity, we ensured that any answer from Stani would also have to be sworn to under penalty of perjury by one of the brothers. But we never got a filed answer. Stani filed two motions in an effort to strike our complaint completely, and then strung out the process for as long as they could. Meanwhile, we filed a demand for Stani to give us their business records. They bobbed and weaved for a couple of months – typical legal intransigence – until finally providing information. That spring, Otis, Olivier, then HAP's law student clerk, and I were able to peruse the papers in the plastic bags that Otis finally recovered. We compared what we had about the Pontiac to the documents Stani gave us. And finally, on October 13, 2018, I was able to take the depositions of Hamza and Tariq.

We knew, of course, that Otis had the car in his possession from June 16 to July 22, 2017. And by then we knew the supposed lien sale date: July 18. Stani needed to have possession of the car to do a lien sale, because it had to be available for prospective buyers to see it. So, I asked Hamza where the car was between May 30 and July 17, 2017. Not surprisingly, he lied and said it was at his shop that entire time. I asked him whether anyone had driven the car after it was repaired, and he said only for a few blocks to make sure it was working. Then I asked him to compare the odometer reading when Otis brought the car in and at the time Tariq re-registered the car, and asked, "Do you want to tell me how the car was driven 1000 miles while it remained in your shop?"

Until that question, nothing had seemed to faze Hamza. He had no answer, but by then we had his unequivocal testimony that the car had been in his shop continually from May 30 through the morning of the sale. And we knew that Otis had gotten a smog check and renewed the car's registration during that period. So, in the midst of the depo, I asked Otis whether he might have the receipt for the smog check in his plastic bag of papers and sent Olivier and Otis into another room to check. Olivier came back in the depo room a few minutes later and whispered that we might want to take a five-minute break. As soon as we were in a private space, Otis and Olivier showed me what they'd found. Sure enough, Otis had the receipt for the smog check. Not only that, but Otis found a receipt for an oil and lube job in Oakland on the very day of the lien sale in San Francisco. It's not often you get a smoking gun that hot. I asked Stani's lawyer to join me for a little chat.

I consulted with my friend, an insurance-savvy lawyer named Jane Tishkoff, who'd been sitting in at the depo, on what settlement strategy we should follow at this point. We wound up demanding, and getting, title to the car, a year's payment of insurance that Otis had wasted paying Geico, an additional $7,000, half of which Otis had paid to Chase Auto and half as "general" damages for his trouble, and, most importantly, the car, but only once the brothers did further repairs, painted it, and gave it to him in tip-top shape. Rather than wait to write a settlement agreement, I insisted that we put the settlement on the record, recorded by the certified shorthand reporter, which under California law is as effective as a signed agreement. Five days later, as we'd agreed, Otis and I showed up at Stani to take delivery of a white 2008 Grand Prix in mint condition.

I confess that before letting the Stani brothers leave the depo room, I exercised a bit of preachy white privilege. In my defense, I'd just had a very rare *Perry Mason* moment, exposing a lie in the middle of testimony. Plus, I'd discussed with Otis whether he was interested in going after these guys criminally and, when he said "nah," whether he'd like me to give them a little lecture. "Yes, indeed," he replied. So, I told the brothers that I was sure that they, as people of color, had suffered discrimination and would likely experience it again. Then I told them how Otis had been humiliated by being slammed to the pavement facedown, and that they had a lot of damn nerve doing what they did to Otis and putting him in the same vulnerable position that they might find themselves in. And I told them I'd be keeping an eye on them. Preachy? Certainly. But my job, as always, was to do the best for my client, and Otis loved it!

Dealing with the brothers was not quite the end of things. We had to get Geico's agreement to reinstate insurance and give Otis back credit, and to get Chase Auto to kick in a little something ($2,500) once we learned that Chase had a written chronology that included my advising them that the car was no longer in Otis's name, which they ignored while continuing to demand payments. Finally, Jane told me Otis had something called a GAP policy, which turns out to be insurance against any failure by Otis to pay that car loan. Since the loan was now paid in full, Otis was entitled to a prorated refund of his premium, and Jane got to work negotiating his recovery, another $274. Finally, with that payment in April 2019, the case was over.

It would have been easier for us to just forget about that last $274 instead of spending the fifteen hours of time, mostly Jane's, that it took to get it refunded. But we both knew that it wasn't so much about the money as it was about why Otis should accept even a penny less than what he was entitled to. It was a matter of simple dignity. He had the right to be made completely whole. Except, of course, for being slammed to the pavement by the cops.

Looking back, I realized that a lot of this case had to do with the way the system saw Otis: the cops, the mechanic brothers, Chase, Progressive, and Geico. I went back to our case file to see how we at HAP saw him. Was it the same? The intake person's notes were a straightforward paragraph of Otis's assertions in a tone that assumed they were truthful. My notes after our first meeting said, "This is a weird case." True enough. But then I wrote, "Otis Benton seems perfectly nice and completely credible." And he was. Here was a guy without a permanent address of his own who nevertheless religiously paid his car loan and insurance premium every month, who kept good records of his transactions (in that plastic bag), and who, importantly, assumed the goodness of other people.

Around the time of the deposition, Otis had secured an apartment in safe senior housing in the Western Addition. A few months after the case was finally over, I was driving down Turk Street past the senior houses when I saw a familiar white Pontiac. It was Otis, so I stopped to exchange hugs and chat. Otis wanted me to check out the car, which was washed, polished, and detailed. It looked like it would last another 100,000 miles, easy.

Acknowledgements

I first want to thank the wonderfully rich assortment of people – clients and their families, judges, co-counsel, opposing counsel, law students, and witnesses – who made my life as a trial lawyer endlessly interesting, and who proved to me that truth is, indeed, often stranger than fiction. But more than that, the people I encountered taught me beyond measure – about how best to practice law and also how to live life. Each experience, whether positive or negative, joyful or tragic, added a little to my cumulative understanding and thus to the lawyer and person I became. I am endlessly grateful.

The creation of this book benefitted from the help of many people, including all those who read bits and pieces of drafts and made wise suggestions: Jeff Nussbaum, Steve Pearlmutter, Arlene Popkin, Jonathan Powers, Steve Rosenfield, Naomi Weinstein, Karl Wustrack, and a cluster of Zitrins: Deborah, Gabriel, Jesse, Maya, and Victoria. The terrific editor Doris Ober read several early chapters and gave me her valuable time and incisive analysis. Special thanks to my oldest friend, Gerry Rosen, who read every pre-final draft page with a proof-reader's eye and didn't miss a thing, fixing myriad grammatical and typographical mistakes along the way.

Thanks to Dennis Riordan, who helped me re-connect with my first client, Johnny Spain, and to David Stull, who helped me connect with Steve Rubin, publisher extraordinaire.

And thanks also to Steve himself, who was always willing to offer suggestions, and for introducing me to Serena Jones, an editor generous with her time, who more than once was willing to give me her expert advice.

From Gerry Schwartzbach, one of the best trial lawyers I've ever known, I received many pearls of wisdom about how to approach a memoir like this. From Holley Newmark, I received the kind and helpful assistance that a great personal assistant brings. From Steve Piser, I received not only his reader's critique but an introduction to his friend and colleague Jotham Stein, who in turn suggested reaching out to his publisher. I so appreciate this help from each of you. I owe eternal thanks to the late historian and author Jules Tygiel, who more than anyone taught me about the craft of writing.

To my publisher, Political Animal Press, my thanks for being a perfect fit for me and the stories I was trying to get down on paper. Thanks to Alex Wall of PAP and, especially, to Lewis Slawsky, an editor and wordsmith of the highest order who made our collaboration both easy and extraordinarily helpful.

Finally, my profound gratitude to some very special people: Eva Paterson, who extended an invitation to me, an older white privileged guy, to write about issues of systemic racism, caste-ism, and elitism; Virginia Fink, who with perception and caring has helped keep me sane for over a quarter century; Bill Balin, my Zoom writing partner, who insisted that I write about my very first case and then, with patience and kindness, read every word and critiqued every page; and my wife Victoria, for the love and support I receive every day.

About the Author

RICHARD ZITRIN has been licensed to practice law in California and New York for four decades and has tried over fifty cases to verdict, from murder cases to products liability and malpractice. He has been certified in California as a trial specialist in both criminal law and legal malpractice law. In parallel with his career as a practicing attorney, Richard has spent over forty years teaching Legal Ethics at two Bay Area law schools, and also taught Trial Practice for several years. He has written three previous books, including *The Moral Compass of the American Lawyer: Truth, Justice, Power, and Greed*, and over one hundred published articles, appearing in periodicals such as *New York Times*, *Los Angeles Times* and *San Francisco Chronicle* to the *National Law Journal*, the *Sporting News*, and *NINE: A Journal of Baseball History & Culture*.

In 2019, Richard was awarded California Bar's state-wide Harry Sondheim Award for "outstanding long-term contribution to the advancement of attorney professional standards in California." Other awards include the national American Bar Association's *Pro Bono Publico* award for service in support of the public good, and statewide and local awards for his pro bono work and for promoting equality and diversity. He was the founding director of the University of San Francisco's Center for Applied Legal Ethics, Chair and Special Advisor to the California State Bar's ethics committee, and spent ten weeks as technical advisor to the feature film *Class Action,* snagging a SAG card and an eleven-word role in a scene with Gene Hackman. He is a graduate of Oberlin College and New York University School of Law.

Richard was born in Brooklyn and has lived in San Francisco since 1973. In his free time, he can be found playing saxophone or full-court basketball, at the ballpark or in his Italian restaurant, or hanging out with his wife or three adult children and two grandchildren, all of whom live in the Bay Area.